Tel: 01543 473073 between 1pm and 9pm	**J. WELSH** P.O. Box 150, Burton-on-Trent, Staffs DE13 7LB Callers by appointment only as all coins banked	Est. 1968 Fax No. (24 hrs) 01543 473234

COINS FOR SALE

HAMMERED GOLD

EDW III Noble S1502 A/UNC..............**£700**
EDW IV Ryal UNC **£750**
H VIII Angel S2300 A/UNC **£575**
JMS I Laurel S26388 VF **£350**
JMS I ½ Unite S2623 A/UNC Rare **£595**

£5 + £2 PIECES

1937 PR £5 GJM FDC.........................**£650**
1937 PR £2 GJM FDC.........................**£325**

GUINEAS ETC

1787 NEF Nice **£160**
1799 Nice ABT UNC Very rare............**£225**
1797 ⅓ GN Nice UNC Square............**£135**
1800 ⅓ UN BU GEM **£140**
1803 ⅓ UN BU GEM **£140**
1804 ⅓ UN BU GEM **£140**
1806 ⅓ UN BU GEM **£140**
1809 ⅓ UN BU GEM **£140**
1810 ⅓ UN BU GEM **£125**

SOVEREIGNS

1817 VF **£125**
1817 BU GEM **£495**
1818 BU GEM Rare **£595**
1822 Nice BU **£550**

1826 BU..**£495**
1829 BU Scarce **£550**
1838 BU Very Rare **£395**
1872 L ST GED BU GEM....................**£150**
1880 L ST GED BU GEM....................**£150**
188M JUB HD BU GEM **£110**
1901 M BU GEM **£85**
1909 L BU GEM **£85**
1911 L BU GEM **£70**
1912 S BU GEM Scarce **£85**
1913 L BU GEM **£68**
1914 L BU GEM Scarce **£70**
1915 P BU GEM Rare **£90**
1917 P BU GEM Rare **£85**
1918 I BU Rare **£95**
1920 P BU GEM Very Rare **£125**
1925 SA BU GEM **£70**
1927 SA BU GEM **£70**
1929 SA BU..**£68**
1930 SA BU..**£70**
1931 SA BU..**£70**
1931 SA BU GEM **£75**

HALF SOVEREIGNS

1837 WILL IV BU GEM Extra rare **£595**
1842 BU GEM Rare **£295**
1884 BU GEM **£140**
1937 PR GEM FDC **£150**
1987 ¹/₁₀ Brit PR FDC...........................**£40**

**ABOVE IS A SMALL SELECTION FROM OUR LARGE STOCK OF
ENGLISH AND FOREIGN GOLD COINS. WE CAN ALSO OFFER YOU ON OUR MONTHLY SALES
LIST A VERY WIDE RANGE OF ENGLISH SILVER, COPPER COINS, GOLD AND SILVER PROOF
SETS AT COMPETITIVE PRICES**

**IF YOU WOULD LIKE TO RECEIVE MY FREE MONTHLY SALES
LIST OF ENGLISH, GOLD, SILVER AND COPPER COINS,
(A VERY WIDE RANGE 1100AD-1997.)
PLEASE WRITE, TELEPHONE OR FAX ME**

BRITISH
COINS
MARKET VALUES

CONTENTS

Executive Editor:
Richard West

Group Advertisement Manager:
Gary Ashburn

Production Assistant:
Keith Rivers

Publishing Director
Peter Warwick

Published by:
Link House
Magazines Ltd
Link House
Dingwall Avenue
Croydon CR9 2TA
Tel: 0181 686 2599
Fax: 0181 781 6044

Distributed by:
USM Distribution Ltd
85-86 Newman Street
London W1P 3LD
Tel: 0171 396 8000
Fax: 0171 392 8002

ISBN 0-86296-145-9

A LINK HOUSE
ANNUAL

Market Trends

WE now have such an active numismatic world in Great Britain and Ireland that the last year has simply flashed past. There seems to have been an important coin auction, or coin fair somewhere each month; the two main numismatic societies boast strong membership and offered excellent programmes of lectures and the British Museum now has an exhibition of coins of which we can all feel proud.

Credit must also go to the professional coin dealers in the country, headed by the BNTA, for maintaining standards. We feel that the presentation and general marketing of coins has improved dramatically in the last few years, and there are now so many good and well illustrated books and catalogues.

Our strong competitive community of auctioneers continue to prosper (Baldwin, Bonhams, Dix-Noonan-Webb, Glendinings, Sotheby, Spink, Vecchi), bringing overseas business to London and possibly making it currently the coin auction capital of the world.

In COINS MARKET VALUES though we concentrate only on the domestic material covered by our catalogue section later on, and it has become our tradition to look at each of the main series.

A superb sovereign of Elizabeth I offered for sale by Dolphin Coins recently

Ancient British

The problems of forgery and stolen hoards now seem to be happily behind us, and there is now developing a small group of keen and knowledgeable collectors. In our opinion they are still enjoying an underpriced market, where the range and availability of material is not as great as is ofte assumed.

This year, we feel the new Seaby Standar Catalogue (newly 'revamped' by Spink tha is) will have an impact on this market. Th compiler has breathed fresh life into th Celtic section with a new presentation an more information on tribes and rulers. W also note that the catalogue prices for coin in VF+ have been increased in price.

A very stable market then and we als note that Philip De Jersey's *Celtic Coinage i Britain* (Shire Archaeology, £4.99) has sol very well over the last year. We fully expec some of the purchasers of this book t develop into keen collectors, and we ca also see the demand for Celtic coin strengthening over the next few years.

English Hammered Gold

Nobles, angels, ryals, sovereigns, a rol call of some of the famous denomination we find in this series. Good quality ham mered gold are now increasing in deman and there seems to be more collectors tha there were even five years ago. Prices hav stood up well at auction, but sadly there ha not been any important offerings of mater ial, and now we could do with the sale o Beresford-Jones or a Strauss collection t test the strength of the market.

There is no doubt that the keen receptio given to Volume I of the Herbert Schneide collection (the best private collection eve assembled), has encouraged collectors With the next volume on the horizon, inter est can only increase.

Milled Gold

This area has in the past attracted peopl looking for alternative investment during th term of a Labour government. Will it happe again? Unfortunately there seems to be lack of top quality pieces, and we confidentl predict a big rise in price for anything in E condition in the next twelve months.

Hammered Silver

This is the largest area in the whole Britis series, starting with the small stubby sceat of the Anglo-Saxon period, and ending wit the often badly struck hammered coins o Charles II. There are many people who col lect by denomination, the penny, the groat, e sixpence and shilling being very popular, while others collect by type or reign, or even mint. At present the crown is strong again as ilustrated by the successful Spink sale of the r Rees-Jones collection in November. The aldwin auctions in May showed that the interest in rare late Anglo-Saxon coins is still here, since in recent years many people hought that demand was at best dormant, fter the halcyon years of the seventies. The ale of Owen Parson's small collection also emonstrated the thirst there is for fresh, interesting material.

This spectacular 1644 crown of Oxford which realised £33,000 in the Rees-Jones ale at Spink

Milled Silver

This is traditionally the area which attracts the most interest from domestic dealers and it has proved consistently stable. There is always a demand for top quality material and dealers in the know, both here and in the USA, can place choice coins instantly. However, this year we have changed many of the prices for coins in the lower categories, showing that there is more interest here as well. We have also noted a renewed interest in collecting date coins. An interesting example of this was the 1667 halfcrown which sold for £1,540 at Bonhams in June. A high price, but there was no specimen of this date in Hamilton, Manville, Norweb or Willis.

Copper and Bronze

Each year we make the same comments about the lack of good material and so it con-

1667 halfcrown which realised £1,540 at Bonhams

tinues. This used to be one of the hottest areas of collecting during the change-checking boons of the 1960s, and a number of important collections were formed at that time.

There is no doubt that copper and bronze needs to be very carefully stored, otherwise they can deteriorate (see our section on keeping your coins), but is that the reason for the decrease in the numbers of collectors interested? Whatever, it is still a wonderful area to collect. We suggest an investment in a second hand copy of Peck's superb British Museum catalogue of copper, tin and bronze coins (why doesn't the BM reprint it?) and a whole new world will open up.

Scottish Coins

We have noted a lot more interest in Scottish coins over the last twelve months, and in particular from within Scotland. Strangely enough in the 60s, 70s and 80s many of the prominent collectors were in England and the USA, so maybe the talk of devolution is encouraging Scots to look more at their history. Certainly it is a wonderful series to collect, and over the past twelve months we have two interesting auctions to look at. First of all the highly important sale of the Douglas collection at Spink in March. The superb gold coins in this collection were the best in private hands and it will

A highly important James IV half-unicorn which sold for £17,600 inthe Douglas auction at Spink

be a long time before it is equalled. Prices held up very well considering the number of pieces on offer with £77,000 being paid for a Francis and Mary ducat. At the other end of the scale, Glendining, in June, held a more modest auction of over 200 lots of Scottish, surprisingly put together by the owner in less than ten years. Quite an achievement, but the quality was rather patchy, although it is unusual nowadays to see so much offered for sale in one go nevertheless they were all absorbed.

Irish Coins

There has again been a slight but noticeable strengthening of the Irish market. In Ireland, Whyte's auctions are featuring good material more frequently and also attracting some good prices. The most important sale since the last edition of COINS MARKET VALUES was Baldwin's auction of the Conte collection in May. This included a particularly strong run of Hiberno-Norse pennies which realised quite firm prices, and will be a useful guide to prices for a while.

Incidentally, as with Scottish and Anglo-Gallic series, COINS MARKET VALUES offers the only up-to-date guide to prices.

Anglo-Gallic Coins

The demand for Anglo-Gallic coins continues to be small but enthusiastic. It appears that there are a small number of keen aficionados spread thinly around the world. Prices can be quite strong when a rarely offered piece comes on the market, but there is no in depth support to buy numbers of these pieces. It is worth noting that collectors of purely English hammered coins like to have one example of Edward the Black Prince's reign in their collection, as well as a denier of Richard the Lionheart because they read 'RICARDUS' while his English coins have the name of his father.

The peak of the market remains the sale of the Elias collection in 1990, and all newcomers to the series must obtain the catalogue which is still available.

COIN MARKET VALUES

Some Useful Books

Here is a small selection of books dealing with coins which are covered in COINS MARKET VALUES. Included are the prices you can expect to pay; some of the books are now out of print, but can still often be obtained second-hand (indicated in the list by SH).

Bateson , J.D. Coinage in Scotland. 1997. **£20.**

Besly, E. Coins and Medals of the English Civil War (1991). **£18.50.**

Blunt, C.E., Stewart, B.H.I.H., Lyon, C.S.S. Coinage in Tenth Century England 1989. **£60.**

Boon, G. Welsh Hoards 1979-1981 (1986) . **£28.**

Boon, G. Coins of the Anarchy 1135-1154 (1988). **£4.**

Brand, J.D. Periodic Change of Type in the Anglo-Saxon and Norman Periods (1984). **£3.**

British Academy (Publisher) Sylloge of Coins of the British Isles. 44 volumes mostly in print available individually. [See List on p.20].

Brooke, G.C. English Coins. (Reprint edition, London 1966). **£12.**

Challis, C. A new History of the Royal Mint, 1992. **£95.**

Coincraft's Standard Catalogue of English and UK Coins, 1996. **£19.50.**

Cooper. D.R. The Art and Craft of Coinmaking. 1988. **£30.**

Dolley, M. Viking coins in the Danelaw and Dublin (London 1965). **SH.**

Dolley, M. Anglo Saxon Pennies (Reprint, London 1970). **SH.**

Dolley, M. The Norman Conquest and English Coinage (London 1966). **£2.**

Dowle, A. and Finn, P. The Guide Book to the Coinage of Ireland (London 1969). **SH.**

Elias, E.R.D. The Anglo-Gallic coins (Paris/London 1984). **£20.**

Freeman, A. The Moneyer and Mint in the Reign of Edward the Confessor 1042-1066. 2 parts (1985). **£40.**

Gouby, Michael. The British Bronze Penny (1986). **£19.95.**

Grueber, H.A. Handbook of the Coins of Great Britain and Ireland (Revised edition London 1970). **SH.**

Hobbs, Richard. British Iron Age Coins in the British Museum. **£40.**

Ie Jersey. P. Celtic Coinage in Britain (Shire Archaeology). **£4.99.**

Linecar, H.W.A. British Coin Designs and Designers (London 1977). **SH.**

Manville, H.E. and Robertson, T.J. British Numismatic Auction Catalogues, 1710-1984 (1986). **£25.**

Manville, H.E. Numismatic Guide to British and Irish periodicals 1731-1991. Part 1. (Archaeological). **£60.**

Mays, M. (Editor). Celtic Coinage: Britain and Beyond. BAR Series 222 1992. **£32.**

McCammon, A.L.T. Currencies of the Anglo-Norman Isles (London 1984). **£25.** Supplement with much new information. **£8.**

North, J.J. English Hammered Coins. Two volumes. Volume 1, **£35;** and Volume 2, **£30.**

North, J.J. and Preston-Morley. P.J. The John G. Brooker Collection – Coins of Charles 1. (Sylloge of Coins of the British Isles, Number 33). **£19.50.**

O'Sullivan, W. The Earliest Anglo-Irish Coinage (second edition, Dublin 1964). **SH.**

Peck, C.W. English Copper, Tin and Bronze Coins in the British Museum 1558-1958 (London 1960). **SH.**

Pridmore, F. The Coins of the British Commonwealth of Nations: 1-European Territories (London 1960). **SH.**

Rayner, P.A. English Silver Coins Since 1649, 1992. **£19.95.**

Robinson, B. Silver Pennies and Linen Towels: The Story of the Royal Maundy (1991). **£29.95.**

Seaby Standard Catalogue of British Coins, 1998. Now produced by Spink. New and revised. **£15.**

Spink and Son (Publishers). Milled Coinage of England 1662-1946 (1958) reprinted. **£5.**

Stewart, I.H. The Scottish Coinage (Second edition, London 1967). **SH.**

Sutherland, C.H.V. English Coinage 600-1900 (London 1973). **SH.**

Thompson, J.D.A. Inventory of British Coin Hoards AD 600-1500 (London 1956). **SH.**

Van Arsdell, R.D. Celtic Coinage of Britain (London 1989). **£40.**

Withers, P and B. British Coin Weights. **£95.**

Woodhead, P. The Herbert Schneider Collection of English Gold Coins. Part 1. Henry III-Elizabeth I. **£60.**

Wren. C.R. The Voided Long Cross Coinage 1247-1279, 1993. **£9.**

Wren. C.R. The Short Cross Coinage 1180-1247, 1992. **£8.75.**

Abbreviations and Terms

used in the Market Price Guide Section

* – Asterisks against some dates indicate that no firm prices were available at the time of going to press.

2mm – P of PENNY is 2mm from trident. On other 1895 pennies the space between is only 1mm.

AE – numismatic symbol for copper or copper alloys.

Arabic 1, Roman I – varieties of the 1 in 1887.

Arcs – decorative border of arcs which vary in number.

B (on William III coins) – minted at Bristol.

1866 shilling lettered BBITANNIAR in error

BBITANNIAR – lettering error.

Bank of England – this issued overstruck Spanish dollars for currency use in Britain 1804-1811.

black – farthings 1897-1918, artificially darkened to avoid confusion with half sovereigns.

briit – lettering error.

B. Unc, BU – Brilliant Uncirculated condition.

C (on milled gold coins) – minted at Ottawa (Canada).

C (on William III coins) – minted at Chester.

close colon – colon close to DEF.

crosslet 4 – having upper and lower serifs to horizontal bar of 4 (see plain 4).

cu-ni – cupro-nickel.

dashes (thus –) following dates in the price list indicate that some particular characteristic of a coin is the same as that last described. Two dashes mean that two characters are repeated, and so on.

debased – in 1920 the silver fineness in British coins was debased from .925 to .500.

diag – diagonal.

'Dorrien and Magens' – issue of shillings by a group of bankers. Suppressed on the day of issue.

DRITANNIAR – lettering error.

E (on William III coins) – minted at Exeter.

E, E* (on Queen Anne coins) – minted at Edinburgh.

Edin – Edinburgh.

EEC – European Economic Community.

EF (over price column) – Extremely Fine condition.

E.I.C. – East India Co (supplier of metal).

Elephant and castle

eleph, eleph & castle – elephant or elephant and castle provenance mark (below the bust) taken from the badge of the African ('Guinea') Company, which imported the metal for the coins.

Eng – English shilling. In 1937, English and Scottish versions of the shilling were introduced. English versions: lion standing on crown (1937-1951); three leopards on a shield (1953-66).

exergue – segment below main design, usually containing the date.

On this penny the exergue is the area containing the date

ext – extremely.

F – face value only.

F (over price column) – Fine condition.

(F) – forgeries exist of these pieces. In some cases the forgeries are complete fakes, in others where the date is rare the date of a common coin has been altered. Collectors are advised to be very cautious when buying any of these coins.

Fair – rather worn condition.

Fantasies – non-currency items, often just produced for the benefit of collectors.

far colon – colon father from DEF than in close colon variety.

FDC – Fleur de coin. A term used to describe coins in perfect mint condition, with no flaws, scratches or other marks.

fig(s) – figure(s).

fillet – hair band.

flan – blank for a coin or medal.

GEOE – lettering error.

Florin of Victoria with the design in the Gothic style

Gothic – Victorian coins featuring Gothic-style portrait and lettering.

guinea-head – die used for obverse of guinea.

H – mintmark of The Mint, Birmingham, Ltd.

hd – head.

hp, harp (early, ord etc.) – varieties of the Irish harp on reverse.

hearts – motif in top RH corner of Hanoverian shield on reverse.

illust – illustration, or illustrated.

im – initial mark.

inc, incuse – incised, sunk in.

inv – inverted.

JH – Jubilee Head.

The Jubilee Head was introduced on the coinage in 1887 to mark Victoria's Golden Jubilee

KN – mintmark of the Kings Norton Metal Co Ltd.

L.C.W. – Initials of Leonard Charles Wyon, engraver.

lge – large.

MA – coins bearing this word were struck from bullion captured by British ships from foreign vessels carrying South American treasure, some of which may have come from Peru (capital Lima).

1902 pennies showing the low horizon variety (A) and the normal horizon (B)

w horizon – on normal coins the horizon meets the point where Britannia's left leg crosses behind the right. On this variety the horizon is lower.

VIII etc – regnal year in Roman numerals on the edge.

att – type of proof without mirror-like finish.

M (on gold coins) – minted at Melbourne (Australia).

military' – popular name for the 1813 guinea struck for the payment of troops fighting in the Napoleonic Wars.

m – mintmark.

Mod eff – modified effigy of George V.

ule – coin struck from wrongly paired dies.

N (on William III coins) – minted at Norwich.

William III shilling with N (for Norwich mint) below the bust

o. – number.

bv – obverse, usually the 'head' side of a coin.

OH – Old Head.

rd – ordinary.

OT – ornamental trident.

P (on gold coins) – minted at Perth (Australia).

attern – trial piece not issued for currency.

piedfort – a coin which has been specially struck on a thicker than normal blank. In France, whence the term originates, the Kings seem to have issued them as presentation pieces from the 12th century onwards. In Britain medieval and Tudor examples are known, and their issue has now been reintroduced by the Royal Mint, starting with the 20 pence piedfort of 1982.

plain (on silver coins) – no provenance marks in angles between shields on reverse.

plain 4 – with upper serif only to horizontal bar of 4 (see crosslet 4).

pln edge prf – plain edge proof.

plume(s) – symbol denoting Welsh mines as source of metal.

proof, prf – coin specially struck from highly polished dies. Usually has a mirror-like surface.

prov, provenance – a provenance mark on a coin (e.g. rose, plume, elephant) indicates the supplier of the bullion from which the coin was struck.

PT – plain trident.

raised – in relief, not incuse.

RB – round beads in border.

rev – reverse, 'tail' side of coin.

r – right.

r & p – roses and plumes.

Roses and plumes provenance marks

rose – symbol denoting west of England mines as source of metal.

RRITANNIAR – lettering error.

rsd – raised.

S (on gold coins) – minted at Sydney (Australia).

SA (on gold coins) – minted at Pretoria (South Africa).

Scottish shilling 1953-66

Scot – Scottish shilling. Lion seated on crown, holding sword and sceptre (1937-51); lion rampant, on shield (1953-66).

SS C – South Sea Company (source of metal).

1723 shilling bearing the South Sea Company's initials

SEC – SECUNDO, regnal year (on edge).

sh – shield(s).

sm – small.

'spade' – refers to spadelike shape of shield on George III gold coins.

'Spade' guinea, reverse

TB – toothed beads in border.

TER – TERTIO, regnal year (on edge).

trnctn, truncation – base of head or bust where the neck or shoulders terminate.

Unc – Uncirculated condition.

var – variety.

VF – Very Fine condition.

VIGO – struck from bullion captured in Vigo Bay.

VIP – 'very important person'. The so-called VIP crowns were the true proofs for the years of issue. Probably most of the limited number struck would have been presented to high ranking officials.

W.C.C. – Welsh Copper Co (supplier of metal).

wire type – figure of value in thin wire-like script.

W.W. – initials of William Wyon, engraver.

xxri – lettering error.

y, Y (on William III coins) – minted at York.

YH – Young Head.

Victoria Young Head Maundy fourpence

Coin Grading

IT IS MOST important that newcomers to collecting should get to know the various grades of condition before attempting to buy or sell coins.

The system of grading most commonly used in Britain recognises the following main classes in descending order of quality: Brilliant Uncirculated (B.Unc,BU), Uncirculated (Unc), Extremely Fine (EF), Very Fine (VF), Fine (F), Fair, Poor.

It is not surprising that beginners get confused at their first encounter with these grades. The word 'FINE' implies a coin of high quality, yet this grade turns out to be very near the bottom of the scale and is in fact about the lowest grade acceptable to most collectors of modern coinage in Britain.

American grading

It is not really necessary to go into the details of American grading here, since it is only on a very few occasions that a British collector will order the coins he wants directly from an American dealer. However, across the Atlantic their grading system is quite different from ours, and whilst it purports to be a lot more accurate, it is actually much more prone, in our opinion, to be abused, and we prefer the English dealers' more conservative methods of grading. American dealers use many more terms than we do, ranging from Mint State to About Good. The latter could be described as 'very heavily worn, with portions of lettering, date and legend worn smooth. The date may be partly legible'. In England we would simply say 'Poor'.

Numerical method

The other area which British collectors will find difficult to evaluate is the American numerical method of describing coins as, for example, MS 70, MS 65. The MS simply stands for Mint State and an MS 65 would be described as 'an above average Uncirculated coin which may be brilliant or lightly toned but has some surface marks'. The MS system seemed to be acceptable at first but there now appear to be two schools of thought in America and you will quite frequently see coins graded in the more traditional manner as well as the MS style in sale catalogues. Fortunately American grades have not come into use in this country, although dealers have followed the American manner of embellishing coin descriptions to make them more desirable, which is understandable and in many ways can be an improvement on the old method of saying simply that the coin is 'Fine', which, of course, might not do justice to it.

Full mint lustre

There are two schools of thought on the use of the terms Brilliant Uncirculated and Uncirculated. The former is often considered to be the most useful and descriptive term for coins of copper, bronze, nickel-brass or other base metals, which display what is known as 'full mint lustre'. When this term is being used it is often necessary in the same context to employ the grade Uncirculated to describe coins which have never been in circulation but have lost the original lustre of a newly minted coin. However, some dealers and collectors tend to classify as Uncirculated all coins which have not circulated, whether they are brilliant or toned, and do not use the term Brilliant Uncirculated.

Fleur de coin

Sometimes FDC (fleur de coin) is used to define top grade coins, but this really only applies to pieces in perfect mint state, having no flaws or surface scratches. With modern methods of minting, slight damage to the surface is inevitable, except in the case of proofs, and therefore Brilliant Uncirculated or Uncirculated best describe the highest grade of modern coins.

The word 'proof' should not be used to denote a coin's condition. Proofs are pieces struck on specially prepared blanks from highly polished dies and usually have a mirror-like finish.

Opinions differ

In all this matter of condition it might be said that the grade 'is in the eye of the beholder', and there are always likely to be differences of opinion as to the exact grade of a coin. Some collectors and dealers have tried to make the existing scale of definitions more exact by adding letters such as N (Nearly), G (Good, meaning slightly better than the grade to which the letter is added), A (About or Almost) and so on. To be still more accurate in cases where a coin wears more on one side than the other, two grades are shown, the first for the obverse, the second for the reverse thus GVF/EF.

Additional description

Any major faults not apparent from the use of a particular grade are often described separately. These include dents and noticeable scratches, discoloration, areas of corrosion, edge knocks, holes on otherwise good quality pieces, and the like.

Middle range of grades

One should always look for wear on the highest points of the design, of course, but these vary from coin to coin. To present a comprehensive guide to exact grading one would have to illustrate each grade of every coin type in a given series, on the lines of the famous *Guide to the Grading of United States Coins*, by Brown and Dunn. This is a complete book in itself (over 200 pages) and obviously such a mammoth task could not be attempted in the space available here. Therefore on the following page we present representative examples from three different periods in the British series, to illustrate the 'middle' range of coin conditions.

Still in mint state

We have already dealt with the grades BU and Unc; they both describe coins which are still in the state in which they left the Mint, and which have never passed into general circulation. They are likely to show minor scratches and edge knocks due to the mass handling processes of modern minting.

Fair and Poor

At the other end of the scale we have Fair, a grade that is applied to very worn coins which still have the main parts of the design distinguishable and Poor which denotes a grade in which the design and rim are worn almost flat and few details are discernible.

Here we show (enlarged) examples of the grades EF, VF and F. On the left are hammered long cross pennies of Aethelred II; in the centre, from the later hammered series, are groats of Henry VIII; on the right are shillings of William IV.

Extremely Fine. This describes coins which have been put into circulation, but have received only the minimum of damage since. There may be a few light marks or minute scratches in the field (flat area around the main design), but otherwise the coin should show very little sign of having been in circulation.

Very Fine. Coins in this condition show some amount of wear on the raised surfaces, but all other detail is still very clear. Here, all three coins have had a little wear as can be seen in the details of the hair and face. However, they are still in attractive condition from the collector's viewpoint.

Fine. In this grade coins show noticeable wear on the raised parts of the design; most other details should still be clear. The penny and the groat show a lot of wear over the whole surface. On the shilling the hair above the ear has worn flat.

Extremely Fine (EF)

Very Fine (VF)

Fine (F)

Keeping your Coins

ONCE you have started to collect coins make sure you know how to look after them properly.

Storage

Careful thought should be given to the storing of coins, for a collection which is carelessly or inadequately housed can suffer irreparable damage. Corrosion depends essentially on the presence of water vapour, and therefore coins should not be stored in damp attics or spare bedrooms, but where possible in evenly heated warm rooms. We should also point out here that one must be very careful only to pick up coins by the edges, for sweaty fingerprints contain corrosive salt. The following are suitable methods of storage.

Wooden cabinets

A collection carefully laid out in a wood cabinet is seen at its most impressive. Unfortunately, though, the modern wooden cabinets which are custom-built especially for coins are not cheap. Their main advantages are the choice of tray and hole sizes, and the fact that because the manufacturer is often himself a collector, he takes care to use only well matured woods, which have no adverse reactions on coins. Among the makers of wood cabinets are H. S. Swann, of Newcastle (01661 853129) and Peter Nichols of St Leonards, East Sussex (01424 436682).

If one cannot afford a new cabinet, then a second-hand version may be the answer. These can sometimes be purchased at coin auctions, or from dealers, and can be very good value. However, it is not always easy to find one with the tray hole sizes to suit your coins.

Do-it-yourself cabinet makers should also be careful not to use new wood which will contain corrosive moisture. In this case the best method would be to use wood from an old piece of furniture.

Albums, plastic cases and carrying cases

There are many of these on the market and some of them are both handsome and inexpensive. There are also very attractive Italian and German-made attaché-type carrying cases for collectors with velvet lining and different sizes of trays, and so on. These can be obtained from a number of dealers, but Collectors Gallery, 6-7 Castle Gates, Shrewsbury SY1 2AE (tel: 01743 272140) makes a speciality of them. We would also recommend the coin album, which claims to prevent oxidization. The coins are contained in cards with crystal clear film windows enabling the collector to see both sides of the coins. The cards then slide into pages in an album, and might be a convenient method of storage, especially for the new collector. Coins International of 1-2 Melbourne Street

A beautiful traditional style hand-made cabinet.

eeds LS2 7PS (0113 2468855) also offer a large range of albums, envelopes, plastic boxes and capsules etc. Lindner Publications Ltd, 26 Queen Street, Cubbington, Leamington Spa CV32 7NA (01296 425026) supply very useful coin and collecting boxes as well as albums. In central London, probably the best place to visit is Vera Trinder, 38 Bedford Street, WC1 (0171 836 2365/6) who does appear to keep a very good stock. Stanley Gibbons, 399 Strand, London (0800 611622) also produce large size coin albums. Phone them for a free brochure.

Envelopes

Plastic envelopes, being transparent, are very useful for exhibition, but we never recommend them for long-term storage purposes. They tend to make the coins 'sweat', which with copper and bronze in particular can lead to corrosion.

Manilla envelopes are much more suitable, since the paper is dry, unlike ordinary paper, and consequently they are ideal for the storage of coins. Most collectors use them in conjunction with a cardboard box, which makes for simple unobtrusive storage. This is the most inexpensive method of storing coins.

Still the best article we have seen on the storage of coins and medals, which deals with all the materials which are used, was by Mr L.R. Green, who is a Higher Conservation Officer at the Department of Coins and Medals at the British Museum. This appeared in the May 1991 issue of Spink's *Numismatic Circular.*

Magnifiers

New collectors will need to have a good magnifying glass to examine coins, and these can be obtained from W.H. Smith or most other stationers; many opticians also offer very good magnifying glasses. There is now also an excellent and inexpensive binocular microscope on the market, manufactured in the USA and available for less than £200 from Allan Davison of Cold Spring, MN (Fax 001 320 685 8636).

Cleaning coins

In the course of each week dealers examine many coins which some poor unfortunates have unwittingly totally ruined by cleaning. They are, therefore, usually the best people to ask about the subject. One dealer tells of a bright-eyed expectant gentleman who offered his late father's very useful collection of copper coins, with he proudly said he had 'brightened up' the previous day, so as to be certain of a good offer! The dealer did not enjoy his customer's sad disappointment when he found himself unable to make any offers, but then the coins had been cleaned with harsh metal polish and looked like soldiers' buttons.

We always advise people never to clean coins unless they are very dirty or corroded. Also by 'dirt' we do not mean oxide which, on silver coins, can give a pleasing bluish tone favoured by many collectors. The following simple instructions may be of some help, but do not, of course, apply to extremely corroded coins which have been found in the ground, for if important they are the province of a museum conservationist.

Gold coins

Gold should cause collectors few problems, since it is subject to corrosion only in extreme conditions. For example, a gold coin recovered from a long spell in the sea might have a dull, rusty appearance. However, in the normal course of events a little bath in methylated spirits will improve a dirty coin. A word of warning – gold coins should not be rubbed in any way.

Silver coins

Silver will discolour easily, and is particularly susceptible to damp or chemicals in the atmosphere. A gentle brushing with a soft non-nylon bristle brush will clear loose surface dirt, but if the dirt is deep and greasy, a dip in ammonia and careful drying on cotton wool should do the trick. We should once again stress that there is no need to clean a coin which simply has a darkish tone.

Copper and bronze coins

There is no safe method of cleaning copper or bronze coins without actually harming them, and we would only recommend the use of a non-nylon, pure bristle brush to deal with dirt. There is no way of curing the ailments peculiar to these metals, namely verdigris (green spots) or bronze disease (blackish spots) permanently, and we would advise collectors not to buy pieces in such condition, unless they are very inexpensive.

How to Collect Coins

A FEW words of advice for those who have recently discovered coin collecting.

How much is it worth?

There was a time when newcomers to coin collecting would ask the question 'What is it?'. Nowadays certainly the most common question dealers hear is 'What is it worth?'. It is a sign of the times that history takes second place to value. The object of COINS MARKET VALUES is to try to place a value on all the coins produced in what is known geographically as the British Isles, in other words England, Wales, Scotland and Ireland, and the Channel Islands, as well as the Anglo-Gallic series.

This is a difficult task because many coins do not turn up in auctions or lists every year even though they are not really rare. However, we make a stab at a figure so that you the collector can at least have an idea of what you will have to pay.

How to sell your coins

Auction

In England we are well served with a number of auction houses, giving the potential seller considerable choice. In London alone we have, in alphabetical order, Baldwins, Bonhams, Dix Noonan Webb, Glendinings, Sothebys, Spink and Vecchi; while there are small companies up and down the country, such as Croydon Coin Auctions. In Ireland Whyte's of Dublin hold the pole position.

The best approach for the seller is first of all to compare all their catalogues and if possible attend the auctions so that you can see how well they are conducted. Talk it over with their experts, for you may have special cataloguing requirements and you could find that one of the firms might look after them better than the others.

An obvious coin, like say an 1887 £5, requires little expertise and will probably sell at a certain price in almost any auction; however, if you require expert cataloguing of countermarked coins or early medieval, then you need to know what the company is capable of before you discuss a rate for the job.

You should remember though that while it is not complicated to sell by auction you may have to wait at least three or four months from the time you consign the coins to the auctioneers before you receive any money. There are times when auctions manage to achieve very high prices, and other times when, for some inexplicable reason, they fail to reach even a modest reserve. You should also bear in mind that the best deal in the long term is not always the lowest commission rate. Finally, auctioneers will usually charge you at least 10 per cent of the knock-down price, and you should bear in mind that some buyers may also be inhibited from paying a top price by a buyer's premium also of 10 per cent. (Some firms are now charging 15%.)

Dealers

The function of a dealer is to have a stock of coins for sale at marked prices. However, they will naturally only wish to buy according to the ebb and flow of their stocks. It is also true to say that dealers infinitely prefer fresh material, and if you strike at the right time it is possible that you could achieve a better price than by waiting for auction, since of course you will receive the money immediately. Generally speaking both dealers and auctioneers will not make any charge for a verbal valuation, but you should allow for the dealer to be making a profit of at least 20 per cent.

Bullion coins

Relating to Krugerrands, sovereigns, and so on, most newspapers carry the price of gold, which is fixed twice daily

by a group of leading banks. Anyone can buy sovereigns, and Krugerrands and other bullion coins, and it is better these days now that there is no VAT on top. Normally when you sell the bullion coin you expect the coin dealer to make a few pounds profit on each coin, but don't expect a good price for a mounted coin attached to grandfather's watch chain, which will not be worth anything like the same price as an undamaged item.

How to collect coins

You should obviously purchase your coins only from a reputable dealer. How do you decide on a reputable dealer? You can be sure of some protection if you choose one who is a member of the British Numismatic Trade Association or the International Association of Professional Numismatists. Membership lists of these organisations can be obtained from the respective secretaries: Mrs Carol Carter, PO Box 474A, Thames Ditton, Surrey KT7 0WJ (tel: 0181 398 4290; fax: 0181 398 4291) and Jean-Luc Van Der Schueren, 14 Rue de la Bourse, B 1000 Brussels. However, many dealers are not members of either organisation, and it does not mean that they are not honest and professional. The best approach is simply to find one who will unconditionally guarantee that the coins you buy from him are genuine and accurately graded.

As a general rule you should only buy coins in the best condition available, and on this subject you will at first have to rely on the judgement of the dealer you choose. However, remember it will not always be possible to find pieces in Extremely Fine condition, for example, and it can sometimes be worth buying coins which are not quite Very Fine. In the case of great rarities, of course, you might well have to make do with a coin that is only Fine, or even Poor. If there are only six known specimens of a particular piece, and four are in museums, it seems pointless to wait 20 years for another one to be found in the ground. Over the last few years condition has become too important in many ways, and has driven away collectors, because obviously you cannot buy coins only in top condition, since in certain series that would rule out at least 50 per cent of the available specimens. It depends on the type of coin, the reign and so on, so be realistic.

It is worth taking out subscriptions with auction houses so that you can receive copies of all their catalogues, because this is an excellent way to keep up with prices as well as the collections that are being offered.

However, one should not overlook the fact that a number of dealers produce price lists, which in many ways are most useful to the collector, because he can choose coins at his leisure by mail order, and can more easily work out what he can afford to buy than when in the hot-house atmosphere of the auction room. The most famous list is *Spink's Numismatic Circular* first published in 1892, and still going strong with ten issues a year. It is much more than a price list being an important forum for numismatic debate and the reporting of new finds, etc (annual subscription £15).

There are also many expert dealers who produce excellent lists, many of them advertise in this publication and obviously we cannot mention them all here, but a good cross section of those who list domestic coins, and not listed in any order of preference, is as follows:

Lloyd Bennett, PO Box 2, Monmouth, Gwent NP5 3YE. Hammered, Milled, Tokens.

B.J. Dawson, 52 St Helens Road, Bolton, Lancs BL3 3NH. Hammered, Milled, Tokens, Medals.

Dolphin Coins, 2c Englands Lane, Hampstead, London NW3 4TG. All British.

Patrick Finn, PO Box 26, Kendal, Cumbria LA9 7AB. Hammered English, Irish, Scottish.

Format, 18/19 Bennetts Hill, Birmingham B2 5QJ. All British.

Grantham Coins, PO Box 60, Grantham, Lincs. Milled, good on Maundy.

K.B. Coins, 50 Lingfield Road, Martins Wood, Stevenage, Herts SG1 5SL. Hammered and Milled.

C.J. Martin, 85 The Vale, Southgate, London N14 6AT. Celtic and Hammered.

Peter Morris, PO Box 223, Bromley,

Kent BR1 4EQ. Hammered, Milled, Tokens.

S.R. Porter, 18 Trinity Road, Headington Quarry, Oxford OX3 8LQ. Milled and Hammered.

Chris Rudd, PO Box 222, Aylsham, Norfolk NR11 6TY. The only specialist dealer in Celtic Coins.

Seaby Coins, 14 Old Bond Street, London W1X 4JL. Hammered, some Milled.

Simmons & Simmons, PO Box 104, Leytonstone, London E11 1ND.

Also don't forget there are specialist dealers who do not produce lists, for example, Chelsea Coins (Dimitri Loulakakis, 0181 879 5501) who is the man for maundy coins.

Societies

You should consider joining your local numismatic society, there being quite a number of these throughout the country. To find if there is one near you, contact the British Association of Numismatic Societies, Mr P. H. Mernick, c/o Bush, Boake, Allen Ltd, Blackhorse Lane, London E17 5QP (tel 0181 523-6531) The BANS organises annual congresses and seminars, and it is a good idea for the serious collector to consider attending one of these. Details are usually well publicised in the numismatic press.

Those collectors who wish to go a little further can apply for membership of the British Numismatic Society, and for their annual membership fee they will receive a copy of the *British Numismatic Journal* which incorporates details of current research and many important articles, as well as book reviews. Another useful facet of membership of this Society is that you can borrow books from its library in the Warburg Institute. Londoners might like to consider joining the London Numismatic Society, which is the best society after the Royal and the British, and is always looking for new members. Newcomers will be sure of a very friendly reception. The secretary is Mrs Stella Greenall, c/o P. Rueff, 2 King's Bench Walk, The Temple, London EC4Y 7DE.

Museums and where to see Coins

London

The British Museum has a new wonderful gallery devoted to money. The display ranges over an enormous number of coins and other objects which have been used as money over the last four and a half thousand years. There are nineteen specially designed cases displaying many choice pieces, beautifully presented and making the best use of modern lighting techniques.

Edinburgh

The Royal Museum of Scotland in Queen Street houses the premier collection of Scottish coins, but has very important Anglo-Saxon and English coins also. The Museum began in 1781 as the collection of the Society of Antiquaries of Scotland.

Glasgow

A new permanent gallery devoted to numismatics has been opened at the Hunterian Museum. It is situated in an upstairs mezzanine gallery off the main hall and features over 2000 items. There are on display many superb specimens from the original collection of the founder, William Hunter.

Cardiff

There is an excellent general exhibition of coins, medals, decorations and tokens in the National Museum. There are many superb pieces on display, presented with excellent lighting in good show cases.

Cambridge

The Fitzwilliam in Cambridge now houses both the famous Grierson collection and the legendary collection of Christopher Blunt, and many other delights. It is under the curatorship of Mark Blackburn, one of the most respected numismatists in the country.

Oxford

The Ashmolean Museum contains

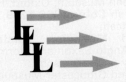
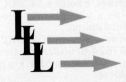

the oldest public collection in Great Britain; it was designed to serve the purposes of teaching. It is a very large and all embracing collection and like Cambridge, very important for serious students. It is currently under the curatorship of the eminent Dr Michael Metcalf, probably most famous as far as British collectors are concerned for his important work on thrymsas and sceattas.

Ireland

The Ulster Museum in Belfast has some very interesting display techniques and certainly makes the most of a relatively small collection. Most of this was done under the directorship of Bill Seaby in the 70s, but the present coin specialist, Robert Heslip, will always be very helpful. The National Museum of Ireland in Dublin has a very important collection but is presently being rehoused. The man in charge there, Michael Kenny, is particularly helpful, and hopefully will have more time for coins when his busy move is completed.

Some other important Museums

There are many other museums up and down the country which have excellent collections of British coins. The following are well worth a visit:
City Museum and Art Gallery, Chamberlain Square, Birmingham B3 3DH. (0120 235 2834). Especially good for coins produced in Birmingham.
Blackburn Museum, Museum Street, Blackburn, Lancs (01254 867170). Has a good reputation for numismatics.
City Museum, Queen's Road, Bristol, BS8 1RL (01179 223571). Especially good on coins of the Bristol mint.
Royal Albert Memorial Museum, Queen Street, Exeter EX4 3RX (01392 265858). Has a very good collection of Exeter mint coins.
Manx Museum, Douglas, Isle of Man (01624 675522). Particularly excellent for students of Viking and Hiberno-Norse.
City Museum, Municipal Buildings, The Headrow, Leeds, W. Yorkshire (01132

478279). An excellent all round collection.
Manchester Museum, The University, Manchester M13 (0161 275634). Another excellent all round collection.
Reading Museum and Art Gallery, Blagrave Street, Reading, Berks (01735 399809). Good medieval and interesting local finds.
The Yorkshire Museum, Museum Gardens, York YO1 2DR (01904 629745). Good for medieval and later English.

Many of our museums have co-operated with the British Academy to produce a wonderful series of books under the heading of Sylloge of coins of the British Isles which now runs to over 40 volumes. Some of these volumes refer to coins held in Museums overseas, but we list here the ones which deal with coins in these islands, and this will give students a better idea of some of the material they have for study.

1   Fitzwilliam Museum, Cambridge. Ancient British and Anglo-Saxon Coins, by P. Grierson.
2   Hunterian Museum, Glasgow. Anglo-Saxon Coins, by A.S. Robertson.
5   Grosvenor Museum, Chester. Coins with the Chester Mint-Signature, by E.J.E. Pirie.
6   National Museum of Antiquities of Scotland, Edinburgh. Anglo-Saxon Coins, by R.B.K. Stevenson.
8   British Museum. Hiberno-Norse Coins, by R.H.M. Dolley.
9   Ashmolean Museum, Oxford, Part 1, Anglo-Irish coins, John-Edward III, by M. Dolley and W. Seaby.
10   Ulster Museum. Belfast. Part 1, Anglo-Irish Coins, John-Edward III, by M. Dolley and W. Seaby.
11   Reading University, Anglo-Saxon and Norman Coins, by C.E. Blunt and M. Dolley.
12   Ashmolean Museum, Oxford, Part II. English Coins 1066-1279, by D.M. Metcalf.
17   Midland Museums, Ancient British, Anglo-Saxon and Norman Coins, by A.J.H. Gunsone.
19   Bristol and Gloucester Museums, Ancient British Coins, and Coins of the British and Gloucestershire

Mints, by L.V. Grinsell, C.E. Blunt and M. Dolley.

Coin Fairs

Whilst it is always important to visit museums to see coins, it is worth remembering that there is often a fine array on show at coin fairs around the country, and most dealers do not mind showing coins to would-be collectors, even if they cannot buy them on the spot.

The BNTA have been very successful with the COINEX shows, and the annual event at the Marriott Hotel should not be missed (10/11 October 1997). Likewise COINEX held each Spring (for further details contact BNTA Secretary 0181 398 4290).

Howard and Frances Simmons are the popular organisers of the Cumberland Coin shows, held at the Cumberland Hotel, London, since the late 1960s, (for details ring 0171 831 2080).

The Croydon team of Davidson/Monk organise the monthly shows at the Commonwealth Institute, Kensington, London W8 (ring 0181 656 4583).

David Fletcher organises the monthly Midland Coin & Stamp Fair, second Sunday every month (enquiries 01203 716160).

There are also fairs held at York racecourse in January and August. For information ring 01268 726687.

Finally for details of the successful Irish coin shows in Dublin ring Peter Sheen (003531 496 4390); and for the annual show in conjunction with the Irish Numismatic Society ring Ian Whyte (003531 874 6161).

British Coin Prices

ANCIENT BRITISH

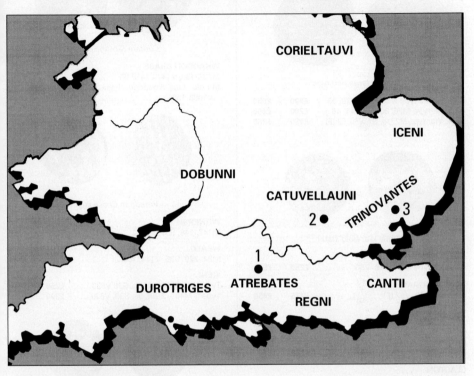

*The distribution of the tribes in Britain
based on the map in 'The coinage of
Ancient Britain', by R.P. Mack, published
by Spink and Son Ltd and B.A. Seaby Ltd.*

Key to towns:
1. Calleva Atrebatum (Silchester)
2. Verulamium (St Albans)
3. Camulodunum (Colchester)

It is always difficult to produce a priced catalogue of coins, but none is more difficult than the early British series. The market has developed considerably since the publication of R.D. Van Arsdell's *Celtic Coinage of Britain,* which is an essential book for collectors (584 pages, 54 plates and many other illustrations, maps and diagrams).

A word of caution, though; quite a number of forgeries exist, some of relatively recent production, and unfortunately also numerous items from undeclared hoards are on the market, which makes it essential to buy from a reputable dealer.

We are very grateful for the help of Robert Van Arsdell since he produced the synopsis of the material which we have used. We have kept this very basic, and simply linked it up for easy reference with *The Coinage of Ancient Britain* by R. P. Mack, third edition, London 1975 (now out of print), and with Seaby's *Standard Catalogue* Part 1. In the following lists Mack types are indicated by 'M' and Seaby types by 'S'. The V numbers relate to the Van Arsdell catalogue. The existence of forgeries is indicated by **(F).**

Gold staters without legends

AMBIANI

	F	VF
Large flan type M1, 3, S1, V10, 12	£500	£1600

Ambiani large flan type

	F	VF
Defaced die type M5, 7, S3, V30, 33	£300	£650
Abstract type M26, 30, S5, V44, 46	£200	£450
Gallic War type M27, a, S7, V50, 52 (F)	£130	£260

Gallic War gold stater

SUESSIONES

	F	VF
Abstract type M34a, S8, V85	£250	£500

VE MONOGRAM

	F	VF
M82, a, b, S9, V87 (F)	£275	£450

WESTERHAM

	F	VF
M28, 29, S19, V200, 202	£250	£450

CHUTE

	F	VF
M32, S20, V1205 (F)	£140	£240

CLACTON

	F	VF
Type I M47, S24, V1458	£260	£475
Type II M46, a, S25, V30, 1455	£250	£450

CORIELTAUVI

	F	VF
Type I M50-51a, S26 , V800	£200	£450
Type II M52-57, S27, V804	£275	£475

Norfolk Wolf stater VA610-3

NORFOLK

	F	VF
Wolf type M49, a, b, S28, V610 ...	£200	£450

	F	VF

CORIELLTAUVI

	F	VF
South Ferriby type, M449-450a, S.30, V.811	£180	£350

Coritani (South Ferriby)

WHADDON CHASE

	F	VF
M133-138, V1470-1478 (F)	£140	£320
Middle , Late Whaddon Chase V1485-1509	£220	£450

Whaddon Chase stater

WONERSH

	F	VF
M147, 148, S37, V1522	£275	£550

WEALD

	F	VF
M84, 229, S35, V144, 150	£350	£750

ICENI

	F	VF
Type I M397-399, 403b, S38 V620 ...	£250	£450
Type II M401, 2, 3a, 3c, S39, V626 ...	£300	£500

Iceni gold stater

ATREBATIC

	F	VF
M58-61, S41-2, V210-216	£250	£450

Atrebatic stater

SAVERNAKE FOREST

	F	VF
M62, S42, V1526	£150	£350

DOBUNNIC

	F	VF
M374, S43, V1005	£250	£550

Gold quarter staters without legends

Ambiani quarter stater

AMBIANI	F	VF
Large flan type M2, 4, S2, V15, 20	£250	£650
Defaced die type M6, 8, S4, V35, 37	£200	£450
GEOMETRIC		
M37, 39, 41, 41A, 42, S6, V65, 146, 69, 67	£75	£190
SUSSEX		
M40, 43-45, S49, V143, 1225-1229	£70	£160
VE MONOGRAM		
M83, S10, V87 (F)	£160	£350

Atrebatic quarter stater, Bognor Cog Wheel

ATREBATIC		
M63-67, 69-75, S51, V220-256	£100	£270

Caesar's trophy, quarter stater VA145

KENTISH		
Caesar's Trophy type V145	£100	£200
ATREBATIC		
M63-67, 69-75, S51, V220-256	£100	£275

Gold staters with legends

COMMIUS	F	VF
M92, S85, V350	£800	£2000
TINCOMARUS		
M93, 93, S86, V362, 363	£600	£1500
VERICA		
Equestrian type M121, S98, V500 ...	£350	£800
Vine leaf type M125, S99, V520 ...	£500	£950

Verica gold stater

EPATICCUS		
M262, S112, V575	£600	£1500

	F	VF
DUBNOVELLAUNUS		
In Kent M283, S118, V176	£400	£900
In Essex M275, S152, V1650	£450	£950
EPPILLUS		
In Kent M300-1, S127-8, V430	£600	£1500
ADDEDOMAROS		
M266, 7, S148, V1605 (F)	£200	£500
TASCIOVANUS		
Bucranium M149, S157, V1680 (F)	£250	£600

VOLISIOS DUMNOCOVEROS

Equestrian M154-7, S158, V1730-1736	£275	£500
TASCIO/RICON M184, S161, V1780	£700	£1600
ANDOCO		
M197, S202, V1860	£500	£1100

Tasciovanus Celtic Warrior

CUNOBELINE		
Two horses M201, S207, V1910 ...	£700	£1500
Corn ear M203 etc. S208, V2010 (F)	£240	£500

ANDOCO Stater

ANTED of the Dobunni		
M385-6, S260, V1062-1066 (F)	£450	£900
EISU		
M388, S262, V1105 (F)	£700	£1500
INAM		
M390, S264, V1140 (F)	extremely rare	
CATTI		
M391, S265, V1130 (F)	£450	£800
COMUX		
M392, S266, V1092 (F)	£650	£1500
CORIO		
M393, S267, V1035	£450	£800

ANCIENT BRITISH

	F	VF
BODVOC		
M395, S269, V1052 (F) … … … … …	**£650**	**£1400**

Bodvoc

	F	VF
VEP CORF		
M459-460, S291, V940, 930 (F) … …	**£350**	**£750**
DUMNOC TIGIR SENO		
M461, S299, V972 (F) … … … … …	**£750**	**£1500**
VOLISIOS DUMNOCOVEROS		
M463, S301, V978 … … … … … …	**£450**	**£850**

Cunobeline quarter stater V.1913-1

Gold quarter staters with legends

	F	VF
TINCOMARUS	F	VF
Abstract type M95, S87, V365 … …	**£275**	**£500**
Medusa head type M97, S89, V387	**£300**	**£600**
Tablet type M101-4, S90, V387-390	**£170**	**£350**

Tincommius Medusa head gold quarter stater

	F	VF
EPPILLUS		
CALLEVA M107, S95, V407 … … …	**£130**	**£250**

Eppillus CALLEVA type

	F	VF
VERICA	F	VF
Horse type M111-114, S100,		
V465-468 … … … … … … … … …	**£120**	**£250**
TASCIOVANUS		
Horse type M152-3, S163, V1690,		
1692 … … … … … … … … … …	**£130**	**£275**
CUNOBELINE		
Various types, from … … … … … …	**£150**	**£350**

Silver coins without legends

DUROTRIGES		
Silver stater M317, S60, V1235 **(F)**	**£35**	**£110**
Geometric type M319, S61, V1242	**£35**	**£85**
Starfish type M320, S61A, V1270 …	**£50**	**£100**

Starfish Unit

DOBUNNIC		
Face M374a, b, 5, 6, 8, S63, V1020	**£25**	**£60**
Abstract M378a-384d, S64, V1042	**£15**	**£45**
CORIELTAUVI		
Boar type M405a, S66, V855 … …	**£75**	**£160**
South Ferriby M410 etc, S68, V875	**£50**	**£100**

Coritani, showing boar and horse

ICENI		
Boar type M407-9, S72, V655-659 …	**£35**	**£90**
Wreath type M414, 5, 440, S75, V679,		
675 … … … … … … … … … …	**£15**	**£45**
Face type M412-413e, S74, V665 …	**£40**	**£100**
QUEEN BOUDICA		
Face type M413, 413D, V790, 792 …	**£70**	**£150**

Silver coins of Boudica (left) and Commius (right)

COMMIUS		
Head left M446b, V355, 357 … … …	**£50**	**£125**

Silver coins with legends

	F	VF
EPPILLUS	F	VF
CALLEVA type M108, S96, V415 …	**£55**	**£120**
EPATICCUS		
Eagle type M263, S113, V580 … …	**£30**	**£95**
Victory type M263a, S114, V581 …	**£35**	**£120**

Silver unit, Epaticcus

CARATACUS	F	VF
Eagle Type M265, S117, V593 (F) ...	£150	£350

TASCIOVANUS		
Equestrian M158, S167, V1745	£90	£250
VER type M161, S170, V1699	£90	£220

CUNOBELINE		
Equestrian M216-8, S215, 6, V1951, 1953, 2047	£70	£160
Bust right M236, S221, VA2055 ...	£100	£250

ANTED of the Dobunni		
M387, S261, V1082	£80	£160

EISU		
M389, S263, V1110	£90	£200

BODVOC		
M396, S270, V1057 (F)	£130	£400

ANTED of the Iceni		
M419-421, S273, V710, 711, 715 ...	£15	£30

ECEN		
M424, S275, V730	£18	£35

EDNAM		
M423, 425b, S277, V740, 734	£40	£80

ECE		
M425a, 426, 7, 8, S278-280, V761, 764, 762, 766	£20	£40

AESU		
M432, S282, V775	£70	£150

PRASUTAGUS		
King of the Iceni (husband of Boudica)	£650	£1100

ESUP ASU		
M4566, S289, VA924	£400	*

VEP CORF		
M460b, 464, S292, V394, 950	£150	£300

DUMNOC TIGIR SENO		
M462, S300 V974	£150	£350

VOLISIOS DUMNOCOVEROS		
M463a, S302, V978, 980	£150	£350

ALE SCA		
M469, S285, V996	£300	*

Bronze, base metal coins without legends

POTIN	F	VF
Experimental type M22a, S83, V104	£60	£100

Potin coin class II

	F	VF
Class I M9-22, S83, V122-131	£20	£65
Class II M23-25, S84, V136-139	£35	£95
Thurrock Types V1402-1442	£25	£50

ARMORICAN		
Billon stater S12-17	£30	£75
Billon quarter stater S18	£40	£100

DUROTRIGES		
Bronze stater M318, S81, V1290 ...	£25	£50
Cast type M332-370, S82 V1322-1370	£45	£90

NORTH THAMES		
M273, 274, 281, S77, V1646 1615, 1669	£45	£120

NORTH KENT		
M295, 296, S80, V154	£80	£170

Bronze coins with legends

DUBNOVELLAUNUS in Essex	F	VF
M277, 8, S154, V1665, 1667	£50	£140

TASCIOVANUS		
Head, beard M168, 9, S179, V1707	£50	£150
VERLAMIO M172, S183, V1808	£50	£150
Head, VER M177, S189, V1816	£70	£200
Boar, VER M179, S191, V1713	£80	£250
Equestrian M190, S195, V1892	£70	£200
Centaur M192, S197, V1882	£80	£250

ANDOCO		
M200, S205, V1871	£150	£400

CUNOBELINE		
Victory, TASC M221, S233, V1971 ...	£60	£150
Victory, CUN M22, a, S234, V1973 ...	£50	£100
Winged animal, M225, S237, V2081	£60	£120

Cunobeline bronze with Centaur reverse

Head, beard, M226, 9, S238, V2131, 2085	£70	£150
Panel, sphinx, M230, S241, V1977 ...	£70	£150
Winged beast, M231, S242, V1979	£70	£150
Centaur, M242, S245, V2089	£50	£200
Sow, M243, S246, V2091	£50	£120
Warrior, M244, S247, V2093	£40	£120
Boar, TASC M245, S248, V1983 ...	£75	£200
Bull, TASC M246, S249, V2095 ...	£50	£100
Metal worker, M248, S251, V2097 ...	£60	£150
Pegasus, M249, S252, V2099	£70	£150
Horse, CAMV, M250, S253, V2101 ...	£65	£150
Jupiter, horse, M251, S254, V2103 ...	£65	£200
Janus head, M252 S255, V2105 ...	£80	£250
Jupiter, lion, M253, S256, V1207 ...	£60	£150
Sphinx, fig, M260, a, S257, V2109	£65	£200

ENGLISH HAMMERED
Gold from 1344 and Silver from *circa* 600

Prices in this section are approximately what collectors can expect to pay for the commonest types of the coins listed; for most other types prices will range upwards from these amounts. Precise valuations cannot be given since they vary from dealer to dealer and, in any case, have to be determined by consideration of a number of factors eg, the coin's condition (which is of prime importance in deciding its value).

For more detailed information refer to English Hammered Coins, *Volumes 1 and 2, by J.J. North and published by Spink and Son Ltd. Any serious collectors should also obtain a copy of the important new volume,* The Herbert Schneider Collection, Volume One, English Gold Coins 1257-1603, *published by Spink and Son, 1996.*

GOLD COINS
The Plantagenet Kings

Henry III gold penny

HENRY III 1216-1272 ... ... F VF
Gold Penny   ... ...
This specimen sold for £159,500 (including buyers premium) at a Spink auction on 9 July 1996.

Edward III quarter noble

EDWARD III 1327-77	F	VF
Third coinage		
Florins or Double leopard	ext. rare	
Half florins or leopard...	ext. rare	
Quarter florins or helms	ext. rare	
Nobles ... ... from	£800	£2000
Half nobles	£1300	£3500
Quarter nobles	£300	£800
Fourth coinage		
Pre-treaty with France (i.e. before 1315) with French title		
Nobles	£325	£650
Half nobles	£200	£450
Quarter nobles	£125	£300
Transitional treaty period, 1361. Aquitaine title added		
Nobles	£390	£700
Half nobles	£190	£450
Quarter nobles	£130	£300
Treaty period 1361-9 omits FRANC		
Nobles, London	£290	£600

Nobles, Calais		
(C in centre of rev.)	£320	£700
Half nobles, London	£190	£350
Half nobles, Calais	£290	£650
Quarter nobles, London	£120	£270
Quarter nobles, Calais	£150	£300

Post-treaty period 1369-77 French title resumed

Nobles, London	£320	£650
Nobles, Calais		
(flag at stern or C in centre)	£375	£700
Half nobles, London	ext. rare	
Half nobles, Calais	£400	£900

There are many other issues and varieties in this reign. These prices relate to the commoner pieces.

Richard II London half noble

RICHARD II 1377-99		
Nobles, London	£500	£900
Nobles, Calais		
(flag at stern)	£550	£1100
Half nobles, London	£550	£1250
Half nobles, Calais		
(flag at stern)	£650	£1800
Quarter nobles	£300	£700

There are many different varieties and different styles of lettering.

HENRY IV 1399-1413		
Heavy coinage		
Nobles (120grs) London	£3000	*
Nobles, Calais (flag at stern)	ext. rare	
Half nobles, London	ext. rare	
Half nobles, Calais	ext. rare	
Quarter nobles, London	£950	£2000
Quarter nobles, Calais	£1000	£2500
Light coinage		
Nobles (108grs)	£750	£1800
Half nobles	£2500	*
Quarter nobles	£450	£950

Henry V noble

HENRY V 1413-22

	F	VF
Nobles, many varieties, from	£380	£650
Half nobles	£350	£750
Quarter nobles	£190	£350

This reign sees an increase in the use of privy marks to differentiate issues.

Henry VI noble, Annulet issue

HENRY VI 1422-61
Annulet issue (1422-27)

	F	VF
Nobles, London	£300	£600
Nobles, Calais (flag at stern)	£400	£900
Nobles, York	£475	£950
Half nobles, London	£220	£450
Half nobles, Calais	£400	£850
Half nobles, London	£450	£850
Quarter nobles, London	£140	£280
Quarter nobles, Calais	£200	£450
Quarter nobles, York	£250	£475

Rosette-mascle issue 1427-30

	F	VF
Nobles, London	£575	£1250
Nobles, Calais	£650	£1500
Half nobles, London	£750	£1500
Half nobles, Calais	£900	£1800
Quarter nobles, London	£275	£550
Quarter nobles, Calais	£350	£650

Pinecone-mascle issue 1430-4

	F	VF
Nobles, London	£600	£1250
Half nobles, London	ext. rare	
Quarter noble	unique	

Henry VI quarter noble, leaf-mascle

	F	VF
Leaf-mascle issue 1434-5		
Nobles	£1500	£3000
Half nobles	ext. rare	
Quarter nobles	£1250	£2500
Leaf-trefoil issue 1435-8		
Nobles	ext. rare	
Quarter noble	unique	
Trefoil issue 1438-43		
Nobles	£1500	£3500
Leaf-pellet issue 1445-54		
Nobles	£1500	£3500

Henry VI noble, leaf-pellet

	F	VF
Cross-pellet issue 1454-60		
Nobles	unique	
EDWARD IV 1st reign 1461-70		
Heavy coinage 1461-64/5		
Nobles (108grs)	£3500	*
Quarter noble	unique	

Edward IV noble, heavy coinage

Light coinage 1464-70

	F	VF
Ryals or rose nobles (120grs),		
London	£300	£600
Flemish copy	£275	£475
Ryals, Bristol (B in waves)	£400	£800
Ryals, Coventry (C in waves))	£650	£1500
Ryals, Norwich (N in waves)	£700	£1600
Ryals, York (E in waves)	£350	£800
Half ryals, London	£275	£450
Half ryals, Bristol (B in waves) ...	£350	£850
Half ryals, Coventry (C in waves) ...	£1000	*
Half ryals Norwich (N in waves) ...	£1250	*
Half ryals, York (E in waves)	£300	£650
Quarter ryals	£190	£400
Angels	£3500	*

HAMMERED GOLD

Edward IV angel, first reign

HENRY VI (restored) 1470-71

Angels, London	£600	£1350
Angels, Bristol (B in waves)	£800	£2000
Half angels, London	£1500	£3500
Half angels, Bristol (B in waves) ...		unique

EDWARD IV 2nd reign 1471-83

Angels, London	£240	£500
Angels, Bristol (B in waves)	£800	£2000
Half angels, some varieties	£200	£480

EDWARD IV or V

mm halved sun and rose

Angels	£950	£2500

EDWARD V 1483

mm boar's head on obverse, halved sun and rose on reverse.

Angels	£7000	*
Half angel		ext. rare

RICHARD III 1483-5

Angel, reading EDWARD, with R over E by mast		unique
Angels, as before, but *mm* boar's head		unique
Angels, reading RICARD or RICAD	£700	£1500
Half angels	£3500	*

Richard III half angel

The Tudor Monarchs

Henry VII sovereign

HENRY VII 1485-1509

	F	VF
Sovereigns of 20 shillings (all ext. rare) from	£5000	£9500
Ryals	£8000	£16000

Angels, varieties, different *mm* from	£275	£500
Half angels	£200	£425

HENRY VIII 1509-47

First coinage 1509-26

Sovereigns of 20 shillings *mm*

crowned portcullis only	£3000	*
Angels (6s 8d) ... ... from	£275	£600
Half angels	£200	£450

Second coinage 1526-44

Sovereigns of 22s 6d, various *mm* ...	£2500	£6000
Angels (7s 6d)	£300	£650
Half angels *mm* lis	£450	£950
George-nobles *mm* rose	£2500	£6000
Half-George noble		unique
Crowns of the rose *mm* rose		ext. rare

(Very seldom on the market – one fetched £10,000 + 10% at Sotheby's in May 1994)

Crowns of the double-rose

HK (Henry and Katherine of Aragon)	£250	£500
HA (Henry and Anne Boleyn) ...	£300	£700
HI (Henry and Jane Seymour) ...	£350	£600
HR (HENRICUS REX)	£200	£450

Halfcrowns of the double-rose

HK	£250	£650
HI	£250	£650
HR	£375	£750

Third coinage 1544-47

Sovereigns of 20s, London ... from	£1800	£5000
Sovereigns of 20s, Southwark	£1600	£3500
Sovereigns of 20s, Bristol	£2750	£6000
Half sovereigns, London	£295	£575
Half sovereigns, Southwark	£350	£700
Half sovereigns, Bristol	£400	£950

Henry VIII Angel, 3rd coinage

Angels	£250	£450
Half angels	£250	£450
Quarter angels	£250	£475
Crowns, HENRIC 8, London	£200	£450
Crowns, Southwark	£250	£475
Crowns, Bristol	£250	£500
Halfcrowns, London	£200	£450
Halfcrowns, Southwark	£250	£500
Halfcrowns, Bristol	£300	£600

EDWARD VI 1547-53

Posthumous coinage in name of Henry VIII (1547-51)

Sovereigns, London	£2000	£4750
Sovereigns, Bristol	£2250	£5000
Half sovereigns, London	£300	£650
Half sovereigns, Southwark	£300	£650
Crowns, London	£350	£700
Crowns, Southwark	£450	£900
Halfcrowns, London	£300	£650
Halfcrowns, Southwark	£300	£650

Coinage in Edward's own name

First period 1547-49

Half sovereigns, Tower, read EDWARD 6	£450	£950

Edward VI sovereign, posthumous coinage

	F	VF
Half sovereigns, Southwark	£450	£950
Crown	ext. rare	
Halfcrowns	ext. rare	

Second period 1549-50

	F	VF
Sovereigns	£1800	£4500
Half sovereigns, uncrowned bust London	ext. rare	
Half sovereigns, SCUTUM on obv. ...	£500	£1250
Half sovereigns, Durham House MDXL VII	ext. rare	
Half sovereigns, crowned bust, London	£500	£1250
Half sovereigns, half-length bust, Durham House	£4000	£8500
Crowns, uncrowned bust	£800	£1500
Crowns, crowned bust	£650	£1350
Halfcrowns, uncrowned bust	£550	£1250
Halfcrowns, crowned bust	£750	£1250

Edward VI fine sovereign of 30s third period

Third period 1550-53

	F	VF
'Fine' sovereigns of 30s, king enthroned	£7500	£20000
Sovereigns of 20s, half-length figure ...	£950	£2500
Half sovereigns, similar to last ...	£550	£1400
Crowns, similar but SCUTUM on rev ...	£650	£1600
Halfcrowns, similar	£750	£1800
Angels	£4000	£9000
Half angel	unique	

MARY 1553-4

	F	VF
Sovereigns, different dates, some undated, some *mms*	£1600	£4000
Ryals, dated MDUI (1553)	£7500	£15000
Angels, *mm* pomegranate	£650	£1400
Half angels	£2000	£6500

Mary Gold Sovereign of 1553

PHILIP AND MARY 1554-8 ... ...

	F	VF
Angels, *mm* lis	£1350	£3000
Half angels	ext. rare	

Philip and Mary angel

Elizabeth I 1558-1603
Hammered issues

	F	VF
'Fine' sovereigns of 30s, different issues from	£1700	£4000
Ryals	£3000	£9000
Angels, different issues	£300	£500
Half angels	£220	£475
Quarter angels	£200	£400

Elizabeth I quarter angel

HAMMERED GOLD

	F	VF
Pounds of 20 shillings, only one issue	£650	£1400
Half pounds, different issues	£425	£850
Crowns —	£300	£650
Halfcrowns —	£250	£600

Elizabeth I hammered halfcrown

Milled issues

	F	VF
Half pounds, one issue but different marks	£700	£1800
Crowns —	£800	£2000
Halfcrowns —	£1200	£3000

The Stuart Kings

James I gold Spur-ryal

JAMES I 1603-25
1st coinage 1603-4

	F	VF
Sovereigns of 20 shillings two bust	£800	£1800
Half sovereigns	£2000	£4000
Crowns	£800	£2500
Halfcrowns	£250	£700

2nd coinage 1604-19

	F	VF
Rose-ryals of 30 shillings	£750	£2000
Spur-ryals of 15 shillings	£2000	£4000
Angels	£500	£1250
Half angels	£1500	£4000
Unites, different busts	£200	£450
Double crowns —	£160	£400
Britain crowns —	£130	£275

James I Rose-ryal of 30 shillings

	F	VF
Halfcrowns —	£120	£240
Thistle crowns, varieties	£135	£275

James I Thistle crown

3rd coinage 1619-25

	F	VF
Rose-ryals, varieties	£950	£2500
Spur-ryals	£2200	£4500
Angels	£600	£1500
Laurels, different busts	£200	£450
Half Laurels	£170	£350
Quarter laurels	£130	£220

James I laurel

CHARLES I 1625-49
Tower Mint 1625-43
Initial marks: lis, cross calvary, negro's head, castle, anchor, heart, plume, rose, harp, portcullis, bell, crown, tun, triangle, star, triangle in circle

	F	VF
Angels, varieties	£700	£1800
Angels, pierced as touchpieces	£400	£800
Unites –	£210	£450
Double Crowns –	£170	£375
Crowns –	£135	£250

Tower Mint under Parliament 1643-8
Initial marks: (P), (R), eye, sun, sceptre

Unites, varieties	£325	£700
Double crowns –	£400	£900
Crowns –	£250	£475

Briot's milled issues 1631-2 (ext. rare)
Initial marks: anemone and **B**, daisy and **B, B**

Angels	£5000	*
Unites	£900	£2000
Double crowns	£650	£1500
Crowns	ext. rare	

Coins of provincial mints
Aberystwyth 1638-42

Unite		unique

Shrewsbury 1642

Triple unite (£3 piece)	£30000	£60000

Oxford 1642-46

Triple unites, varieties from ...	£2250	£5000
Unites –	£650	£1250
Half unites –	£500	£1000

Charles I Oxford triple unite, 1643

Bristol 1643-45

Unites		ext. rare
Half unites		ext. rare

Truro 1642-43

Unites		ext. rare

Chester

Unites		ext. rare

Siege pieces 1645-49
Colchester besieged 1648

Ten shillings **(F)**		ext. rare

Pontefract besieged 1648-49

Unites **(F)**		ext. rare

Commonwealth 1649-60 gold unite

COMMONWEALTH 1649-60	F	VF
Unites *im* sun	£400	£850
– *im* anchor	£1250	£3000
Double crowns *im* sun	£350	£700
– *im* anchor	£1000	£2500
Crowns *im* sun	£275	£550
– *im* anchor	£1250	*

Commonwealth crown

CHARLES II 1660-85
Hammered Coinage 1660-62

Charles II gold unite

Unites, two issues from	£500	£1400
Double crowns –	£500	£1200
Crowns –	£450	£950

SILVER COINS

In this section column headings are mainly F (Fine) and VF (Very Fine), but for pe nies of the early Plantagenets – a series in which higher-grade coins are seldom ava able – prices are shown under the headings Fair and F. Again it should be noted th throughout the section prices are approximate, for the commonest types only, a are the amounts collectors can expect to pay – not dealers' buying price Descriptions of some early Anglo-Saxon coins are, of necessity, brief because pressure on space. Descriptions such as 'cross/moneyer's name' indicate that a cro appears on the obverse and the moneyer's name on the reverse. For more details s Standard Catalogue of British Coins – Volume 1 published by B. A. Seaby Ltd, ai English Hammered Coins, Volumes 1 and 2, by J. J. North, published by Spink a Son Ltd. (A new edition of Volume 2 was published in 1991 and a new edition Volume 1 was published in 1994).

Anglo-Saxon Sceats and Stycas

Two superb sceats

	F	VF
EARLY PERIOD c 600-750		
Silver sceats ... ...from	£60	£150

A fascinating series with great variation of styles of early art. Large numbers of types and varieties.

NORTHUMBRIAN KINGS c 737-867		
Silver sceats c 737-796 ...from	£150	£350
Copper stycas c 810-867 ...from	£12	£35

Struck for many kings. Numerous moneyers and different varieties. The copper styca is the commonest coin in the Anglo-Saxon series.

ARCHBISHOPS OF YORK c 732-900		
Silver sceats ... ...from	£75	£160
Copper stycas ... ...from	£35	£75

From here onwards until the reign of Edward I all coins are silver pennies unless otherwise stated

Kings of Kent

	F	VF
HEABERHT c 764		
Monogram/cross	ext. rare	

One moneyer (EOBA).

ECGBERHT c 765-780		
Monogram/cross	£1700	£4000

Two moneyers (BABBA and UDD)

EADBERHT PRAEN 797-798		
EADBERHT REX/moneyer	£2000	£4500

Three moneyers

Penny of Eadberht Praen

CUTHRED 789-807		
Non-portrait, various designs from	£450	£950
Bust right	£550	£1250

Different moneyers, varieties etc.

BALDRED c 825		
Bust right	£900	£2750
Cross/cross	£700	£2000

different types and moneyers

Baldred penny, bust right

ANONYMOUS c 823	F	V
Bust right	£600	£17

Different varieties and moneyers.

Archbishops of Canterbury

JAENBERHT 766-792	F	
Various types (non-portrait) from	£1250	£26
AETHELHEARD 793-805		
Various types (non-portrait) from	£1250	£25
WULFRED 805-832		
Various groups (portrait types) from	£600	£12
CEOLNOTH 833-870		
Various groups (portrait types) from	£300	£7

Ceolnot penny

AETHERED 870-889		
Various types (portrait, non-portrait)	ext. ra	
PLEGMUND 890-914		
Various types (all non-portrait) from	£375	£9

Kings of Mercia

Offa portrait penny

OFFA 757-796	F	V
Non-portrait from	£370	£75
Portrait from	£650	£14

Many types and varieties

HAMMERED SILVER

Cynethryth
(wife of Offa)
portrait
penny

Eadwald penny

CYNETHRYTH (wife of Offa)	F	VF
Portraits	£2500	£5500
Non-portrait	£2500	£4500

COENWULF 796-821
Various types (portrait, non-portrait) from £300 £650

Coenwulf portrait penny.

CEOLWULF I 821-823		
Various types (portrait)	£650	£1600

BEORNWULF 823-825		
Various types (portrait)	£900	£2500

Beornwulf penny

LUDICA 825-827
Two types (portrait) (F) ... ... ext. rare

WIGLAF 827-829, 830-840
Two groups (portrait, non-portrait) £1800 £4500

BERHTWULF 840-852
Two groups
(portrait, non-portrait) £750 £2000

Berhtwult penny

BURGRED 852-874
One type (portrait), five variants £95 £200

CEOLWULF II 874-c 877
Two types (portrait)) ... ... £3750 *

Kings of East Anglia

BEONNA c 758	F	VF
Silver sceat	£450	£950

AETHELBERHT LUL (died 794)
Portrait type (F) ... ... ext. rare

EADWALD c 796	F	
Non-portrait types	£1250	£30

AETHELSTAN I c 850
Various types (portrait, non-
portrait) £375 £8

AETHELWEARD c 850
Non-portrait types £500 £12

EADMUND 855-870
Non-portrait types £300 £6

Viking Invaders 878-954

ALFRED F
Imitations of Alfred pennies etc. from £300 £5
(Many different types, portrait and non portrait)

ANGLIA
AETHELSTAN II 878-890
Cross/moneyer ... ... very ra

OSWALD (Unknown in history except from coins)
A/cross ... ... very ra

ALFDENE (uncertain c 900)
Penny and halfpenny ... ... ext. ra

ST EADMUND
Memorial coinage, various
legends etc. £80 £1
Many moneyers.
Halfpenny, similar £400 £12

St Eadmund memorial penny

ST MARTIN OF LINCOLN c 925
Sword/cross £2000

AETHELRED c 870
Temple/cross ... ... ext. ra

YORK
SIEVERT-SIEFRED-CNUT c 897
Crosslet/small cross £95 £1
Many different groups and varieties
Halfpenny, similar £450 £9

EARL SIHTRIC (unknown)
Non-portrait ... ... ext. ra

REGNALD c 919-921
Various types, some blundered £2000 £45

SIHTRIC I 921-927
Sword/cross ... ... ext. ra

ANLAF GUTHFRITHSSON 939-941
Raven/cross £2750 £60
Cross/cross ... ... ext. ra
Flower/cross ... ... ext. ra

LAF SIHTRICSSON 941-944, 948-952 | F | VF
ious types ... ... | **£2000** | **£6000**

TRIC II c 942-943
eld/standard ... ... | ext. rare

GNALD II c 941-943
ss/cross ... ... | **£3500** | *
eld/standard ... ... | **£3500** | *

C BLOODAXE 948, 952-954
ss/moneyer ... ... | ext. rare
ord/cross ... ... | **£3250** | **£6500**

St Peter of York halfpenny

PETER OF YORK c 905-927
ious types ... ...from | **£250** | **£650**
fpenny, similar ... ... | **£750** | *

ings of Wessex

ORHTRIC 786-802 ... ... | F | VF
o types (non-portrait) ... ... | ext. rare

GBERHT 802-839
UR GROUPS (portrait, non-portrait) | **£850** | **£2500**
nts of Canterbury, London, Rochester, Winchester

THELWULF 839-858
ur phases (portrait, non-portrait) | **£250** | **£575**
m Mints of Canterbury, Rochester (?)

THELBERHT 858-866
o types (portrait) ... ...from | **£220** | **£500**
ny moneyers.

THELRED I 865-871
rtrait types ... ...from | **£275** | **£750**
ny moneyers.

FRED THE GREAT 871-899
rtrait in style of Aethelred I ... | **£350** | **£800**
ur other portrait types commonest being those
h the London monogram reverse | **£650** | **£1500**
fpennies ... ... | **£700** | **£1500**

Alfred the Great penny, London monogram

n-portrait types ... ...from | **£250** | **£500**
ny different styles of lettering etc.
lfpennies ... ... | **£450** | **£975**

WARD THE ELDER 899-924
n-portrait types:
oss/moneyer's name in two lines | **£130** | **£275**
lfpennies as previous ... ... | ext. rare

HAMMERED SILVER

Rare penny of Edward the Elder

Portrait types: ... ... | F | VF
Bust/moneyer's name ... ... | **£350** | **£950**
Many types, varieties and moneyers.

Kings of all England

AETHELSTAN 924-39 ... ... | F | VF
Non-portrait types:
Cross/moneyer's name in two lines | **£200** | **£450**
Cross/cross ... ... | **£200** | **£400**

Portrait types:
bust/moneyer's name ... ... | **£475** | **£1400**
Bust/small cross ... ... | **£425** | **£1200**
Many other issues. There are also different mints
and moneyer's names.

Aethelstan portrait penny

EADMUND 939-46
Non-portrait types:
Cross or rosette/moneyer's name
in two lines ... ... | **£160** | **£400**
Silver halfpenny, similar ... ... | **£800** | **£2000**

Eadmund penny, two-line type

Portrait types:
Crowned bust/small cross ... ... | **£300** | **£1250**
Helmeted bust/cross crosslet ... | **£750** | **£2500**
Many other issues and varieties; also different
mint names and moneyers.

EADRED 946-55
Non-portrait types:
Cross/moneyer's name in two lines | **£130** | **£325**
Silver halfpenny similar ... ... | **£700** | **£1500**
Rosette/moneyer's name ... ... | **£150** | **£400**

HAMMERED SILVER

Eadred penny, portrait type

Portrait types:	F	VF
Crowned bust/small cross	£350	£1200

Again many variations and mint names and moneyers.

HOWEL DDA (King of Wales), died c948
Small cross/moneyer's name in two lines (GILLYS)		unique

EADWIG 955-59
Non-portrait types:
Cross/moneyer's name ... from	£190	£500

Many variations, some rare.
Silver halfpennies, similar		ext. rare

Portrait types:
Bust/cross		ext. rare

EADGAR 959-75
Non-portrait types:
Cross/moneyer's name ... from	£110	£260
Cross/cross ... ... from	£110	£220
Rosette/rosette ... ... from	£150	£300
Halfpennies		ext. rare

Eadgar non-portrait penny

Portrait type:
Pre-Reform	£450	£1250
Halfpenny, diademed bust/London monogram		ext. rare
Post Reform	£475	£1000

Many other varieties.

EDWARD THE MARTYR 975-78
Portrait types:
Bust left/small cross	£650	£1500

Many different mints and moneyers.

AETHELRED II 978-1016
First small cross ... ... from	£400	£1250
First hand ... ... from	£90	£200
Second hand ... ... from	£80	£140
Benediction hand ... from	£450	£1200
CRUX ... ... from	£80	£140

Aethelred II CRUX type penny

	F	
Long Cross	£80	£1.
Helmet	£85	£1¦
Agnus Dei		ext. ra

Other issues and varieties, many mint names an moneyers.

Aethelred II long cross penny

CNUT 1016-35
Quatrefoil ... ... from	£80	£1·

Cnut quatrefoil type penny

Pointed helmet ... ... from	£80	£1·

Cnut pointed helmet type

Small cross ... ... from	£80	£1:
Jewel cross ... ... from	£650	

Other types, and many different mint names and moneyers.

HAROLD I 1035-40
Jewel cross ... ... from	£190	£4¦
Long cross with trefoils ... from	£175	£3¦
Long cross with fleurs-de-lis from	£175	£3¦

Many different mint names and moneyers.

HARTHACNUT 1035-42
Jewel cross, bust left	£750	£18(
– bust right	£700	£16(
Arm and sceptre types	£800	£17(
Different mint names and moneyers.		
Scandinavian types struck at Lund	£200	£4·

EDWARD THE CONFESSOR 1042-66
PACX type ... ... from	£150	£4(
Radiate crown/small cross from	£80	£1¦
Trefoil quadrilateral	£80	£14
Small flan ... ... from	£80	£12
Expanding cross types ... from	£85	£14

Edward the Confessor expanding cross penny

COINS MARKET VALU

	F	VF
...inted helmet types	£80	£140
...vereign/eagles	£100	£175
...ammer cross	£80	£135
...st facing	£80	£130
...oss and piles	£95	£150
...rge bust, facing, with sceptre	£1000	£2500

...her issues, including a unique gold penny; many ...fferent mint names and moneyers.

AROLD II 1066

...owned head left with sceptre	£350	£650

Harold II, bust left, without sceptre

...milar but not sceptre	£400	£800
...owned head right with sceptre	£750	£1500

The Norman Kings

...ILLIAM I 1066-87

	F	VF
...ofile/cross fleury ... ...from	£140	£360
...onnet ... ...from	£110	£200
...anopy ... ...from	£200	£400
...vo sceptres ... ...from	£135	£350
...vo stars ... ...from	£120	£200
...word ... ...from	£200	£450

William I profile/cross fleury penny

...ofile/cross and trefoils ...from	£300	£650
...AXS ... ...from	£100	£150

...ILLIAM II 1087-1100

...ofile ... ...from	£270	£575
...ross in quatrefoil ... ...from	£220	£475
...ross voided ... ...from	£220	£500
...oss pattee over fleury ...from	£350	£700
...ross fleury and piles ... ...from	£400	£800

Henry I penny; small bust/cross and annulets

...ENRY I 1100-1135

...nnulets ... ...from	£250	£600
...ofile/cross fleury ... ...from	£200	£400
...AX ... ...from	£250	£450
...nnulets and piles ... ...from	£300	£600
...oided cross and fleurs ...from	£500	£975
...ointing bust and stars ... ...from	£650	£1250
...uatrefoil and piles ... ...from	£275	£500
...ofile/cross and annulets from	£600	£1400
...ross in quatrefoil ... ...from	£470	£900

HAMMERED SILVER

	F	VF
Full face/cross fleury	£170	£350
Double inscription	£325	£650
Small bust/cross and annulets	£250	£500
Star in lozenge fleury	£250	£500
Pellets in quatrefoil	£130	£290
Quadrilateral on cross fleury ...	£110	£230
Halfpennies	£1500	£3000

STEPHEN 1135-54

Cross moline (Watford) ...from	£95	£190

Stephen 'Watford' penny

Cross moline PERERIC	£350	£700
Voided cross and mullets	£170	£400

Stephen penny, voided cross pattée with mullets

Profile/cross fleury	£300	£750
Voided cross pommée (Awbridge)	£200	£420

There are also a number of irregular issues produced during the Civil War, all of which are very rare. These include several extremely rare and attractive pieces bearing the names of barons, such as Eustace Fitzjohn and Robert de Stuteville.

The Plantagenet Kings

HENRY II 1154-89

	Fair	F
Cross and crosslets ('Tealby' coinage)	£25	£50

The issue is classified by bust variants into six groups, struck at 32 mints.

Henry II Tealby penny

	F	VF
Short cross pennies	£30	£70

The 'short cross' coinage was introduced in 1180 and continued through successive reigns until Henry III brought about a change in 1247. HENRICVS REX appears on all these coins but they can be classified into reigns by the styles of the busts and lettering. We recommend a copy of C.R. Wren's illustrated guide The Short Cross Coinage 1180-1247, *as the best guide to identification.*

RICHARD I 1189-99

Short cross pennies	£40	£80

HAMMERED SILVER

JOHN 1199-1216

Short cross pennies £35   £70

John short cross penny

HENRY III 1216-72

Short cross pennies	£20	£35
Long cross pennies no sceptre	£15	£35
Long cross pennies with sceptre	£15	£35

Henry III long cross penny, no sceptre

The 'long cross' pennies, first introduced in 1247, are divided into two groups: those with sceptre and those without. They also fall into five basic classes, with many varieties. We recommend C.R. Wren's, The Voided Long Cross Coinage, 1247-79 *as the best guide to identification.*

EDWARD I 1272-1307
1st coinage 1272-78

Long cross pennies ... ...from   £25   £70
similar in style to those of Henry III but with more realistic beard.

Edward I Durham penny

New coinage 1278-1307

Groats	£1000	£2750
Pennies, various classes, mints from	£10	£30
Halfpennies – ... ...from	£25	£65
Farthings – ... ...from	£65	£160

Any new collector wishing to become serious about this area should obtain a copy of Edwardian English Silver Coins 1279-1351. Sylloge of coins of the British Isles 39 (The JJ North collection)

EDWARD II 1307-27

Pennies, various classes, mints from	£12	£50
Halfpennies ... ...from	£50	£125
Farthings ... ...from	£65	£160

EDWARD III 1327-77
1st and 2nd coinages 1327-43

Pennies (only 1st coinage) various types and mints	£200	£450
Halfpennies, different types and mints	£50	£150
Farthings	£70	£150

3rd coinage 1344-51 (Florin Coinage)

Pennies, various types and mints   £15   £65

Halfpennies –	£15	£45
Farthings	£50	£120

A superb Edward III penny

	F	VF
4th coinage 1351-77		
Groats, many types and mints from	£35	£95

Edward III groat

Halfgroats –	£20	£55
Pennies –	£18	£50
Halfpennies, different types ...	£95	£200
Farthings, a few types	£120	£250

Richard III groat

RICHARD II 1377-99

Groats, four types from	£200	£475
Halfgroats	£190	£450
Pennies, various types, London	£190	£450
Pennies, various types, York ...	£50	£120
Pennies, Durham	£190	*
Halfpennies, three main types ...	£30	£80
Farthings, some varieties	£150	£375

HENRY IV 1399-1413

Groats, varieties ... ...from	£1500	£4000
Halfgroats –	£500	£1600
Pennies	£250	£750
Halfpennies	£170	£400
Farthings –	£500	*

Henry V groat

HENRY V 1413-22

Groats, varieties ... ...from   £70   £150

	F	VF
alfgroats	£75	£160
·nnies	£35	£90
alfpennies	£30	£75
·rthings	£160	£375

·ENRY VI 1422-61
·nnulet issue 1422-1427

·oats	£30	£70
alfgroats	£25	£60
·nnies	£20	£50
alfpennies	£20	£50
·rthings	£160	£350

·osette-Mascle issue 1427-1430

·oats	£35	£100
alfgroats	£30	£70
·nnies	£30	£70
alfpennies	£20	£50
·rthings	£120	£250

·necone-Mascle 1430-1434

·oats	£35	£90
alfgroats	£30	£70
·nnies	£25	£60
alfpennies	£25	£50
·rthings	£120	£250

·eaf-Mascle issue 1434-1435

·oats	£50	£150
alfgroats	£40	£95
·nnies	£40	£90
alfpennies	£25	£60

·af-Trefoil 1435-1438

·oats	£50	£120
alfgroats	£35	£90
·nnies	£40	£80
alfpennies	£25	£60
·rthings	£120	£300

·efoil 1438-1443

·oats	£60	£140
alfgroats	£275	*
alfpennies	£40	£90

·efoil-Pellet 1443-1445

·oats	£60	£180

·eaf-Pellet 1445-1454

·oats	£40	£130
alfgroats	£40	£95
·nnies	£40	£90
alfpennies	£30	£65
·rthings	£150	£300

·nmarked 1445-1454

·oats	£200	£650
alfgroats	£200	£450

·ross-Pellet 1454-1460

·oats	£90	£200
alfgroats	£190	£450
·nnies	£60	£120
alfpennies	£60	£120
·rthings	£150	*

·s-Pellet 1454-1460

·oats	£175	£450

·here are many different varieties, mintmarks and ·ints in this reign. These prices are for the com- ·onest pieces in each issue.

HAMMERED SILVER

EDWARD IV 1st Reign 1461-1470
Heavy coinage 1461-4

	F	VF
Groats, many classes, all London	£70	£180
Halfgroats, many classes, all London	£250	*
Pennies, different classes. London, York and Durham	£150	*
Halfpennies, different classes, all London	£60	*
Farthings. London	£600	*

Light coinage 1464-70

Groats, many different issues, varieties, mms and mints from	£35	£80
Halfgroats, ditto	£35	£65
Pennies, ditto	£30	£65
Halfpennies, ditto	£40	£80
Farthings Two issues	£400	*

HENRY VI (restored) 1470-71

Groats, different mints, mms from	£120	£250
Halfgroats – from	£250	£500
Pennies – from	£220	£500
Halfpennies – from	£170	£350

EDWARD IV 2nd reign 1471-83

Groats, different varieties, mints etc	£35	£85
Halfgroats	£30	£70
Pennies	£30	£75
Halfpennies	£25	£70

EDWARD V 1483
(The coins read EDWARD but are now considered to be attributable to Richard III)
(Mintmark boar's head)

Groats	£2000	*
Halfgroats (?)		
Penny (?)		

RICHARD III 1483-85

Groats, London and York mints, various combinations of mms	£230	£475
Halfgroats	£700	£1400
Pennies, York and Durham (London mint unique)	£250	£500
Halfpennies	£175	£400

PERKIN WARBECK, PRETENDER

Groat, 1494 [cf. BNJ XXVI, p. 125]	£650	£2000

The Tudor Monarchs

HENRY VII 1485-1509
Facing bust issues:

Henry VII Groat London open crown type

Groats, all London		
Open crown without arches	£75	£250
Crown with two arches unjewelled	£50	£120
Crown with two jewelled arches	£55	£120

HAMMERED SILVER

	F	VF
Similar but only one arch jewelled	£40	£80
Similar but tall thin lettering ...	£40	£110
Similar but single arch, tall thin lettering	£40	£90
Halfgroats, London		
Open crown without arches, tressure unbroken	£300	£700
Double arched crown	£50	£150
Unarched crown	£35	£70
Some varieties and different *mms.*		
Halfgroats, Canterbury		
Open crown, without arches ...	£35	£80
Double arched crown	£30	£65
Some varieties and different *mms.*		
Halfgroats, York		
Double arched crown	£35	£80
Unarched crown with tressure broken	£30	£70
Double arched crown with keys at side of bust	£25	£60
Many varieties and different mms.		
Pennies, facing bust type		
London		rare
Canterbury, open crown		rare
– arched crown	£45	£120
Durham, Bishop Sherwood (S on breast)	£60	£200
York	£40	£90
Many varities and mms.		
Pennies, 'sovereign enthroned' type		
London, many varieties	£35	£90
Durham –	£45	£120
York –	£35	£90
Halfpennies, London		
Open crown	£65	£150
Arched crown	£35	£120
Crown with lower arch	£25	£100
Some varieties and mms.		
Halfpennies, Canterbury		
Open crown	£150	*
Arched crown	£150	*
Halfpennies, York		
Arched crown and key below bust	£120	£250
Farthings, all London	£250	*
Profile issues:		
Testoons im lis, three different legends	£3750	£8000

Henry VII profile issue testoon

	F	VF
Groats, all London		
Tentative issue (double band to crown)	£135	£400
Regular issue (triple band to crown)	£40	£140
Some varieties, and *mms*		
Halfgroats		
London	£45	£140

	F	VF
– no numeral after king's name	£375	*
Canterbury	£30	£80
York, two keys below shield ...	£30	£75
– XB by shield	£500	*

HENRY VIII 1509-47
With portrait of Henry VII
1st coinage 1509-26

	F	VF
Groats, London	£80	£200
Groats, Tournai	£300	£850
Groats, Tournai, without portrait	*	ext. rare
Halfgroats, London	£60	£175
Halfgroats, Canterbury, varieties	£40	£120
Halfgroats, York, varieties	£35	£120
Halfgroats, Tournai		unique
Pennies, 'sovereign enthroned' type, London	£35	£90
Pennies, Canterbury, varieties ...	£75	*
Pennies, Durham, varieties ...	£40	£100
Halfpennies, facing bust type, London	£35	£80
Canterbury	£70	£150
Farthings, portcullis type, London	£400	£900

Henry VIII second coinage groat,
with Irish title HIB REX

With young portrait of Henry VIII
2nd coinage 1526-44

	F	VF
Groats, London, varities, *mms*	£35	£120
Groats, Irish title, HIB REX	£350	£850
Groats, York *mms*	£70	£200
Halfgroats, London *mms*	£35	£90
Halfgroats, Canterbury *mms* ...	£30	£80
Halfgroats, York *mms*	£30	£80
Pennies 'sovereign enthroned' type		
London, varieties, *mms*	£30	£90
Canterbury, varieties, *mms* ...	£60	£150
Durham –	£30	£90
York	£90	£200
Halfpennies, facing bust type		
London, varieties, *mms*	£35	£90
Canterbury	£60	£150
York	£70	£140
Farthings, portcullis type	£400	*

With old bearded portrait
3rd coinage 1544-47
Posthumous issues 1547-51

	F	VF
Testoons (or shillings)		
London (Tower mint), varieties, *mms*	£400	£1000
Southwark, varieties, *mms* ...	£400	£1000
Bristol, varieties, *mms*	£500	£1300
Groats, six different busts, varieties, *mms*		
London (Tower mint)	£50	£160
Southwark	£50	£160
Bristol	£65	£190
Canterbury	£65	£180
London (Durham House)	£170	£500

Henry VIII third coinage groat

Halfgroats, only one style of
bust (except York which has
two), varieties, mms

	F	VF
London (Tower mint)	£45	£140
Southwark	£70	£250
Bristol	£65	£180
Canterbury	£35	£130
York	£60	£160
London (Durham House)		very rare

Pennies (facing bust) varieties, mms

	F	VF
London (Tower mint)	£40	£120
Southwark	£75	£175
London (Durham House)		very rare
Bristol	£50	£160
Canterbury	£40	£140
York	£45	£140

Halfpennies (facing bust) varieties, mms

	F	VF
London (Tower mint)	£50	£150
Bristol	£90	£200
Canterbury	£50	£120
York	£40	£120

EDWARD VI 1547-53
1st period 1547-49

	F	VF
Shillings, London (Durham House), mm bow, patterns (?)		ext. rare
Groats, London (Tower), mm arrow	£400	£900
Groats, London (Southwark), mm E, none	£425	£1200
Halfgroats, London (Tower), mm arrow	£350	£800
Halfgroats, London (Southwark), mm arrow, E	£350	£750
Halfgroats, Canterbury, mm none	£200	£600
Pennies, London (Tower), mm	£275	£650
Pennies, London (Southwark), mm E	£295	£700
Pennies, Bristol, mm none	£200	£600
Halfpennies, London (Tower), mm uncertain	£375	£800
Halfpennies, Bristol, mm none	£300	£650

Edward VI 2nd period shilling. Tower mint

HAMMERED SILVER

	F	VF

2nd period 1549-50

	F	VF
Shillings, London (Tower) various mms	£95	£300
Shillings, Bristol, mm TC	£600	£1400
Shillings, Canterbury, mm T or t	£100	£400
Shillings, London (Durham House), mm bow, varieties	£250	£650

3rd period £550-53
Base silver (similar to issues of 2nd period)

	F	VF
Shillings, London (Tower), mm lis, lion, rose	£130	£350
Pennies, London (Tower), mm escallop	£90	£200
Pennies, York, mm mullet	£75	£190
Halfpennies, London (Tower) ...	£200	*

Fine Silver

	F	VF
Crown 1551 mm Y, 1551-53 mm tun	£240	£600
Halfcrown, walking horse, 1551, mm Y	£160	£450
Halfcrowns, galloping horse, 1551-52, mm tun	£200	£800

Edward VI 1552 halfcrown galloping horse

	F	VF
Halfcrowns, walking horse, 1553, mm tun	£650	£1500
Shillings, mm Y, tun	£50	£170
Sixpences, London (Tower), mm y, tun	£55	£170
Sixpences, York, mm mullet ...	£100	£350
Threepences, London (Tower), mm tun	£130	£450
Threepences, York mm mullet ...	£250	£650
Pennies, sovereign type	£700	£1500
Farthings, portcullis type	£700	*

Mary groat, pomegranate after MARIA

MARY 1553-54

	F	VF
Groats, mm pomegranate	£55	£175
Halfgroats, similar	£550	*
Pennies, rev VERITAS TEMP FILIA ...	£400	*
Pennies, rev CIVITAS LONDON	£400	*

HAMMERED SILVER

PHILIP AND MARY 1554-58

	F	VF
Shillings, full titles, without date	£130	£450
– also without XII	£160	£600
– dated 1554	£130	£450
– dated 1554, English titles ...	£150	£500
– dated 1555, English titles only	£150	£500
– dated 1554, English titles only also without XII	£300	*
– 1555, as last	£400	*
– 1554 but date below bust ...	£350	*
– 1555 but date below bust ...	£350	*
– 1555 similar to previous but without ANG	£450	*
Sixpences, full titles, 1554	£140	£400
– full titles, undated	*	*
– English titles, 1555	£150	£450
– similar but date below bust, 1554	£500	*
– English titles, 1557	£170	£550
– similar, but date below bust, 1557	£650	*
Groats, *mm* lis	£50	£200
Halfgroats, *mm* lis	£450	£1250

Philip and Mary Shilling, 1554

Pennies, *mm* lis	£400	*
Base pennies, without portrait	£50	£160

ELIZABETH I 1558-1603
Hammered coinage, 1st issue 1558-61
Shillings ELIZABETH

Wire-line circles	£250	£750
Beaded inner circles	£120	£320
ET for Z	£50	£160

Edward VI shilling greyhound countermark (reign of Elizabeth), and Elizabeth I hammered groat

Groats

Wire-line inner circles	£110	£375
Beaded inner circles	£45	£140
ET for Z	£30	£130
Halfgroats		
Wire-line inner circles	£150	£350
Beaded inner circles	£30	£75
Pennies		
Wire-line inner circles	£160	£400
Beaded inner circles	£15	£60

Countermarked shillings of Edward VI, 1560-61

With portcullis mark (Current for 4½d)	£1250	*
With greyhound mark (current for 2½d)	£1400	*

Hammered coinage, 2nd issue 1561-82

	F	VF
Sixpences, dated 1561-82	£30	£95
Threepences, 1561-82	£20	£75
Halfgroats, undated	£35	£90
Threehalfpences, 1561-62, 1564-70, 1572-79, 1581-82	£25	£90
Pennies, undated	£25	£70
Threefarthings, 1561-62, 1568, 1572-78, 1581-82	£60	£150

Elizabeth I Halfcrown, 1601

Hammered coinage, 3rd issue 1583-1603

Crowns, im **1**	£400	£900
Crowns, im **2**	£475	£1350
Halfcrowns, im **1**	£250	£550
Halfcrowns, im **2 (F)**	£800	£2000
Shillings ELIZAB	£45	£170
Sixpences, 1582-1602	£35	£130
Halfgroats, E D G ROSA etc	£15	£80
Pennies	£18	£70
Halfpennies, portcullis type ...	£25	£80

There are many different mintmarks, such as lis, bell, lion etc., featured on the hammered coins of Elizabeth I, and these marks enable one to date those coins which are not themselves dated. For more details see J.J. North's English Hammered Coinage, *Volume 2.*

Milled Coinage
Shillings

large size	£250	£600
Intermediate	£130	£375
Small	£110	£350
Sixpences		
1561	£35	£120
1562	£30	£100
1563-64, 1566	£55	£180
1567-68	£55	£180
1570-71	£95	£275
Groats, undated	£120	£400
Threepences, 1561, 1562-64 ...	£100	£300
Halfgroats	£90	£300
Threefarthings		ext. rare

The Stuart Kings

JAMES I 1603-25

	F	VF
1st coinage 1603-04		
Crowns, rev EXURGAT etc	£425	£950
Halfcrowns –	£475	£1400
Shillings, varieties	£45	£190
Sixpences, dated 1603-04, varieties	£35	£150
Halfgroats, undated	£25	£75
Pennies –	£30	£80

2nd coinage 1604-19

		F	VF
Crowns rev QVAE DEVS etc	...	£375	£750
Halfcrowns –	... ...	£600	1400

James I 2nd coinage shilling

		F	VF
Shillings, varieties	... ...	£35	£150
Sixpences, dated 1604-15,			
varieties etc.	... ...	£30	£95
Halfgroats, varieties	... ...	£15	£60
Pennies	... ...	£15	£40
Halfpennies	... ...	£15	£45

3rd coinage 1619-25

		F	VF
Crowns		£250	£550
– Plume over reverse shield	...	£300	£650
Halfcrowns	... ...	£100	£280
– Plume over reverse shield	...	£170	£450

James I halfcrown (reverse) plume over shield

		F	VF
Shillings	... ...	£35	£150
– Plume over reverse shield	...	£75	£250
Sixpences dated 1621-24	... ...	£30	£120
Halfgroats	... ...	£15	£35
Pennies	... ...	£15	£30
Halfpennies	... ...	£15	£40

James I sixpence of 1622

CHARLES I 1625-1649
Tower Mint 1625-1643
Crowns
(Obv. King on horseback. Rev. shield)

		F	VF
1st horseman/square shield			
im lis, cross calvary	... ...	£220	£550
As last/plume above shield			
im lis, cross calvary, castle	...	£500	£1000
2nd horseman/oval shield			
im plume, rose harp.			
Some varieties, from	... ...	£200	£500

HAMMERED SILVER

	F	VF
3rd horseman/round shield		
im bell, crown, tun, anchor,		
triangle, star, portcullis, triangle		
in circle. Some varieties, from	£200	£500

Halfcrowns
(Obv. King on horseback. Rev. shield)

	F	VF
1st horseman/square shield		
im lis, cross calvary, negro's		
head, castle, anchor.		
Many varieties, from	£95	£300
2nd horseman/oval shield		
im plume, rose, harp, portcullis.		
Many varieties, from	£80	£200
3rd horseman/round shield		
im bell, crown, tun, portcullis,		
anchor, triangle, star		
Many varieties, from	£60	£150
4th horseman/round shield		
im star, triangle in circle	£35	£100

Charles I Tower halfcrown: first horseman

Shillings

	F	VF
1st bust/square shield		
im lis, cross calvary		
Some varieties	£50	£160
2nd bust/square shield		
im cross calvary, negro's head,		
castle, anchor, heart, plume		
Many varieties, from	£45	£140
3rd bust/oval shield		
im plume, rose	... ...	£35	£120
4th bust/oval or round shield		
im harp, portcullis, bell, crown,		
tun		
Many varieties, from	£40	£140
5th bust/square shield		
im tun, anchor, triangle		
Many varieties, from	£30	£120
6th bust/square shield		
im anchor, triangle, star, triangle		
in circle		
Some varieties, from	£30	£120
Sixpences		
(early ones are dated)		
1st bust/square shield, date above		
1625 im lis, cross calvary		
1626 *im* cross calvary	£45	£170
2nd bust/square shield, date above		
1625, 1626 im cross calvary		
1626, 1627 im negro's head		
1626, 1628 im castle		
1628, 1629 im anchor		
1629 im heart		
1630 im heart, plume	£60	£160
3rd bust/oval shield		
im plume, rose	£40	£150
4th bust/oval or round shield		
im harp, portcullis, bell,		
crown, tun	£30	£120

HAMMERED SILVER

Charles I Tower sixpence mm bell

	F	VF
5th bust/square shield		
im tun, anchor, triangle		
Many varieties, from	£30	£130
6th bust/square shield		
im triangle, star	£30	£130
Halfgroats		
Crowned rose both sides		
im lis, cross calvary,		
blackamoor's head	£15	£50
2nd bust/oval shield		
im plume, rose	£18	£60
3rd bust/oval shield		
im rose, plume	£15	£60
4th bust/oval or round shield,		
im harp, crown, portcullis, bell,		
tun, anchor, triangle, star		
Many varieties from	£15	£60
5th bust/round shield		
im anchor	£25	£100
Pennies		
Uncrowned rose both sides		
im one or two pellets, lis,		
negro's head	£12	£40
2nd bust/oval shield		
im plume	£15	£60
3rd bust/oval shield		
im plume, rose	£15	£60
4th bust/oval shield		
im harp, one or two pellets,		
portcullis, bell, triangle	£15	£60
5th bust/oval shield		
im one or two pellets, none ...	£15	£45
Halfpennies		
Uncrowned rose both sides		
im none	£15	£45

Tower Mint, under Parliament 1643-48
Crowns
(Obv. King on horseback, Rev. shield)

	F	VF
4th horseman/round shield		
im (P), (R), eye sun	£270	£650
5th horseman/round shield		
im sun, sceptre	£300	£700

Halfcrowns
(Obv. King on horseback, Rev. shield)
3rd horseman/round shield

	F	VF
im (P), (R), eye sun	£70	£275

Charles I Parliament shilling, mm eye

	F	VF
4th horseman/round shield		
im (P)	£150	*
5th horseman (tall)/round shield		
im sun, sceptre	£75	£300
Shillings (revs. all square shield)		
6th bust (crude)		
im (P), (R), eye, sun	£40	£200
7th bust (tall, slim)		
im sun, sceptre	£40	£200
8th bust (shorter, older)		
im sceptre	£40	£250
Sixpences (revs. all square shield)		
6th bust		
im (P), (R), eye sun	£80	£200
7th bust		
im (R), eye, sun, sceptre ...	£75	£200
8th bust, (crude style)		
im eye, sun	£90	*
Halfgroats		
4th bust/round shield		
im (P), (R), eye sceptre ...	£30	£80
7th bust (old/round shield)		
im eye, sun, sceptre	£25	£70
Pennies		
7th bust/oval shield		
im one or two pellets	£20	£50

Charles I Briot's crown

Briot's 1st milled issued 1631-32
im: flower and **B**

	F	VF
Crowns	£300	£800
Halfcrowns...	£190	£480
Shillings	£130	£300
Sixpences	£70	£200
Halfgroats	£35	£70
Pennies	£30	£70

Briot's 2nd milled issue 1638-39
im: anchor, anchor and B, anchor and mullet

	F	VF
Halfcrowns	£160	£380
Shillings	£80	£200
Sixpences	£40	£100

Sixpence of Briot's 2nd milled issue

Briot's hammered issues 1638-39	F	VF
im: anchor, triangle over anchor		
Halfcrowns	£600	£1250
Shillings	£350	£900

Charles I
Crown
of Exeter

PROVINCIAL MINTS
York 1642-44
im: lion

	F	VF
Halfcrowns, varieties from	£90	£250
Shillings –	£80	£200
Sixpences –	£150	£375
Threepences	£40	£95

Aberystwyth 1638-42
im: open book

Halfcrowns, varieties from	£400	£1000
Shillings –	£180	£450
Sixpences –	£180	£500
Groats –	£35	£80

Aberystwyth groat

Threepences –	£30	£60
Halfgroats –	£40	£90
Pennies –	£70	£200
Halfpennies	£150	£350

Aberystwyth – Furnace 1647-48
im: crown

Halfcrowns from	£1000	£2500
Shillings		ext. rare
Sixpences		ext. rare
Groats	£200	£450
Threepences	£250	£600
Halfgroats	£250	£600
Pennies	£600	£1250

Shrewsbury 1642
mm: plume without band

Pounds, varieties from	£800	£3000
Halfpounds –	£375	£900
Crowns –	£350	£800
Halfcrowns –	£220	£600
Shillings –	£500	£1250

Oxford 1642-46
mm: plume with band

Pounds, varieties from	£800	£3000
Halfpounds –	£350	£700
Crowns –	£350	£650

HAMMERED SILVER

	F	VF
Halfcrowns –	£90	£250
Shillings –	£100	£250
Sixpences –	£130	£300
Groats –	£50	£160
Threepences –	£40	£150
Halfgroats –	£80	£200
Pennies –	£100	£250

Bristol 1643-45
im: Bristol monogram, acorn, plumelet

Halfcrowns, varieties from	£130	£350

Charles I halfcrown of York

Shillings –	£120	£300
Sixpences –	£150	£400
Groats –	£120	£280
Threepences –	£140	£400
Halfgroats –	£200	£450
Pennies –	£320	*

A, B, and plumes issues
Associated with Thomas Bushell; previously
assigned to Lundy

Halfcrowns, varieties from	£450	£1250
Shillings –	£250	£650
Sixpences –	£150	£400
Groats –	£90	£200
Threepences –	£90	£170
Halfgroats –	£300	£700

Truro 1642-43
im: rose, bugle

Crowns, varieties	£200	£450
Halfcrowns –	£425	£900
Shillings –		ext. rare

Bristol shilling 1644

Exeter 1643-46
im Ex, rose, castle

Halfpounds –		ext. rare
Crowns, varieties	£170	£400
Halfcrowns	£160	£350
Shillings	£170	£450
Sixpences	£170	£500
Groats	£60	£175

HAMMERED SILVER

	F	VF
Threepences	£80	£180
Halfgroats –	£120	£350
Pennies	£250	£475

Worcester 1643-4
im: castle, helmet, leopard's head, lion, two lions, lis, rose, star

		F	VF
Halfcrowns, many varieties	...	£375	£850

Salopia (Shrewsbury) 1644
im: helmet, lis, rose (in legend)

		F	VF
Halfcrowns, many varieties	...	£550	£2000

Worcester or Salopia (Shrewsbury)
im: bird, boar's head, lis, castle, cross, and annulets, helmet, lion, lis, pear, rose, scroll

		F	VF
Shillings, varieties	...	£500	£1750
Sixpences	...	£800	£1500
Groats	...	£400	£1250
Threepences	...	£350	£850
Halfgroats	...	£400	£900

'HC' mint (probably Hartlebury Castle, Worcester 1646)
im: pear, three pears

		F	VF
Halfcrowns	...	£1250	£3000

Chester 1644
im: cinquefoil, plume, prostrate gerb, three gerbs

		F	VF
Halfcrowns, varieties	...	£550	£1250
Shillings	...	ext. rare	
Threepences	...	very rare	

Welsh Marches mint? 1644

	F	VF
Halfcrowns...	£450	*

Welsh Marches mint, halfcrown

SIEGE PIECES
Carlisle besieged 1644-45

		F	VF
Three shillings	£2500	£6000
Shillings (**F**)	£1700	£3500

Newark besieged many times
(surrendered May 6, 1646)

		F	VF
Halfcrowns, 1645-46 (**F**)	£325	£750

Newark siege halfcrown

	F	VF
Shillings, 1645-46, varieties (**F**)	£220	£600
Ninepences, 1645-46	£200	£550
Sixpences	£200	£600

Pontefract besieged 1648-49

	F	VF
Two shillings, 1648		ext. rare
Shillings, 1648, varieties	£575	£1250

Pontefract siege shilling

Scarborough besieged 1644-45
Many odd values issued here, all of which are extremely rare. The coin's value was decided by the intrinsic value of the piece of metal from which it was made.
Examples: 5s 8d, 2s 4d, 1s 9d, 1s 3d, 7d etc. (**F**).
Collectors could expect to pay at least £2000 or more in F and £4000 in VF for any of these.

COMMONWEALTH 1649-60

	F	VF
Crowns, *im* sun 1649,51-54, 56 ...	£350	£600
Halfcrowns, *im* sun 1649, 1651-6	£130	£350
—*im* anchor 1658-60	£400	*
Shillings, *im* sun 1649, 1661-87	£70	£170
—*im* anchor 1658-60	£350	*

A superb 1651 sixpence

	F	VF
Sixpences, *im* sun 1649, 1651-7	£80	£170
—*im* anchor 1658-6	£400	*
Halfgroats undated	£25	£60
Pennies undated	£25	£50
Halfpennies undated	£25	£60

CHARLES II 1660-85
Hammered coinage 1660-62

		F	VF
Halfcrowns, three issues ... from	£200	£500
Shillings— ... ... from	£80	£350

Charles II hammered issue shilling

		F	VF
Sixpences—	£60	£200
Fourpences, third issue only ...	£20	£70
Threepences— ... ... from	£25	£65
Twopences, three issues from	£10	£50
Pennies— ... ... from	£25	£50

'ROYAL' AND 'ROSE' BASE METAL FARTHINGS

Until 1613 English coins were struck only in gold or silver — the monarchy considered that base metal issues would be discreditable to the royal prerogative of coining. However, silver coins had become far too small, farthings so tiny that they had to be discontinued. So to meet demands for small change James I authorised Lord Harington to issue copper farthing tokens. Subsequently this authority passed in turn to the Duke of Lennox, the Duchess of Richmond and Lord Maltravers. It ceased by order of Parliament in 1644.

	Fair	F	VF	EF
JAMES I **Royal farthing tokens**				
Type 1 Harington (circa 1613). Small copper flan with tin-washed surface, mint-mark between sceptres below crown … … … … …	£10	£35	£120	*
Type 2 Harington (circa 1613). Larger flan, no tin wash … … … …	£12	£25	£75	*
Type 3 Lennox (1614-25). IACO starts at 1 o'clock position … … …	£8	£20	£50	*
Type 4 Lennox (1622-25). Oval flan, IACO starts at 7 o'clock … … …	£12	£30	£75	*
CHARLES I **Royal farthing tokens**				
Type 1 Richmond (1625-34). Single arched crown … … … … …	£8	£15	£40	*
Type 2 Transitional (circa 1634). Double arched crown … … … …	£8	£20	£60	*
Type 3 Maltravers (1634-36). Inner circles … … … … … …	£8	£20	£45	£95
Type 4 Richmond (1625-34). As Type 1 but oval … … … … …	£8	£30	*	*
Type 5 Maltravers (1634-36). Double arched crown … … … … …	£15	£50	*	*
Rose farthing tokens (rose on reverse)				
Type 1 Small thick flan … … … … … … … … … … … … …	£7	£15	£35	*
Type 2 Same, but single arched crown … … … … … … … …	£7	£15	£40	*
Type 3 Same, but sceptres below crown … … … … … … …	£15	£50	*	*

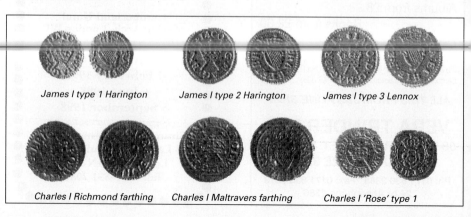

James I type 1 Harington   James I type 2 Harington   James I type 3 Lennox

Charles I Richmond farthing   Charles I Maltravers farthing   Charles I 'Rose' type 1

MILLED COINAGE from 1656

Again it must be stressed that the prices shown in this guide are the approximate amounts collectors can expect to pay for coins — they are not dealers' buying prices. Information for this guide is drawn from auction results and dealers' lists, with the aim of determining firm valuations. Prices still vary enormously from sale to sale and from one dealer's list to another. Allowance must also be made for the variance in the standards of grading. The prices given here aim at a reasonable assessment of the market at the time of compilation, but they are not the product of computers, which would, in any case, provide only average (not necessarily accurate) prices. It is not possible to forecast such values because of the erratic fluctuations that can occur, not only in boom conditions but also during times of economic uncertainty, and an annual catalogue of this type cannot be up to date on the bullion prices of common sovereigns, for example. If you are buying or selling bullion gold coins, refer to current quotations from bullion dealers.

With some denominations in the silver and copper series, column headings indicating condition change at the beginning of the lists of George III coins. The condition (grade) of a coin is of great importance in determining its market value. Notes on grading and on abbreviations etc. used in these price guides appear elsewhere in this publication.

Cromwell gold patterns

These were struck by order of Cromwell, with the consent of the Council. The dies were made by Thomas Simon, and the coins were struck on Peter Blondeau's machine. The fifty shillings and the broad were struck from the same dies, but the fifty shillings has the edge inscription PROTECTOR LITERIS LITERAE NUMMIS CORONA ER SALUS, while the broad is not so thick and has a grained edge. No original strikings of the half broad are known, but some were struck from dies made by John Tanner in 1738. All three denominations are dated 1656.

Cromwell half broad

	F	VF	EF	Unc
Fifty shillings	*	*	£15000	*
Broad	*	£2500	£5000	£7000
Half broad	*	*	*	£8500

Five guineas

CHARLES II	F	VF	EF	Unc
1668-78 pointed end to trnctn of bust ...	£1100	£1750	£6500	*
1668, 69, 75—eleph below bust	£1100	£1750	£6500	*
1675-8—eleph & castle below bust	£1100	£1750	£6500	*
1678-84 rounded end to trnctn	£1100	£1650	£5000	*
1680-4—eleph & castle	£1450	£1950	£7000	*
JAMES II				
1686 sceptres in wrong order on rev ...	£1100	£1750	£5000	£8500
1687-8 sceptres correct	£1100	£1750	£5000	*
1687-8 eleph & castle	£1100	£1950	£5500	*
WILLIAM AND MARY				
1691-4 no prov mark	£1200	£1950	£4750	£8500
1691-4 eleph & castle	£1350	£2000	£5500	*
WILLIAM III				
1699-1700 no prov mark	£1000	£1650	£4000	*
1699 eleph & castle	£1100	£2000	£5000	*
1701 new bust 'fine work'	£1350	£2000	£4750	£7000

Charles II 1676 five guineas, elephant and castle

FIVE GUINEAS

George II 1729 five guineas

*Charles II 1664 two guineas
elephant below bust*

James II 1687 two guineas

ANNE

	F	VF	EF	Unc
Pre-Union with Scotland				
1703 VIGO below bust	*	*	£37500	*
1705-6 plain below	£1350	£2250	£5000	£8000
Post-Union with Scotland				
1706	£1250	£1950	£4500	£7500
1709 Larger lettering, wider shield and crowns	£1250	£1750	£4250	*
1711, 1713-4 broader bust	£1250	£1750	£4250	£6500

Pre-Union reverses have separate shields (top and right) for England and Scotland. Post-Union reverses have the English and Scottish arms side by side on the top and bottom shields.

GEORGE I

	F	VF	EF	Unc
1716, 17, 20, 26	£1750	£2500	£7000	*

GEORGE II

	F	VF	EF	Unc
1729, 31, 35, 38, 41 YH	£1350	£1850	£3250	£6500
1729 E,I,C, below head	£1350	£1950	£3500	£7000
1746 OH, lima below	£1350	£2000	£4000	£7500
1748, 53 plain below	£1350	£2000	£3750	£7500

GEORGE III

	F	VF	EF	Unc
1770, 73, 77 patterns only	*	*	£40000	£50000

Two guineas

CHARLES II

	F	VF	EF	Unc
1664, 5, 9, 71 pointed end to trnctn	£700	£1100	£4000	*
1664 elephant below	£700	£1100	£3500	*
1675-84 rounded end to trnctn	£650	£900	£3000	*
1676, 78, 82-84 eleph & castle below bust	£800	£1350	£4500	*
1678 elephant below				ext. rare

JAMES II

	F	VF	EF	Unc
1687	£900	£1750	£4500	*
1688/9	£900	£1750	£5000	*

WILLIAM AND MARY

	F	VF	EF	Unc
1691, 3, 4 eleph & castle	£750	£1250	£3500	£5500
1693, 4 no prov mark	£700	£1000	£3000	*

WILLIAM III

	F	VF	EF	Unc
1701	£1000	£1750	£3500	*

ANNE

(none struck before Union)

	F	VF	EF	Unc
1709, 11, 13, 14	£600	£850	£1850	*

GEORGE I

	F	VF	EF	Unc
1717, 20, 26	£700	£1000	£1850	£3250

GEORGE II

	F	VF	EF	Unc
1734, 5, 8, 9, YH (F)	£350	£500	£1100	£1950
1739, 40 intermediate head (F)	£325	£600	£1250	£2500
1748, 53 OH	£375	£650	£1450	£2750

GEORGE III

	F	VF	EF	Unc
1768, 73, 77 patterns only	*	*	£15000	£25000

Guineas

CHARLES II

	F	VF	EF	Unc
1663 pointed trnctn	£450	£750	£3000	£6000
1663—eleph	£450	£750	£3500	*
1664 trnctn indented	£450	£750	£3000	*
1664—eleph	*	*	£6000	*

	F	VF	EF	Unc
1664-73 sloping pointed trnctn	£350	£600	£2750	£5500
1664, 5, 8 — eleph	£450	£1000	£3250	*
1672-84 rounded trnctn	£300	£500	£2500	*
1674-84 — eleph & castle	£450	£850	£4000	*
1677, 8 — eleph	*	£1750	*	*

JAMES II

1685, 6 1st bust	£250	£500	£1750	£3000
1685 — eleph & castle	£275	£550	£1900	*
1686-8 2nd bust	£275	£525	£1750	£3000
1686-8 — eleph & castle	£275	£550	£1850	*

WILLIAM AND MARY

1689-94 no prov mark	£300	£475	£1750	£3500
1689-94 eleph & castle	£325	£575	£2000	*
1692 eleph	£550	£1200	*	*

WILLIAM III

1695, 6 1st bust	£250	£400	£1500	£2500
1695, 7 — eleph & castle	*	*	*	*
1697-1701 2nd bust	£250	£400	£1500	*
1698-1701 — eleph & castle	£450	£1100	*	*
1701 3rd bust 'fine work'	£350	£600	£2500	*

*Charles II 1663 guinea
elephant below bust*

ANNE
Pre-Union[1]

1702, 1705-7 plain below bust	£300	£600	£1500	£2750
1703 VIGO below	£500	*	*	*

Post Union[1]

1707, 8 1st bust	£175	£300	£750	£1500
1707 — eleph & castle	£400	£850	£2750	*
1707-9 2nd bust	£175	£300	£750	£1500
1708-9 — eleph & castle	£450	£1100	£3500	*
1710-1714 3rd bust	£175	£275	£700	£1250

[1]See note in prices of five guinea pieces for Anne.

GEORGE I

1714 1st head PR. EL. (Prince Elector) in rev legend	£450	£850	£2000	£3000
1715 2nd head, tie with two ends	£225	£375	£750	£1850
1715 3rd head, hair not curling round trnctn	£200	£350	£1000	*
1716-23 4th head, tie with loop	£150	£275	£750	£1750
1721, 2 — eleph & castle	*	*	*	*
1723-7 5th head, smaller, older bust	£200	£300	£1000	£2250
1726 — eleph & castle	£500	£1350	*	*

Anne 1706 guinea

GEORGE II

1727 1st YH, small lettering	£350	£550	£1800	£2500
1727, 8 — larger lettering	£300	£500	£1800	*
1729-32 2nd YH (narrower)	£200	£300	£1500	*
1729, 31, 2 — E.I.C. below	£200	£375	£1700	£2250
1732-8 — larger lettering	£200	£250	£1350	£1750
1732 — — E.I.C. below	£350	£600	£1750	*
1739, 40, 43 intermediate head	£200	£275	£750	£1500
1739 — E.I.C. below	£350	£750	*	*
1745, 6 — larger lettering	£200	£350	£800	*
1745 — LIMA below	£400	£850	£2500	*
1747-53, 5, 6, 8, 9, 60, OH	£175	£250	£750	£1500

GEORGE III

1761, 1st head	£400	£850	£2500	£3500
1763, 4, 2nd head	£195	£500	£1700	*
1765-73, 3rd head	£100	£175	£600	*
1744-9, 81-6, 4th head	£100	£165	£325	£650
1789-99, 5th head, 'spade' rev (**F**)	£100	£140	£250	£400
1813, 6th head, rev shield in Garter ('Military guinea')	£200	£400	£750	£1000

*George III 1813
'Military guinea'*

Half Guineas

CHARLES II		F	VF	EF	Unc
1669-72 bust with pointed trnctn		£200	£325	£1650	*
1672-84 rounded trnctn...		£200	£325	£1650	*
1676-8, 80, 82-4 — eleph & castle		£250	£500	£2500	*

William and Mary 1691 half guinea

JAMES II					
1686-8 no prov mark		£200	£350	£1500	£2250
1686 eleph & castle		£600	*	*	*

WILLIAM AND MARY					
1689 1st busts		£200	£400	£1500	£2750
1690-4 2nd busts		£200	£350	£1500	*
1691-2 — eleph & castle		£250	£400	£1750	*
1692 — eleph					ext. rare

William III 1695 half guinea

WILLIAM III					
1695 no prov mark		£150	£250	£1000	£1750
1695, 6 eleph & castle		£300	£650	£2000	*
1697-1701 larger harp on rev		£200	£300	£1200	*
1698 — eleph & castle		£275	£450	£2000	*

ANNE					
Pre-Union[1]					
1702, 5 plain below bust		£250	£500	£1500	*
1703 VIGO below		£2500	£3500	*	*
Post-Union[1]					
1707-14 plain		£140	£225	£550	£1250

[1]See note in prices of five guineas for Anne.

George I 1719 half guinea

GEORGE I					
1715, 17-23, 1st head		£150	£250	£600	£1200
1721 eleph & castle		£300	£800	*	*
1724-7, smaller older head		£150	£250	£600	£1200

GEORGE II					
1728-39 YH		£150	£250	£850	£1750
1729-32, 9 — E.I.C. below		£175	£325	£1200	*
1740, 3, 5, 6, intermediate head		£150	£275	£750	*
1745 — LIMA below		£650	£1000	£2750	*
1747-53, 5, 6, 58-60 OH		£125	£150	£500	£800

George I half guinea, 1725

GEORGE III					
1762, 3, 1st head		£200	£375	£1000	*
1764-6, 8, 9, 72-5, 2nd head		£100	£150	£400	£750
1774, 5, 3rd head		£250	£600	£1500	*
1775-9, 81, 83-6, 4th head		£75	£100	£250	£450
1787-91, 93-8, 1800, 5th head		£60	£80	£175	£350
1801-3, 6th head		£60	£75	£165	£300
1804, 6, 8-11, 13, 7th head		£60	£75	£165	£300

George III 1786 half guinea

Third guineas

GEORGE III	F	VF	EF	Unc
1797-1800 1st head	£40	£60	£100	£195
1801-3 — date close to crown on reverse	£40	£60	£100	£195
1804, 6, 8-11, 2nd head	£40	£70	£125	£200

*George III 1788 half guinea
with 'spade' type shield on reverse*

Quarter guineas

GEORGE I	F	VF	EF	Unc
1718	£40	£75	£110	£195

GEORGE III	F	VF	EF	Unc
1762	£45	£75	£150	£250

George I 1718 quarter guinea

It should be noted that all coins less than 100 years old are subject to VAT at the current rate, in addition to the prices given here.

N.B Forgeries exist of pieces marked (F) and if discovered should be reported to the police.

Brittannias
(See under Decimal Coinage)

Five pounds

	F	VF	EF	Unc
GEORGE III				
1820 pattern (F)	*	*	*	£4500
GEORGE IV				
1826 proof	*	*	£5500	£8000
VICTORIA				
1839 proof with 'Una and the Lion' rev (F)	*	£6500	£12500	£17500
1887 JH (F) £300	£425	£550	£700
1887 proof ...	*	*	£950	£1750
1893 OH (F) £400	£550	£750	£1100
1893 proof	*	*	£1000	£2000
EDWARD VII				
1902 (F) £325	£400	£475	£575
1902 proof	*	*	£500	£600
GEORGE V				
1911 proof (F) ...	*	*	*	£1100
GEORGE VI				
1937 proof	*	*	*	£600

ELIZABETH II

In 1984 the Royal Mint issued the first of an annual issue of Brilliant Uncirculated £5 coins. These bear the symbol 'U' in a circle to the left of the date on the reverse to indicate the standard of striking.

1981 proof	£400
1984	£400
1985	£425
1986	£425
1987 new effigy	£425
1988	£425
1989 500th anniversary of the sovereign, BU	£450
1990 Queen Mother's 90th birthday, proof	£575
1990	£435
1991	£450
1992	£450
1993 Coronation, proof	£700
1993	£475
1994	£500
1995	£535
1996 Queen's 70th Birthday, proof	£645
... ...BU	£575
1997 Golden Wedding, proof	£650
1997	£535

Reverse of the gold proof five pounds marking the Queen Mother's 90th birthday (for silver and cupro-nickel versions see Decimal Coinage)

Two pounds

	F	VF	EF	Unc
GEORGE III				
1820 pattern (F)	*	*	£9500	£12500

George III 1820 pattern two pounds
George III 1820 pattern two pounds

	F	VF	EF	Unc
GEORGE IV ...				
1823 St George on reverse (F)£200	£350	£550	£1000
1826 proof, shield reverse	*	*	£1950	£2950

William IV 1831 proof two pounds
William IV 1831 proof two pounds

WILLIAM IV				
1831 proof	*	*	£2500	£4250
VICTORIA				
1887 JH (F) ...£165	£200	£240	£275
1887 proof	*	*	£450	£800
1893 OH (F) ...£175	£250	£375	£495
1893 proof	*	*	£500	£900
EDWARD VII				
1902 (F) £160	£195	£230	£275
1902 proof	*	*	£240	£295
GEORGE V				
1911 proof (F)	*	*	*	£500

1937 proof two pounds
1937 proof two pounds

GEORGE VI				
1937 proof ...	*	*	*	£375

TWO POUNDS

ELIZABETH II	F	VF	EF	Unc
1983 proof				£225
1986 Commonwealth Games, proof				£225
1987 proof				£250
1988 proof				£250
1989 500th anniversary of the sovereign, proof				£275
1990 proof				£250
1991 proof				£250
1993 proof				£250
1994 gold proof				£425
1994 gold proof 'mule'				£600
1995 VE day gold proof				£375
1995 50th Anniversary of UN, proof				£300
1996 European Football Championship ...				£350
1997 Bimetal gold proof				£350

Sovereigns

GEORGE III	F	VF	EF	Unc
1817 (F)	£100	£175	£375	£600
1818	£100	£195	£450	£750
1819				ext. rare
1820	£100	£175	£400	£650

GEORGE IV
Type Laureate head/St George

	F	VF	EF	Unc
1821	£100	£165	£375	£600
1822 (F)	£100	£165	£400	£650
1823	£130	£200	£650	*
1824	£100	£165	£375	£600
1825	£125	£350	£950	*

George IV 1826 proof sovereign

Type bare head/shield

	F	VF	EF	Unc
1825 (F)	£95	£150	£375	£650
1826	£95	£150	£395	£700
1826 proof	*	*	£800	£1750
1827 (F)	£95	£150	£395	£700
1828 (F)	£500	£1500	£3750	*
1829	£95	£150	£375	£650
1830	£95	£150	£375	£650

WILLIAM IV

	F	VF	EF	Unc
1831	£100	£165	£450	£750
1831 proof	*	*	£1000	£2500

William IV 1831 proof sovereign

	F	VF	EF	Unc
1832 (F)	£100	£165	£375	£600
1833	£100	£175	£395	£650
1835	£100	£165	£375	£600
1836	£100	£165	£375	£600
1837	£100	£165	£375	£650

VICTORIA
Type 1, YH obv, shield rev

	F	VF	EF	Unc
1838	£70	£90	£200	£550

Victoria 1839 proof sovereign

	F	VF	EF	Unc
1839	£95	£175	£750	£1200
1839 proof	*	*	£1000	£1950
1841	£400	£700	£2750	*
1842	*	*	£125	£400
1843	*	*	£125	£350
1843 narrow shield	£650	£1200	£2000	*
1844	*	*	£125	£300
1845	*	*	£125	£300
1846	*	*	£125	£300
1847	*	*	£125	£300
1848	*	*	£125	£300
1849	*	*	£125	£375
1850	*	*	£125	£250
1851	*	*	£125	£250
1852	*	*	£125	£250
1853	*	*	£110	£250

Victoria 1853 sovereign, shield on reverse

	F	VF	EF	Unc
1853 proof	*	*	*	£4500
1854	*	*	£100	£250
1855	*	*	£100	£250
1856	*	*	£100	£250
1857	*	*	£100	£250
1858	*	*	£300	£750
1859	*	*	£100	£200
1859 'Ansell' ...	£80	£200	£1000	*
1860	*	*	£200	£600
1861	*	*	£95	£200
1862	*	*	£95	£200
1863	*	*	£80	£175
1863 die number below wreath on rev	*	*	£75	£175
1863 '827' on truncation ...	£1000	£1500	£2500	*
1864 die no. ...	*	*	£85	£175
1865 die no. ...	*	*	£85	£175
1866 die no. ...	*	*	£85	£175
1868 die no. ...	*	*	£85	£175
1869 die no. ...	*	*	£85	£175
1870 die no. ...	*	*	£85	£175
1871 die no. ...	*	*	£85	£125
1871 S (Sydney mint) below wreath	*	*	£85	£400
1872	*	*	£80	£150
1872 die no. ...	*	*	£70	£125
1872 M (Melbourne mint) below wreath	*	*	£120	£300
1872 S	*	*	£80	£350
1873 die no. ...	*	*	£80	£175
1873 S	*	*	£85	£325
1874 die no. ...	£250	£650	£2500	*
1874 M	*	*	£85	£325
1875 S	*	*	£85	£325
1877 S	*	*	£85	£100

SOVEREIGNS

	F	VF	EF	Unc
1878 S	*	*	£95	£300
1879 S	*	*	£95	£300
1880 M	£350	£1000	£2000	£3500
1880 S	*	*	£95	£300
1881 M	*	£100	£300	£500
1881 S	*	*	£95	£300
1882 M	*	*	£95	£300
1882 S	*	*	£95	£300
1883 M	*	£350	£800	£1500
1883 S	*	*	£95	£300
1884 M	*	*	£95	£300
1884 S	*	*	£90	£300
1885 M	*	*	£85	£250
1885 S	*	*	£85	£250
1886 M	£500	£1500	£3000	£4000
1886 S	*	*	£80	£250
1887 M	£300	£750	£1750	£2500
1887 S	*	*	£90	£250

Type II. YH obv, St George and Dragon rev

	F	VF	EF	Unc
1871	*	*	£75	£150
1871 S below head	*	£150	£500	£1250
1872	*	*	£75	£250
1872 M below head	*	£150	£500	*
1872 S	*	*	£400	*
1873	*	*	£75	£140
1873 M	*	£150	£650	£1500
1873 S	*	*	£350	*
1874	*	*	£75	£175
1874 M	*	*	£300	£175
1874 S	*	*	£300	*
1875 M	*	*	£300	£850
1875 S	*	*	£250	*
1876	*	*	£75	*
1876 M	*	*	£350	*
1876 S	*	*	£350	*
1877 M	*	*	£300	£750
1878	*	*	£75	£150
1878 M	*	*	£250	£500
1879	£65	£150	£600	*
1879 M	*	*	£250	*
1879 S	*	*	£350	*
1880	*	*	£70	*
1880 M	*	*	£250	*
1880 S	*	*	£150	£350
1881 M	*	*	£200	*
1881 S	*	*	£150	£350
1882 M	*	*	£250	*
1882 S	*	*	£150	£350
1883 M	*	*	£350	£1500
1883 S	*	*	£150	£350
1884	*	*	£70	£150
1884 M	*	*	£200	£400
1884 S	*	*	£200	£400
1885	*	*	£70	£150
1885 M	*	*	£150	£350
1885 S	*	*	£150	£350
1886 M	*	*	£150	£350
1886 S	*	*	£150	£350
1887 M	*	*	£150	£350
1887 S	*	*	£150	£350

Jubilee head coinage

	F	VF	EF	Unc
1887 (F)	*	*	£60	£85
1887 proof	*	*	£300	£450
1887 M on ground below dragon	*	*	£100	£250
1887 S on ground below dragon	*	*	£275	£550
1888	*	*	*	£90
1888 M	*	*	*	£125
1888 S	*	*	*	£125
1889	*	*	*	£90
1889 M	*	*	*	£125

	F	VF	EF	Unc
1889 S	*	*	*	£100
1890	*	*	*	£85
1890	*	*	*	£100
1890 S	*	*	*	£100
1891	*	*	*	£85
1891 M	*	*	*	£100
1891 S	*	*	*	£100
1892	*	*	*	£85
1892 M	*	*	*	£100
1892 S	*	*	*	£100
1893 M	*	*	*	£100
1893 S	*	*	*	£100

Old head coinage

	F	VF	EF	Unc
1893	*	*	*	£85
1893 proof	*	*	£350	£500
1893 M	*	*	*	£85
1893 S	*	*	*	£95
1894	*	*	*	£80
1894 M	*	*	*	£85
1894 S	*	*	*	£95
1895	*	*	*	£80
1895 M	*	*	*	£85
1895 S	*	*	*	£95
1896	*	*	*	£80
1896 M	*	*	*	£85
1896 S	*	*	*	£95
1897 M	*	*	*	£85
1897 S	*	*	*	£95
1898	*	*	*	£80
1898 M	*	*	*	£95
1898 S	*	*	*	£100
1899	*	*	*	£80

1898 Victoria Old Head sovereign

	F	VF	EF	Unc
1899 M	*	*	*	£100
1899 P (Perth mint) on ground below dragon	*	*	*	£200
1899 S	*	*	*	£150
1900	*	*	*	£75
1900 M	*	*	*	£90
1900 P	*	*	*	£110
1900 S	*	*	*	£125
1901	*	*	*	£85
1901 M	*	*	*	£85
1901 P	*	*	*	£110
1901 S	*	*	*	£100

EDWARD VII

	F	VF	EF	Unc
1902	*	*	*	£75
1902 proof	*	*	£80	£125
1902 M	*	*	*	£75
1902 P	*	*	*	£75
1902 S	*	*	*	£75
1903	*	*	*	£75
1903 M	*	*	*	£75
1903 P	*	*	*	£75
1903 S	*	*	*	£75
1904	*	*	*	£75
1904 M	*	*	*	£75
1904 P	*	*	*	£75
1904 S	*	*	*	£75
1905	*	*	*	£75
1905 M	*	*	*	£75
1905 P	*	*	*	£75

SOVEREIGNS

	F	VF	EF	Unc
1905 S	*	*	*	£75
1906	*	*	*	£75
1906 M	*	*	*	£75
1906 P	*	*	*	£75
1906 S	*	*	*	£75
1907	*	*	*	£75
1907 M	*	*	*	£75
1907 P	*	*	*	£75
1907 S	*	*	*	£75
1908	*	*	*	£75
1908 C (Canada, Ottawa mint) on ground below dragon (F)		*	£1500	£2500
1908 M	*	*	*	£75
1908 P	*	*	*	£75
1908 S	*	*	*	£75
1909	*	*	*	£75
1909 C	*	*	£225	£500
1909 M	*	*	*	£75
1909 P	*	*	*	£75
1909 S	*	*	*	£75
1910	*	*	*	£75
1910 C	*	*	£175	£400
1910 M	*	*	*	£75
1910 P	*	*	*	£75
1910 S	*	*	*	£75

GEORGE V

	F	VF	EF	Unc
1911	*	*	*	£70
1911 proof	*	*	£150	£250
1911 C	*	*	*	£85
1911 M	*	*	*	£70
1911 P	*	*	*	£70
1911 S	*	*	*	£70
1912	*	*	*	£70
1912 M	*	*	*	£70
1912 P	*	*	*	£70
1912S	*	*	*	£70
1913	*	*	*	£70
1913 C (F)	*	£175	£250	£400
1913 M	*	*	*	£70
1913 P	*	*	*	£70
1913 S	*	*	*	£70
1914	*	*	*	£70
1914 C	*	£100	£150	£200
1914 M	*	*	*	£70
1914P	*	*	*	£70
1914 S	*	*	*	£70
1915	*	*	*	£70
1915 M	*	*	*	£70
1915 P	*	*	*	£70
1915 S	*	*	*	£70
1916	*	*	*	£70
1916 C	*	*	£8000	*
1916 M	*	*	*	£70
1916 P	*	*	*	£70
1916 S	*	*	*	£70
1917 (F)	*	£1750	£2500	*
1917 C	*	*	£65	£110
1917 M	*	*	*	£70
1917 P	*	*	*	£70
1917 S	*	*	*	£70
1918 C	*	*	£75	£125
1918 I (Indian mint, Bombay), on ground below dragon	*	*	*	£80
1918 M	*	*	*	£70
1918 P	*	*	*	£70
1918 S	*	*	*	£70
1919 C	*	*	£85	£150
1919 M	*	*	*	£70
1919 P	*	*	*	£70
1919 S	*	*	*	£70
1920 M	*	£2000	£4000	*

	F	VF	EF	Unc
1920 P	*	*	*	£70
1920 S			highest	rarity
1921 M	*	£2000	£4500	£6500
1921 P	*	*	*	£80
1921 S	*	£500	£1200	£1750
1922 M	*	£1750	£400	£6500
1922 P	*	*	*	£80
1922 S	*	£3500	£7000	£12000
1923 M	*	*	*	£80
1923 S	*	£2000	£4500	£7500
1923 SA (South Africa, Pretorial Mint) on ground below dragon	*	£1250	£1750	£2500
1924 M	*	*	£75	£100
1924 P	*	*	*	£85
1924 S	*	£350	£600	£1000
1924 SA	*	*	£1500	£1750
1925	*	*	*	£80
1925 M	*	*	*	£80
1925 P	*	*	£90	£150
1925 S	*	*	*	£80
1925 SA	*	*	*	£75
1926 M	*	*	£75	£110
1926 P	*	*	£250	£350
1926 S	*	£5000	£12000	£17000
1926 SA	*	*	*	£70
1927 P	*	*	£125	£250
1927 SA	*	*	*	£70
1928 M	*	£800	£1750	£2500
1928 P	*	*	£85	£120
1928 SA	*	*	*	£70
1929 M	*	£400	£900	£1500
1929 P	*	*	*	£70
1929 SA	*	*	*	£70
1930 M	*	*	£90	£150
1930 P	*	*	*	£70
1930 SA	*	*	*	£70
1931 M	*	£100	£200	£350
1931 P	*	*	*	£70
1931 SA	*	*	*	£70
1932 SA	*	*	*	£70

GEORGE VI

	F	VF	EF	Unc
1937 proof only		*	*	£375

ELIZABETH II

	F	VF	EF	Unc
1957	*	*	*	£60
1958	*	*	*	£60
1959	*	*	*	£60
1962	*	*	*	£60
1963	*	*	*	£60
1964	*	*	*	£60
1965	*	*	*	£60
1966	*	*	*	£60
1967	*	*	*	£60
1968	*	*	*	£60
1974	*	*	*	£60
1976	*	*	*	£60
1978	*	*	*	£60
1979	*	*	*	£60
1979 proof	*	*	*	£95
1980	*	*	*	£70
1980 proof	*	*	*	£95
1981	*	*	*	£60
1981 proof	*	*	*	£95
1982	*	*	*	£60
1982 proof	*	*	*	£95
1983 proof	*	*	*	£100
1984 proof	*	*	*	£100
1985 proof	*	*	*	£105
1986 proof	*	*	*	£105
1987 proof	*	*	*	£105
1988 proof	*	*	*	£150
1989 500th anniversary of the sovereign, proof	*	*	*	£140

SOVEREIGNS

	F	VF	EF	Unc
1990 proof	*	*	*	£150
1991 proof	*	*	*	£160
1992 proof	*	*	*	£160
1993 proof	*	*	*	£160
1994 proof	*	*	*	£160
1995 proof	*	*	*	£160
1996 proof	*	*	*	£155
1997 proof	*	*	*	£150

Half sovereigns

GEORGE III

	F	VF	EF	Unc
1817	£60	£90	£200	£400
1818	£50	£100	£175	£500
1820	£55	£100	£250	£500

GEORGE IV

Laureate head/ornate shield, date on rev

	F	VF	EF	Unc
1821	£250	£450	£1000	£1750
1823 plain shield	£70	£100	£350	£575
1824	£65	£100	£300	£550
1825	£65	£100	£300	£550

Bare head, date on obv/shield, full legend rev

1826	£65	£90	£300	£550
1827	£65	£90	£300	£600
1828	£65	£90	£325	£650

WILLIAM IV

1834 reduced size	£80	£125	£450	£750
1835 normal size	£80	£125	£400	£650
1836	£200	£500	£1950	£2750
1837	£80	£100	£400	£650

Victoria 1839 proof half sovereign

VICTORIA

Young head/shield rev

	F	VF	EF	Unc
1838	*	£50	£165	£400
1839 proof only	*	*	*	£950
1841	*	£50	£155	£400
1842	*	£50	£165	£425
1843	*	£50	£165	£475
1844	*	£50	£165	£425
1845	*	£150	*	*
1846	*	£60	£175	£475
1847	*	£50	£165	£425
1848	*	£80	£185	£500
1849	*	£60	£175	£450
1850	£80	£150	£550	£1000
1851	*	£50	£165	£450
1852	*	£50	£165	£400
1853	*	£50	£165	£425
1854	£125	£200	*	*
1855	*	£50	£165	£400
1856	*	£50	£165	£400
1857	*	£50	£150	£350
1858	*	£50	£150	£350
1859	*	£50	£150	£350
1860	*	£50	£150	£350
1861	*	£50	£175	£425
1862	£200	£375	£1500	*
1863	*	£50	£150	£375
1863 die no.	*	£50	£145	£325
1864 die no.	*	£50	£145	£300
1865 die no.	*	£50	£145	£325
1866 die no.	*	£50	£145	£325
1867 die no.	*	£50	£145	£325
1869 die no.	*	£50	£145	£325

	F	VF	EF	Unc
1870 die no.	*	£50	£145	£325
1871 die no. ...	*	£50	£125	£325
1871 S below shield	*	£175	£650	£1500
1872 die no. ...	*	£50	£125	£325
1872 S	*	£175	£650	£1500
1873 die no. ...	*	£50	£125	£325
1873 M below shield	*	£175	£650	£1500

Victoria 1874 half sovereign

	F	VF	EF	Unc
1874 die no. ...	*	*	£100	£325
1875 die no. ...	*	*	£100	£325
1875 S	*	*	£650	£1500
1876 die no. ...	*	*	£100	£300
1877 die no. ...	*	*	£90	£250
1877 M	£100	£200	£850	£1650
1878 die no. ...	*	*	£90	£250
1879 die no. ...	*	*	£90	£250
1879 S	£100	£200	£750	£1550
1880	*	*	£90	£225
1880 die no. ...	*	*	£90	£225
1880 S	£150	£250	£900	£2000
1881 S	£150	£250	£900	£2000
1881 M	£150	£300	£900	£2000
1882 S	£200	£650	£3500	£6500
1882 M	*	£175	£750	£1600
1883	*	*	£90	£200
1883 S	£80	£175	£650	£1500
1884	*	*	£90	£200
1884 M	£80	£175	£750	£1500
1885	*	*	£85	£200
1885 M	£150	£400	£1500	£3750
1886 S	£65	£150	£650	£1500
1886 M	£100	£250	£1000	£3250
1887 S	£80	£175	£900	£2500
1887 M	£125	£500	£2500	£4500

Jubilee head/shield rev

1887	*	*	£60	£80
1887 proof	*	*	£200	£375
1887 M	*	£150	£350	£750
1887 S	*	£150	£400	*
1889 S	*	£150	£350	*
1890	*	*	£50	£80
1891	*	*	£50	£80
1891 S	*	*	£400	£750
1892	*	*	£50	£85
1893	*	*	£50	£85
1893 M	*	*	£450	£1000

Old head/St George reverse

1893			£45	£60
1893 proof	*	*	£225	£450
1893 M	£750	*	*	*
1893 S	£60	£120	£300	£800
1894	*	*	£45	£60
1895	*	*	£45	£60
1896	*	*	£45	£60
1896 M	£70	£125	£450	£1000
1897	*	*	£40	£65
1897 S	*	£90	£250	£450
1898	*	*	£40	£65
1899	*	*	£40	£65
1899 M	£70	£125	£450	£1500
1899 P Proof only	*	*	*	£6000
1900	*	*	£40	£60
1900 M	£70	£125	£450	£1500
1900 P	£300	£500	£1200	£2500
1900 S	*	£80	£350	£1000
1901	*	*	£40	£65

64

	F	VF	EF	Unc
1901 P proof only	*	*	*	£6000

1902
matt
proof
half
sovereign

EDWARD VII

	F	VF	EF	Unc
1902	*	*	*	£55
1902 proof	*	*	£75	£100
1902 S	*	*	£150	£450
1903	*	*	*	£60
1903 S	*	*	£90	£250
1904	*	*	*	£55
1904 P	£100	£200	£700	£1200
1905	*	*	*	£58
1906	*	*	*	£55
1906 M	*	*	£90	£350
1906 S	*	*	£85	£225
1907	*	*	*	£55
1907 M	*	*	£80	£200
1908	*	*	*	£55
1908 M	*	*	£80	£200
1908 P	*	£100	£600	*
1908 S	*	*	£80	£200
1909	*	*	*	£48
1909 M	*	*	£80	£275
1909 P	£70	£150	£500	£1500
1910	*	*	*	£48
1910 S	*	*	£80	£250

GEORGE V

	F	VF	EF	Unc
1911	*	*	*	£45
1911 proof	*	*	£100	£200
1911 P	*	*	£40	£80
1911 S	*	*	*	£50
1912	*	*	*	£45
1912 S	*	*	£40	£50
1913	*	*	*	£40
1914	*	*	*	£40
1914 S	*	*	*	£50
1915	*	*	*	£40
1915 M	*	*	£40	£50
1915 P	*	*	£40	£65
1915 S	*	*	*	£40
1916 S	*	*	*	£40
1918 P	*	£200	£500	£800
1923 SA proof...	*	*	*	£165
1925 SA	*	*	*	£40
1926 SA	*	*	*	£40

GEORGE VI

	F	VF	EF	Unc
1937 proof	*	*	*	£150

ELIZABETH II

	F	VF	EF	Unc
1980 proof	*	*	*	£55
1982	*	*	*	£38
1982 proof	*	*	*	£60
1983 proof	*	*	*	£60
1984 proof	*	*	*	£60
1985 proof	*	*	*	£65
1986 proof	*	*	*	£65
1987 proof	*	*	*	£65
1988 proof	*	*	*	£65
1989 500th anniversary of the sovereign, proof	*	*	*	£85
1990 proof	*	*	*	£80
1991 proof	*	*	*	£80
1992 proof	*	*	*	£90
1993 proof	*	*	*	£85
1994 proof	*	*	*	£85
1995 proof	*	*	*	£85
1996 proof	*	*	*	£85
1997 proof	*	*	*	£85

Crowns

CROMWELL

	F	VF	EF
1658	£700	£1200	£1950
1658 Dutch copy	*	£1750	£3000
1658 Tanner's copy	*	£2200	£3750

CHARLES II

	F	VF	EF
1662 1st bust	£95	£300	£2500
1663 –	£100	£395	£2750
1664 2nd bust	£100	£395	£3500
1665 –	£300	£750	*
1666 –	£95	£395	£3500
1666 – eleph	£175	£500	£4000
1667 –	£75	£300	£2500
1668 –	£70	£300	£2000
1668/7 –	£100	£350	£3000
1669 –	£200	£650	*
1669/8 –	£200	£750	£4000
1670 –	£80	£300	£2250
1670/69 –	£120	£350	*
1671 –	£75	£350	£2500
1671 3rd bust	£75	£300	£2250
1672 –	£75	£300	£2200
1673 –	£75	£300	£2250
1673/2 –	£80	£275	£2250
1674 –	£4000	*	*
1675 –	£300	*	*
1675/4 –	£300	*	*
1676 –	£60	£250	£1500
1677 –	£70	£250	£1500
1677/6 –	£70	£250	£1500
1678/7 –	£120	£400	*
1679 –	£65	£250	£1500
1679 4th bust –	£90	£250	£1500
1680 3rd bust –	£140	£450	£2000
1680/79 –	£70	£250	£1750
1680 4th bust –	£70	£250	£2000
1680/79 –	£125	£300	£2250
1681 – elephant & castle	£750	£2250	*
1681 –	£75	£300	£2250
1682 –	£100	£300	£2250
1682/1 –	£70	£300	£2250
1683 –	£175	£450	£2750
1684 –	£95	£350	£2250

JAMES II

	F	VF	EF
1686 1st bust	£85	£350	£1250
1687 2nd bust	£80	£150	£750
1688 –	£80	£150	£700
1688/7 –	£95	£175	£750

WILLIAM AND MARY

	F	VF	EF
1691	£150	£400	£1200
1692	£165	£350	£1000
1692/2 inverted QVINTO	£165	£350	£1000
1692/2 inverted QVARTO	£350	£750	*

WILLIAM III

	F	VF	EF
1695 1st bust	£50	£140	£450
1696 –	£50	£140	£450
1696 – GEI error	£125	£300	*
1696/5 –	£100	£250	£600
1696 2nd bust	*	*	*
1696 3rd bust	£50	£140	£450
1697 –	£350	£900	*
1700 3rd bust variety	£50	£140	£450

ANNE

	F	VF	EF
1703 1st bust VIGO	£200	£500	£2000
1705 –	£450	£850	£2500
1706 –	£125	£325	£800
1707 –	£100	£250	£700
1707 2nd bust	£85	£200	£600
1707 – E	£85	£200	£600
1708 –	£85	£225	£600

	F	VF	EF
1708 – E	£80	£225	*
1708/7 –	£90	£250	*
1708 – plumes	£110	£225	£600
1713 3rd bust	£110	£225	£600

GEORGE I

	F	VF	EF
1716	£175	£300	£1400
1718	£300	£500	£2000
1718/6	£200	£350	£1250
1720	£200	£350	£1250
1720/18	£175	£300	£1300
1723 SS C	£175	£350	£1250
1726 roses & plumes	£225	£475	£1850

GEORGE II

	F	VF	EF
1732 YH	£140	£250	£750
1732 – proof	*	*	£2000
1734	£140	£250	£750
1735	£140	£250	£650
1736	£140	£250	£650
1739	£140	£200	£625
1741	£140	£200	£600
1743 OH	£125	£195	£500

1691 William & Mary Crown

	F	VF	EF	
1746 – LIMA	£125	£195	£500	
1746 – proof	*	*	£1500	
1750	£150	£250	£700	
1751	£200	£300	£850	

GEORGE III

	F	VF	EF	Unc
Oval counter-stamp[1]	£75	£125	£250	£400
Octagonal Counterstamp[1]	£200	£350	£650	£950
1804 Bank of England dollar[1]	£50	£95	£225	£375
1818 LVIII	£10	£45	£175	£400
1818 – error edge	£250	*	*	*
1818 LIX	£10	£45	£150	£350

	F	VF	EF	Unc
1819 –	£10	£45	£175	£400
1819 – no edge stops	£50	£100	£350	*
1819/8 LIX	*	£100	£350	*
1819 LIX	£10	£35	£175	£400
1819 – no stop after TUTAMEN	£30	£50	£275	*
1820 lx	*	*	£175	£400
1820/19	£50	£150	£300	*

[1]Beware of contemporary forgeries. The counter-stamps are usually on Spanish-American dollars.

GEORGE IV

	F	VF	EF	Unc
1821 1st hd SEC ...	*	*	£225	£800
1821 – prf	*	*	*	£1500
1821 – TER error edge	*	*	£1500	£2500
1822 – SEC	*	*	£250	£900
1822 – – prf	*	*	*	*
1822 – TER	*	*	£275	£900
1822 – – prf	*	*	*	£2500
1823 – prf				£11000
1826 2nd hd prf	*	*	£1250	£2250

WILLIAM IV

	F	VF	EF	Unc
1831 w.w.	*	*	£3000	£4750
1831 W.WYON	*	*	£4000	£6500
1834 w.w.	*	*	*	£8500

VICTORIA

	F	VF	EF	Unc
1839 proof	*	*	£1250	£2750
1844 star stops	£20	£75	£600	£1500
1844 – prf	*	*	*	£5500
1844 cinquefoil stops	£20	£75	£600	£1500
1845	£20	£75	£600	£1500
1845 proof	*	*	*	£5000
1847	£20	£75	£700	£1750

Victoria 1847 Gothic crown

	F	VF	EF	Unc
1847 Gothic	£175	£350	£600	£1400
1847 – plain edge ...	*	£450	£750	£1750
1853 SEPTIMO	*	*	£2500	£4000
1853 plain	*	*	£3000	£5000
1887 JH	£12	£15	£25	£65
1887 – proof	*	*	£150	£350
1888 close date	£15	£25	£50	£85
1888 wide date	£20	£40	£95	£175
1889	£12	£15	£35	£75
1890	£12	£15	£35	£80
1891	£12	£15	£50	£100
1892	£12	£15	£50	£100
1893 LVI	£12	£15	£95	£150
1893 – proof	*	*	£150	£350
1893 LVII	£12	£40	£140	£275
1894 LVII	£12	£15	£95	£165
1894 LVIII...	£12	£15	£95	£160
1895 LVIII...	£12	£15	£95	£160
1895 LIX	£12	£15	£90	£140
1896 LIX	£12	£25	£175	£300
1896 LX	£12	£15	£90	£160
1897 LX	£12	£15	£90	£160
1897 LXI	£12	£15	£90	£160
1898 LXI	£12	£15	£125	£250
1898 LXII	£12	£15	£100	£185
1899 LXII	£12	£15	£85	£160
1899 LXIII...	£12	£15	£95	£165
1900 LXIII...	£12	£15	£95	£165
1900 LXIV...	£12	£15	£95	£165

EDWARD VII

	F	VF	EF	Unc
1902	£18	£35	£70	£100
1902 matt proof	*	*	£75	£100

GEORGE V

	F	VF	EF	Unc
1927 proof	*	*	£75	£125
1928	£50	£65	£100	£150
1929	£50	£70	£100	£175
1930	£50	£65	£110	£175
1931	£50	£65	£110	£175
1932	£70	£95	£185	£300
1933	£50	£65	£110	£175
1934	£250	£350	£600	£850
1935	£5	£7	£10	£18
1935 rsd edge prf ...	*	*	£125	£200
1935 gold proof	*	*		*£10000
1935 prf in good silver (.925)	*	*	£650	£1250
1935 specimen	*	*	*	£40
1936	£50	£75	£165	£225

GEORGE VI

	F	VF	EF	Unc
1937	*	*	£8	£15
1937 proof	*	*	*	£25
1937 'VIP' proof	*	*	*	£400
1951	*	*	*	£4
1951 'VIP' proof	*	*	*	£300

ELIZABETH II

	F	VF	EF	Unc
1953	*	*	*	£7
1953 proof	*	*	*	£15
1953 'VIP' proof	*	*	*	£200
1960	*	*	*	£7
1960 'VIP' proof	*	*	*	£350
1960 polished dies ...	*	*	£4	£10
1965 Churchill	*	*	*	£1.50
1965 – 'satin' finish ...	*	*	*	£450

For issues 1972 onwards see under 25 pence in Decimal Coinage section.

Double florins

Victoria 1887 halfcrown

VICTORIA	F	VF	EF	Unc
1887 Roman 1	*	£10	£18	£35
1887 – proof	*	*	£125	£225
1887 Arabic 1	*	£12	£20	£45
1887 – proof	*	*	£90	£175
1888	*	£12	£28	£75
1888 inverted 1	£10	£20	£65	£150
1889	*	£10	£25	£60
1889 inverted 1	£10	£25	£65	£150
1890	*	£12	£25	£70

Three shilling bank tokens

Contemporary forgeries of these pieces, as well as of other George III coins, were produced in quite large numbers. Several varieties exist for the pieces dated 1811 and 1812. Prices given here are for the commonest types of these years.

GEORGE III	F	VF	EF	Unc
1811	*	£18	£45	£75
1812 draped bust ...	*	£18	£45	£75
1812 laureate head	*	£18	£45	£75
1813	*	£18	£45	£75
1814	*	£18	£45	£75
1815	*	£18	£45	£75
1816	£70	£150	£300	£750

Halfcrowns

Cromwell 1658 halfcrown

CROMWELL	F	VF	EF
1656	£500	£1200	£3000
1658	£375	£650	£1000

CHARLES II			
1663 1st bust	£70	£350	£1500
1664 2nd bust	£85	£200	£1650
1666/3 3rd bust	£750	*	*
1666/3 – elephant	£200	£750	£4500
1667/4 –	£1450	*	*
1668/4 –	£125	£275	*
1669 –	£225	£600	*
1669/4 –	£125	£375	*
1670 –	£40	£150	£1000
1671 3rd bust var	£40	£150	£1000
1671/0 –	£60	£150	£1100
1672 –	£65	£160	£1100
1672 4th bust	£90	£250	£1200
1673 –	£40	£150	£1250
1673 – plume below	£1000	*	*
1673 – plume both sides ...	£1750	*	*
1674 –	£95	£350	*
1674/3 –	£110	*	*
1675 –	£40	£125	£750

Charles II 1676 halfcrown

1676 –	£40	£125	£750
1677 –	£40	£125	£750
1678 –	£110	£300	*
1679 –	£40	£95	£750
1680 –	£125	£250	*
1681 –	£50	£150	£1000
1681/0 –	£50	£150	£1000
1681 – eleph & castle	£1250	*	*
1682 –	£100	£250	*
1682/1 –	£125	*	*
1682/79 –	£125	*	*
1683 –	£45	£110	£1250
1683 – plume below	£3000	*	*
1684/3 –	£150	*	*

James III 1687 halfcrown

JAMES II			
1685 1st bust	£65	£185	£750
1686 –	£65	£185	£750
1686/5 –	£125	£350	*
1687 –	£65	£185	£750

	F	VF	EF
1687/6 –	£85	£225	£850
1687 2nd bust	£100	£295	£950
1688 –	£65	£185	£750

WILLIAM AND MARY

	F	VF	EF
1689 1st busts 1st shield ...	£60	£175	£500
1689 – 2nd shield	£60	£175	£500
1690 – –	£75	£200	£600
1691 2nd busts 3rd shield ...	£65	£200	£550
1692 – –	£65	£200	£550
1693 – –	£60	£175	£500
1693 – – 3 inverted	£85	£225	£750
1693 3 over 3 inverted	£80	£200	£600

William and Mary 1693 Halfcrown

WILLIAM III

1696 large shield early harp	£20	£45	£150
1696 – – B	£30	£80	£275
1696 – – C	£35	£80	£275
1696 – – E	£40	£90	£325
1696 – – N	£35	£85	£350
1696 – – Y	£30	£80	£325
1696 – – y/E	£65	*	*
1696 – ord harp	£75	*	*
1696 – – C	£75	*	*
1696 – – E	£85	£200	*
1696 – – N	£85	*	*
1696 small shield	£20	£50	£150
1696 – B	£30	£80	£300
1696 – C	£55	£125	*
1696 – E	£85	*	*
1696 – N	£30	£80	£300
1696 – y	£40	£90	£300
1696 2nd bust	*	*	*
1697 1st bust large shield ...	£20	£50	£125
1697 – – B	£30	£75	£200
1697 – – C	£35	£70	£250
1697 – – E	£35	£70	£250
1697 – – E/C	£80	£150	*
1697 – – N	£30	£70	£300
1697 – – y	£30	£70	£250

1697 Halfcrown of NORWICH: N below bust

1698 – –	£20	£40	£150
1699 – –	£35	£100	£325

	F	VF	EF
1700 – –	£20	£40	£150
1701 – –	£30	£50	£175
1701 – eleph & castle	£500	*	*
1701 – plumes	£100	£300	£750

ANNE

1703 plain	£300	£700	£1600
1703 VIGO	£50	£150	£350
1704 plumes	£100	£200	£650
1705 –	£75	£175	£500
1706 r & p	£35	£100	£225
1707 –	£30	£100	£225
1707 plain	£35	£45	£150
1707 E	£30	£75	£225
1708 plain	£20	£45	£150
1708 E	£30	£75	£300
1708 plumes	£40	£125	£300
1709 plain	£25	£60	£150
1709 E	£150	*	*
1710 r & p	£40	£125	£250
1712 –	£35	£85	£200
1713 plain	£50	£175	£500
1713 r & p	£30	£85	£250
1714 –	£30	£85	£275
1714/3	£85	*	*

GEORGE I

1715 proof	*	*	£2500
1715 r & p	£90	£175	£600
1717 –	£100	£275	£700
1720 –	£150	£350	£800
1720/17 –	£85	£165	£575
1723 SS C	£75	£140	£400
1725 small r & p	£1000		*

Spanish Half Dollar with George III counterstamp (octagonal)

GEORGE II

1731 YH proof	*	*	£1800
1731	£60	£150	£400
1732	£60	£150	£400
1734	£60	£150	£400
1735	£60	£150	£425
1736	£60	£150	£400
1739	£50	£120	£275
1741	£90	£195	£450
1743 OH	£50	£70	£200
1745	£50	£60	£150
1745 LIMA	£40	£75	£175
1746 –	£40	£75	£175
1746 plain, proof	*	*	£750
1750	£75	£175	£350
1751	£40	£185	£400
1741/39	£60	£120	£250

GEORGE III	F	VF	EF	Unc
Oval counterstamp usually on Spanish half dollar	£100	£200	£350	*

HALFCROWNS

	F	VF	EF	Unc
1816 large head	*	£40	£100	£200
1817 –	*	£40	£100	£200
1817 small head ...	*	£40	£100	£185
1818	*	£40	£100	£200
1819	*	£40	£100	£200
1819/8	*	*	*	*
1820	*	£50	£125	£225

George IV halfcrown of 1821

GEORGE IV

	F	VF	EF	Unc
1820 1st hd 1st rev ...	*	£45	£125	£250
1821 –	*	£45	£125	£250
1821 proof	*	*	£450	£750
1823	£300	£750	£2250	*
1823 – 2nd rev	*	£45	£125	£275
1824 – –	£25	£50	£175	£375
1824 2nd hd 3rd rev ...	£1000	*	*	*
1825 – –	*	£25	£90	£200
1826 – –	*	£20	£90	£200
1826 – – proof	*	*	£200	£450
1828 – –	*	£28	£175	£300
1829 – –	*	£28	£125	£250

William IV 1831 halfcrown

WILLIAM IV

	F	VF	EF	Unc
1831	*	*	*	*
1831 proof	*	*	£250	£475
1834 ww	£30	£60	£200	£500
1834 ww in script ...	£12	£35	£95	£250
1835	£25	£60	£175	£400
1836	£12	£35	£95	£250
1836/5	£30	£75	£250	*
1837	£35	£80	£250	£600

VICTORIA

From time to time halfcrowns bearing dates ranging from 1861 to 1871 are found, but except for rare proofs: 1853, 1862 and 1864, no halfcrowns were struck between 1850 and 1874, so pieces dated for this period are now considered to be contemporary or later forgeries.

	F	VF	EF	Unc
1839 plain and ornate fillets, ww	*	£550	£1750	*
1839 – plain edge proof	*	*	£325	£650
1839 plain fillets, ww incuse	*	£750	£1750	£2500
1840	£10	£30	£150	£225
1841	£75	£225	£700	£1000
1842	£10	£20	£150	£250
1843	£40	£95	£250	£475
1844	£10	£20	£125	£250
1845	£10	£20	£175	£300
1846	£14	£25	£175	£300
1848	£75	£175	£450	£850
1848/6	£75	£200	£550	£950
1849 large date	£20	£60	£200	£450
1849 small date	£50	£175	£375	£750
1850	£20	£60	£225	£425
1853 proof	*	£350	£600	£1000
1862 proof	*	*	£1500	£2250
1864 proof	*	*	£1500	£2250
1874	*	£25	£95	£150
1875	*	£15	£75	£140
1876	*	£30	£120	£200
1876/5	*	*	*	*
1877	*	£15	£70	£140
1878	*	£15	£70	£140
1879	*	£18	£85	£120
1880	*	£10	£65	£120
1881	*	£10	£60	£100
1882	*	£10	£60	£120
1883	*	£10	£60	£95
1884	*	£10	£60	£95
1885	*	£10	£60	£95
1886	*	£10	£60	£95
1887 YH	*	£15	£70	£140
1887 JH	*	£5	£15	£35
1887 – proof	*	*	£70	£130
1888	*	£6	£25	£50
1889	*	£5	£25	£45
1890	*	£6	£30	£55
1891	*	£6	£30	£65
1892	*	£6	£30	£65
1893 OH	*	£6	£35	£60
1893 – proof	*	*	£80	£150
1894	*	£6	£35	£60
1895	*	£6	£35	£60
1896	*	£6	£35	£60
1897	*	£6	£35	£60
1898	*	£6	£35	£60
1899	*	£6	£35	£65
1900	*	£6	£35	£60
1901	*	£6	£30	£60

EDWARD VII

	F	VF	EF	Unc
1902	*	£6	£20	£35
1902 matt proof	*	*	*	£40
1903	£20	£65	£300	£600
1904	£15	£45	£185	£425
1905 (F)	£65	£200	£900	£1500
1906	*	£20	£85	£175
1907	*	£25	£85	£200
1908	*	£20	£175	£275
1909	*	£8	£85	£175
1910	*	£6	£35	£70

GEORGE V

	F	VF	EF	Unc
1911	*	£4	£30	£65
1911 proof	*	*	*	£85
1912	£1.20	£3	£35	£80
1913	£1.20	£3	£40	£90
1914	*	*	£10	£30
1915	*	*	£10	£20
1916	*	*	£10	£20

	F	VF	EF	Unc
1917	*	£2	£10	£28
1918	*	*	£10	£20
1919	*	*	£12	£20
1920	*	*	£15	£40
1921	*	*	£17	£40
1922	*	*	£17	£50
1923	*	*	£10	£20
1924	*	*	£10	£30
1925	£4	£15	£150	£250

George V 1926 halfcrown

	F	VF	EF	Unc
1926	*	*	£25	£65
1926 mod eff	*	*	£35	£85
1927	*	*	£12	£40
1927 new rev, proof			*	£25
1928	*	*	£4	£25
1929	*	*	£4	£20
1930	£4	£15	£100	£175
1931	*	*	£4	£20
1932	*	*	£15	£35
1933	*	*	£4	£20
1934	*	*	£17	£35
1935	*	*	£3	£12
1936	*	*	£2	£10

GEORGE VI

	F	VF	EF	Unc
1937	*	*	*	£9
1937 proof	*	*	*	£12
1938	*	*	£4	£20
1939	*	*	*	£14
1940	*	*	*	£8
1941	*	*	*	£7
1942	*	*	*	£7
1943	*	*	*	£7
1944	*	*	*	£7
1945	*	*	*	£7
1946	*	*	*	£4
1947	*	*	*	£4
1948	*	*	*	£4
1949	*	*	*	£8
1950	*	*	*	£8
1950 proof	*	*	*	£10
1951	*	*	*	£8
1951 proof	*	*	*	£10

ELIZABETH II

	F	VF	EF	Unc
1953	*	*	*	£2
1953 proof	*	*	*	£8
1954	*	*	£3	£20
1955	*	*	*	£4
1956	*	*	*	£4
1957	*	*	*	£3
1958	*	*	£2.50	£15
1959	*	*	£4	£35
1960	*	*	*	£3
1961	*	*	*	£1
1962	*	*	*	£1
1963	*	*	*	£1
1964	*	*	*	*
1965	*	*	*	*
1966	*	*	*	*
1967	*	*	*	*

Florins

The first florins produced in the reign of Victoria bore the legend VICTORIA REGINA and the date, omitting DEI GRATIA (By the Grace of God). They are therefore known as 'Godless' florins.

The date of a Victorian Gothic florin is shown in Roman numerals, in Gothic lettering on the obverse for example: mdccclvii (1857). Gothic florins were issued during the period 1851-1887.

VICTORIA	F	VF	EF	Unc
1848 'Godless' proof with milled edge	*	*	*	£1000

Victoria 1849 'Godless' florin

	F	VF	EF	Unc
1849 – ww obliterated by circle	£8	£25	£65	£125
1849 – ww inside circle	£7	£20	£65	£125
1851 proof only	*	*	*	£4000
1852	£5	£30	£65	£125
1853	£5	£30	£65	£130
1853 no stop after date	£5	£30	£70	£135
1853 proof	*	*	*	£750
1854	£250	£500	£800	*
1855	£5	£30	£70	£130
1856	£5	£35	£125	£240
1857	£5	£30	£125	£130
1858	£5	£30	£125	£130
1859	£5	£30	£125	£130
1859 no stop after date	£8	£35	£125	£150
1860	£8	£40	£130	£185
1862	£15	£75	£200	£300
1863	£35	£125	£300	£600
1864	£5	£30	£125	£190
1865	£5	£30	£125	£180
1865 colon after date	£8	£40	£125	£180
1866	£5	£30	£125	£185
1866 colon after date	£8	£30	£140	£200
1867	£10	£40	£150	£200
1868	£5	£30	£140	£190
1869	£5	£30	£125	£200
1870	£5	£30	£135	£185
1871	£5	£30	£125	£185

Victoria 1871 Gothic florin

FLORINS

	F	VF	EF	Unc
1872	£5	£28	£70	£125
1873	£5	£30	£70	£125
1874	£5	£28	£70	£125
1874 xxiv-/ (die 29)	£50	£95	*	*
1875	£5	£30	£70	£125
1876	£5	£30	£70	£125
1877	£5	£30	£75	£140
1877 no ww	£25	*	*	*
1877 42 arcs	£25	*	*	*
1878	£5	£28	£70	£125
1879 ww 48 arcs	£8	£28	£75	£130
1879 die no.	£10	£40	£125	£225
1879 ww. 42 arcs	£10	£40	£40	£130
1879 no ww, 38 arcs	£5	£28	£70	£120
1880	£5	£26	£65	£110
1881	£5	£26	£65	£110
1881 xxri	£8	£28	£70	£120
1883	£5	£26	£65	£110
1884	£5	£26	£65	£110
1885	£5	£26	£65	£110
1886	£5	£28	£65	£110
1887 33 arcs	£8	£30	£70	£130
1887 46 arcs	£8	£40	£130	£175
1887 JH	£2	£5	£12	£20
1887 – proof	*	*	£45	£90
1888	*	£5	£25	£40
1889	*	£5	£25	£40
1890	£5	£15	£40	£80
1891	£20	£50	£110	£195
1892	£20	£50	£100	£165
1893 OH	£2	£4	£24	£50
1893 proof	*	*	*	£110
1894	*	£5	£25	£50
1895	*	£5	£25	£50
1896	*	£5	£25	£50
1897	*	£5	£25	£50
1898	*	£4	£25	£50
1899	*	£4	£25	£50
1900	*	£3	£25	£50
1901	*	£3	£25	£50

Edward VII 1902 florin

EDWARD VII

	F	VF	EF	Unc
1902	*	£5	£18	£30
1902 matt proof	*	*	*	£35
1903	£3	£25	£40	£75
1904	£5	£32	£100	£195
1905	£20	£50	£250	£500
1906	*	£16	£30	£70
1907	*	£16	£40	£90
1908	£2	£18	£60	£135
1909	£3	£24	£70	£150
1910	*	£6	£20	£45

GEORGE V

	F	VF	EF	Unc
1911	*	£2.25	£25	£45
1911 proof	*	*	*	£50
1912	*	*	330	£65

	F	VF	EF	Unc
1913	*	*	£35	£70
1914	*	*	£10	£25
1915	*	*	£8	£18
1916	*	*	£8	£18
1917	*	*	£8	£18
1918	*	*	£8	£15
1919	*	*	£8	£20
1920	*	*	£12	£35
1921	*	*	£10	£28
1922	*	*	£12	£32
1923	*	*	£12	£22
1924	*	*	£12	£35
1925	*	£35	£125	£200
1926	*	*	£25	£60
1927 proof only	*	*	*	£30

George V 1928 florin

	F	VF	EF	Unc
1928	*	*	£5	£12
1929	*	*	£5	£12
1930	*	*	£8	£50
1931	*	*	£4	£20
1932	£10	£45	£120	£200
1933	*	*	£6	£15
1935	*	*	£6	£15
1936	*	*	£2	£8

GEORGE VI

	F	VF	EF	Unc
1937	*	*	£1	£7
1937 proof	*	*	*	£12
1938	*	*	£2	£15
1939	*	*	£1	£6
1940	*	*	£1	£6
1941	*	*	£1	£4
1942	*	*	*	£5
1943	*	*	*	£4
1944	*	*	*	£4
1945	*	*	*	£4
1946	*	*	*	£4
1947	*	*	*	£4
1948	*	*	*	£3
1949	*	*	*	£5
1950	*	*	*	£6
1950 proof	*	*	*	£8
1951	*	*	*	£5
1951 proof	*	*	*	£9

Elizabeth II 1956 florin

ELIZABETH II	F	VF	EF	Unc
1953	*	*	*	£2
1953 proof	*	*	*	£5
1954	*	*	*	£15
1955	*	*	*	£3
1956	*	*	*	£3
1957	*	*	*	£15
1958	*	*	*	£10
1959	*	*	*	£15
1960	*	*	*	£1
1961	*	*	*	£1
1962	*	*	*	*
1963	*	*	*	*
1964	*	*	*	*
1965	*	*	*	*
1966	*	*	*	*
1967	*	*	*	*

One and sixpence bank tokens

GEORGE III	F	VF	EF	Unc
1811	£5	£14	£30	£50
1812 laureate bust ...	£5	£14	£35	£60
1812 laureate head	£5	£14	£35	£60
1813	£5	£14	£35	£60
1814	£5	£14	£35	£60
1815	£5	£14	£35	£60
1816	£5	£14	£35	£60

Shillings

1658 shilling of Cromwell

CROMWELL	F	VF	EF
1658	£250	£500	£700
1658 Dutch copy	*	*	*

Charles II 1671 shilling, plumes below bust

CHARLES II	F	VF	EF
1663 1st bust	£40	£100	£350
1663 1st bust var	£40	£100	£350
1666 –	*	*	*
1666 – eleph	£150	£400	£1500
1666 guinea hd, eleph ...	£500	£1200	*

	F	VF	EF
1666 2nd bust	£500	*	*
1668 1st bust var	£250	*	*
1668 2nd bust	£35	£100	£350
1668/7 –	£50	£110	£425
1669/6 1st bust var	£375	*	*
1669 2nd bust	*	*	*
1670 –	£50	£110	£425
1671 –	£55	£125	£475
1671 – plumes both sides	£175	£375	£950
1672 –	£40	£90	£350
1673 –	£45	£100	£450
1673/2 –	£50	£90	£425
1673 – plumes both sides	£200	£425	*
1674 –	£45	£100	£425
1674/3 –	£50	£150	£400
1674 – plumes both sides	£150	£400	£1000
1674 – plumes rev only ...	£150	£400	*
1674 3rd bust	£250	*	*
1675 –	£300	£650	*
1675/3 –	£300	£650	*
1675 2nd bust	£200	£500	*
1675/4 –	£200	£500	*
1675 – plumes both sides	£200	£450	*
1676 –	£30	£90	£350
1676/5 –	£35	£125	£400
1676 – plumes both sides	£175	£450	£1200
1677 –	£35	£90	£400
1677 – plume obv only ...	£300	*	*
1678 –	£50	£110	£425
1678/7 –	£50	£125	£450
1679 –	£35	£90	£325
1679/7 –	£50	£125	£425
1679 plumes	£250	*	*
1679 plumes obv only ...	£200	*	*
1680 –	£500	*	*
1680 plumes	£175	£450	£1200
1680/79 –	*	*	*
1681 –	£100	£275	*
1681/0 –	£100	£275	*
1681/0 – eleph & castle ...	£850	*	*
1682/1	£175	*	*
1683 –	*	*	*
1683 4th bust	£75	£150	£575
1684 –	£50	£125	£500

James II 1685 shilling

JAMES II	F	VF	EF
1685	£70	£175	£500
1685 no stops on rev	£125	*	*
1685 plume on rev	*	£2000	£7500
1686	£50	£125	£450
1686 V/S	£60	£150	£450
1687	£50	£125	£450
1687/6	£40	£100	£425
1688	£45	£115	£450
1688/7	£60	£125	£475
WILLIAM & MARY			
1692	£60	£150	£425
1693	£55	£125	£400

SHILLINGS

WILLIAM III

	F	VF	EF
1695	£12	£35	£100
1696	£10	£25	£75
1696 no strap on rev ...	£25	£70	£165
1669 in error	£400	*	*
1696 1st bust B	£15	£40	£135
1696 – C	£15	£40	£135
1696 – E	£15	£40	£135
1696 – N	£15	£40	£135
1696 – Y	£15	£40	£135
1696 – Y	£20	£60	£175
1696 2nd bust		highest rarity	
1696 3rd bust C	£60	£150	£375
1696 – E	£125	*	*
1697 1st bust	£10	£20	£65
1697 – no stops on rev ...	£25	£75	£200
1697 – B	£15	£40	£150
1697 – C	£15	£40	£150

1697 Shilling of BRISTOL: B below bust

	F	VF	EF
1697 – E	£15	£60	£160
1697 – N	£20	£45	£160
1697 – Y	£20	£45	£160
1697 – Y	£25	£50	£170
1697 3rd bust	£12	£20	£65
1697 – B	£20	£65	£225
1697 – C	£12	£45	£130
1697 – E	£18	£65	£200
1697 – N	£18	£50	£160
1697 – Y	£18	£50	£160
1697 3rd bust var	£10	£25	£75
1697 – B	£18	£50	£150
1697 – C	£75	£125	£275
1698	£20	£65	£150
1698 – plumes	£75	£125	£400
1698 4th bust	£60	£140	£400
1699 –	£70	£150	£425
1699 5th bust	£40	£75	£200
1699 – plumes	£40	£180	£175
1699 – roses	£85	£175	£375
1700 –	£10	£30	£90
1700 – no stops on rev ...	£30	£65	£150
1700 – plume	£650	*	*
1701 –	£35	£95	£200
1701 – plumes	£60	£120	£275

Anne 1702 shilling, VIGO below bust

ANNE

	F	VF	EF
1702 – 1st bust	£35	£75	£175

1702 – plumes	£45	£95	£30
1702 – VIGO	£35	£65	£17
1703 2nd bust VIGO	£35	£70	£19
1704 –	£150	£450	
1704 – plumes	£50	£125	£30
1705 –	£50	£125	£30
1705 – plumes	£35	£65	£20
1705 – r&p	£35	£65	£20
1707 – r&p	£35	£65	£20
1707 – E	£35	£60	£15
1707 – E★	£65	£100	£25
1707 3rd bust	£15	£25	£8
1707 – plumes	£35	£70	£17
1707 – E	£15	£50	£15
1707 Edin bust E★	*	*	
1708 2nd bust E	£60	£165	
1708 – E★	£40	£70	£22
1708/7 – E★	£45	£125	
1708 – r&p	£45	£140	£35
1708 3rd bust	£12	£25	£9
1708 – plumes	£35	£65	£20
1708 – r&p	£35	£65	£20
1708 – E	£45	£90	
1708 – E	£60	£120	
1708 – Edin bust E★	£30	£65	£22
1709 –	£35	£75	£22
1709 – E	£75	£140	£35
1709 3rd bust	£12	£25	£8
1710 – r&p	£25	£50	£16
1710 4th bust prf	*	*	
1710 – r&p	£30	£65	£18
1711 3rd bust	£55	£90	£22
1711 4th bust	£12	£25	£8
1712 – r&p	£20	£30	£15
1713/2 –	£25	£45	£15
1714 –	£20	£45	£15

George I 1723 SS C shilling

GEORGE I

1715 1st bust r&p	£20	£50	£14
1716 –	£75	£200	£45
1717 –	£20	£50	£16
1718 –	£25	£60	£15
1719 –	£60	£150	£25
1720 –	£20	£40	£14
1720 – plain	£15	£35	£14
1720 – large 0	£15	£35	£14
1721 –	£150	£400	£70
1721 r&p	£15	£40	£14
1721/0 –	£15	£40	£14
1721/19	£20	£45	£14
1721/18 –	£20	£45	£14
1722 –	£15	£45	£14
1723 –	£12	£45	£15
1723 – SS C	£12	£30	£9
1723 – SSC French arms at date	£95	£140	£25
1723 2nd bust SS C	£12	£30	£10
1723 – r&p	£15	£70	£20
1723 – w.c.c.	£150	£300	£80
1724 – r&p	£15	£70	£20
1724 – w.c.c.	£150	£300	£80

	F	VF	EF
1725 – r & p	£20	£70	£200
1725 – no obv stops	£40	£100	£275
1725 – w.c.c.	£250	£400	*
1726 – r & p	*	*	*
1726 – w.c.c.	£300	£500	*
1712 – r & p	£400	*	*
1727 – – no stops on obv	£300	*	*

GEORGE II

	F	VF	EF
1727 YH plumes	£50	£125	£240
1727 – r & p	£40	£90	£200
1728 –	£50	£100	£395
1728 – r & p	£40	£80	£180
1729 – –	£45	£90	£200
1731 – –	£20	£70	£165
1731 – plumes	£45	£125	£350
1732 – r & p	£35	£80	£175
1734 – –	£35	£70	£175
1735 – –	£35	£70	£175
1736 – –	£35	£70	£175
1736/5 – –	£40	£80	£190
1737 – –	£20	£65	£150
1739 – roses	£12	£35	£120
1741 – roses	£12	£40	£120

1763 'Northumberland' Shilling

	F	VF	EF
1743 OH roses	£12	£35	£125
1745 –	£12	£35	£125
1745 – LIMA	£15	£30	£125
1746 – – LIMA	£40	£100	£300
1746/5 – LIMA	£25	£120	£350
1746 – proof	*	£250	£500
1747 – roses	£12	£35	£100
1750 –	£12	£35	£130
1750/6 –	£15	£40	£130
1750 – 5 over 4	£15	£35	£130
1751 –	£20	£45	£145
1758 –	£8	£15	£25

1728 Young Head Shilling

GEORGE III

	F	VF	EF	Unc
1763 'Northumber- land'	£125	£195	£300	£400
1786 proof or pattern	*	*	*	£2500
1787 no hearts	*	£5	£25	£35
1787 – no stop over head	£3	£15	£45	£65
1787 – no stops at date	£3	£20	£40	£70

	F	VF	EF	Unc
1787 – no stops on obv	£100	£300	£600	*
1787 hearts	*	£4	£25	£35
1798 'Dorrien and Magens'	*	*	£3250	£5000
1816	£1	£3	£35	£50
1817	£1	£3	£35	£50
1817 GEOE	£30	£70	£250	*
1818	£4	£20	£45	£90
1819	£1	£4	£40	£55
1819/8	*	*	£90	£90
1820	£1	£4	£40	£75

GEORGE IV

	F	VF	EF	Unc
1820 1st hd 1st rev pattern or prf ...	*	*	*	£1500
1821 1st hd 1st rev	£5	£10	£80	£130
1821 – proof	*	*	£175	£350
1823 – 2nd rev	£5	£30	£85	£185
1824 – –	£5	£12	£70	£130
1825 – –	£5	£12	£70	£130
1825 2nd hd	£5	£10	£70	£140
1826 –	£3	£10	£70	£110

George IV 1826 shilling

	F	VF	EF	Unc
1826 – proof	*	*	£75	£150
1827	£5	£20	£100	£160
1829	£4	£15	£85	£150

WILLIAM IV

	F	VF	EF	Unc
1831 proof	*	*	*	£275
1834	£3	£15	£70	£130
1835	£5	£20	£100	£180
1836	£3	£12	£70	£130
1837	£5	£15	£125	£275

William IV 1837 shilling

VICTORIA

	F	VF	EF	Unc
1838	£2	£12	£50	£90
1839	£2	£12	£65	£110
1839 2nd YH	£2	£9	£60	£80
1839 – proof	*	*	*	£225
1840	£7	£30	£90	£125
1841	£2	£12	£55	£140
1842	£2	£10	£55	£90
1843	£2	£12	£65	£100
1844	£1	£9	£55	£90
1845	£2	£10	£55	£90
1846	£1	£10	£55	£90
1848/6	£20	£70	£275	£425
1849	£2	£10	£65	£120

SHILLINGS

	F	VF	EF	Unc
1850	£150	£450	£900	*
1850/46	£150	£450	£900	*
1851	£15	£50	£200	*
1852	£1	£10	£55	£90
1853	£1	£10	£55	£90
1853 proof	*	*	*	£350
1854	£20	£90	£250	*
1855	£2	£10	£55	£90
1856	£2	£10	£55	£90
1857	£2	£10	£55	£90
1857 F:G:	*	*	*	*
1858	£2	£10	£50	£90
1859	£2	£10	£50	£90
1860	£5	£10	£75	£135
1861	£5	£10	£75	£135
1862	£8	£30	£90	£165

Victoria 1839 shilling

	F	VF	EF	Unc
1863	£8	£35	£150	£250
1864	£4	£9	£50	£90
1865	£4	£9	£50	£90
1866	£4	£9	£50	£90
1866 BBITANNIAR ...	*	*	£350	*
1867	£4	£9	£60	£110
1867 3rd YH, die no.	£150	£250	*	*
1868	£4	£9	£60	£110
1869	£4	£10	£70	£130
1870	£4	£10	£70	£125
1871	£4	£9	£40	£65
1872	£2	£8	£40	£65
1873	£2	£8	£40	£65
1874	£2	£8	£40	£65
1875	£2	£8	£40	£65
1876	£2	£8	£40	£80
1877 die no.	£1	£5	£35	£55
1877 no die no	*	*	*	*
1878	£1	£5	£35	£60
1879 3rd YH	£10	£20	£85	*
1879 4th YH	£3	£10	£35	£70
1880	£1	£5	£25	£55
1880 longer line below SHILLING	*	*	*	*
1881	£1	£5	£25	£60
1881 longer line below SHILLING	£2	£8	£30	£60
1881 – Large rev lettering	£2	£8	£25	£60
1882	£2	£10	£45	£110
1883	£1	£5	£30	£55
1884	£1	£5	£30	£55
1885	£1	£5	£30	£55
1886	£1	£5	£30	£55
1887	£1	£5	£40	£90
1887 JH	*	*	£5	£12
1887 proof	*	*	*	£80
1888	*	£4	£20	£45
1889	£12	£30	£150	£300
1889 large JH	*	£2	£15	£40
1890	*	£2	£20	£50
1891	*	£2	£20	£45
1892	*	£2	£20	£45

Victoria Jubilee Head and Old Head shillings

	F	VF	EF	Unc
1893 OH	*	£2	£12	£20
1893 – proof	*	*	*	£100
1893 small obv letters	*	£2	£15	£30
1894	*	£2	£15	£30
1895	*	£2	£15	£30
1896	*	£2	£15	£30
1897	*	£2	£15	£30
1898	*	£2	£15	£30
1899	*	£2	£15	£30
1900	*	£2	£15	£30
1901	*	£2	£15	£20

EDWARD VII

	F	VF	EF	Unc
1902	*	£2	£12	£18
1902 matt prf	*	*	£15	£20

Edward VII 1905 shilling

	F	VF	EF	Unc
1903	£3	£10	£75	£200
1904	£3	£10	£85	£225
1905	£25	£65	£375	*
1906	*	£2	£20	£45
1907	£1	£5	£25	£60
1908	£3	£10	£75	£200
1909	£1	£9	£90	£175
1910	*	£3	£15	£35

GEORGE V

	F	VF	EF	Unc
1911	*	*	£6	£18
1911 proof	*	*	*	£30
1912	*	*	£3	£45
1913	*	*	£20	£60
1914	*	*	£3	£12
1915	*	*	£2	£10
1916	*	*	£3	£12
1917	*	*	£3	£15
1918	*	*	£3	£15
1919	*	*	£6	£25
1920	*	*	£7	£20
1921	*	*	£7	£25

George V nickel trial shilling, 1924

	F	VF	EF	Unc
1922	*	*	£12	£35
1923	*	*	£7	£25
1923 nickel	*	*	£250	£450
1924	*	*	£7	£20
1924 nickel	*	*	£250	£450
1925	*	*	£12	£60
1926	*	*	£8	£35
1926 mod eff	*	*	£8	£25
1927 –	*	*	£8	£30
1927 new type	*	*	£4	£20
1927 – proof	*	*	*	£20
1928	*	*	£1	£10
1929	*	*	£2	£12
1930	*	*	£7	£20
1931	*	*	£3	£12
1932	*	*	£3	£12
1933	*	*	£3	£12
1934	*	*	£4	£25
1935	*	*	£1	£7
1936	*	*	£1	£5

GEORGE VI

	F	VF	EF	Unc
1937 Eng	*	*	£1	£5
1937 Eng prf	*	*	*	£7
1937 Scot	*	*	£1	£3
1937 Scot prf	*	*	*	£6
1938 Eng	*	*	£2	£15
1938 Scot	*	*	£2	£12
1939 Eng	*	*	£1	£5
1939 Scot	*	*	£1	£5
1940 Eng	*	*	£1	£5
1940 Scot	*	*	£1	£5
1941 Eng	*	*	£1	£4
1941 Scot	*	*	£2	£5
1942 Eng	*	*	£1	£3
1942 Scot	*	*	£1	£4
1943 Eng	*	*	£1	£3
1943 Scot	*	*	£1	£4
1944 Eng	*	*	*	£3
1944 Scot	*	*	*	£3
1945 Eng	*	*	*	£3
1945 Scot	*	*	*	£2
1946 Eng	*	*	*	£2
1946 Scot	*	*	*	£2
1947 Eng	*	*	*	£3
1947 Scot	*	*	*	£3

Reverses: English (left), Scottish (right)

	F	VF	EF	Unc
1948 Eng	*	*	*	£2
1948 Scot	*	*	*	£2
1949 Eng	*	*	*	£4
1949 Scot	*	*	*	£4
1950 Eng	*	*	*	£5
1950 Eng prf	*	*	*	£6
1950 Scot	*	*	*	£5
1950 Scot prf	*	*	*	£6
1951 Eng	*	*	*	£5
1951 Eng prf	*	*	*	£6
1951 Scot	*	*	*	£5
1951 Scot prf	*	*	*	£6

ELIZABETH II

	F	VF	EF	Unc
1953 Eng	*	*	*	£1
1953 Eng prf	*	*	*	£5
1953 Scot	*	*	*	£1

SHILLINGS

	F	VF	EF	Unc
1953 Scot prf	*	*	*	£5
1954 Eng	*	*	*	£1
1954 Scot	*	*	*	£1
1955 Eng	*	*	*	£1
1955 Scot	*	*	*	£1
1956 Eng	*	*	*	£2
1956 Scot	*	*	*	£6
1957 Eng	*	*	*	£2
1957 Scot	*	*	*	£5
1958 Eng	*	*	*	£6
1958 Scot	*	*	*	£1

Reverses: English (left), Scottish (right)

	F	VF	EF	Unc
1959 Eng	*	*	*	£1
1959 Scot	*	*	*	£20
1960 Eng	*	*	*	£1
1960 Scot	*	*	*	£2
1961 Eng	*	*	*	£0.80
1961 Scot	*	*	*	£5
1962 Eng	*	*	*	*
1962 Scot	*	*	*	*
1963 Eng	*	*	*	*
1963 Scot	*	*	*	*
1964 Eng	*	*	*	*
1964 Scot	*	*	*	*
1965 Eng	*	*	*	*
1965 Scot	*	*	*	*
1966 Eng	*	*	*	*
1966 Scot	*	*	*	*

Sixpences

CROMWELL

	F	VF	EF
1658	*	*	of the highest rarity
1658 Dutch copy	£500	£900	*

CHARLES II

	F	VF	EF
1674	£20	£60	£160
1675	£15	£50	£160
1675/4	£25	£75	£185
1676	£25	£75	£185
1676/5	£25	£75	£185
1677	£15	£50	£160
1678/7	£25	£75	£180

Charles II 1678 sixpence

	F	VF	EF
1679	£25	£75	£185
1680	£35	£95	£250

SIXPENCES

	F	VF	EF
1681	£15	£45	£150
1682	£35	£85	£195
1682/1	£15	£55	£150
1683	£12	£55	£135
1684	£20	£65	£180

James II 1688 sixpence

JAMES II

	F	VF	EF
1686 early shields	£45	£100	£300
1687 –	£40	£100	£350
1687/6	£40	£100	£350
1687 later shield	£40	£100	£300
1687/6	£45	£110	£375
1688 –	£50	£125	£400

WILLIAM AND MARY

	F	VF	EF
1693	£45	£125	£325
1693 3 upside down	£55	£150	£350
1694	£70	£175	£375

William and Mary 1694 sixpence

WILLIAM III

	F	VF	EF
1695 1st bust early harp ...	£5	£25	£95
1696 – –	£3	£15	£45
1696 – – no obv stops	£5	£25	£95
1696/5	£10	£40	£125
1696 – – B	£5	£25	£100
1696 – – C	£5	£25	£100
1696 – – E	£10	£40	£110
1696 – – N	£5	£35	£100
1696 – – y	£5	£25	£90
1696 – – Y	£10	£40	£110
1696 – later harp	£10	£60	£165
1696 – – B	£22	£80	£200
1696 – – C	£25	£95	£225
1696 – – N	£22	£85	£200
1696 2nd bust	£100	£225	£475
1697 1st bust early harp ...	£3	£15	£50
1697 – – B	£9	£30	£100
1697 – – C	£9	£40	£100
1697 – – E	£10	£40	£100
1697 – – N	£5	£30	£100
1697 – – y	£10	£40	£100
1697 2nd bust	£30	£110	£250
1697 3rd bust later harp ...	£3	£15	£50
1697 – – B	£10	£35	£120
1697 – – C	£30	£60	£125
1697 – – E	£15	£40	£125
1697 – – Y	£15	£45	£110
1698 – –	£10	£35	£90
1698 – – plumes	£28	£80	£175
1699 – –	£45	£125	£275
1699 – – plumes	£35	£75	£175

William III 1699 sixpence, plumes

	F	VF	EF
1699 – – roses	£50	£100	£225
1700	£10	£20	£60
1701	£15	£25	£110

ANNE

	F	VF	EF
1703 VIGO	£20	£35	£90
1705	£25	£80	£165
1705 plumes	£20	£65	£160
1705 roses & plumes	£20	£55	£130
1707 –	£20	£50	£80
1707 plain	£15	£20	£50
1707 E	£15	£35	£120

Anne 1707 sixpence, E below bust

	F	VF	EF
1707 plumes	£20	£40	£110
1708 plain	£10	£20	£55
1708 E	£20	£55	£150
1708/7 E	£50	£100	£225
1708 E★	£20	£65	£200
1708/7 E★	£50	£100	£195
1708 Edin bust E★	£20	£70	£170
1708 plumes	£20	£50	£150
1710 roses & plumes	£20	£55	£160
1711	£10	£20	£50

George I 1717 sixpence

GEORGE I

	F	VF	EF
1717	£20	£70	£200
1720/17	£20	£70	£200
1723 SS C, Small letters on obv	£10	£20	£75
1723 SS C, large letters on both sides	£10	£20	£70
1726 roses & plumes	£25	£90	£250

GEORGE II

	F	VF	EF
1728 YH	£20	£60	£160
1728 – plumes	£15	£50	£140
1728 – r & p	£15	£45	£125
1731 – –	£15	£45	£125
1732 – –	£15	£45	£125
1734 – –	£20	£60	£140
1735 – –	£20	£50	£125
1736 – –	£15	£40	£125
1739 – roses	£10	£30	£90

	F	VF	EF
1741 – –	£10	£25	£90
1743 OH	£10	£25	£90
1745 – –	£10	£25	£90
1745/3 – –	£20	£35	£125
1745 – LIMA	£8	£18	£65
1746 – LIMA	£8	£18	£65
1746 – plain proof	*	*	£300

George II 1746 sixpence

		F	VF	EF
1750		£8	£15	£65
1751		£12	£25	£80
1757		£3	£5	£15
1757		£3	£5	£15
1758/7		£5	£12	£20

GEORGE III

	F	VF	EF	Unc
1787 hearts	£1	£3	£12	£30
1787 no hearts	£1	£3	£12	£30
1816	£1	£3	£20	£45
1817	£1	£3	£20	£45
1818	£3	£9	£35	£75
1819	£1	£3	£20	£50
1819 small 8	£8	£15	£40	£100
1820	£1	£3	£20	£60
1820 1 inverted	£30	£100	£225	£450

GEORGE IV

	F	VF	EF	Unc
1820 1st hd 1st rev	*	*	*	£850
(pattern or proof)				
1821 1st hd 1st rev	£2	£5	£60	£100
1821 – –				
BBITANNIAR	£50	£100	£250	£400
1824 1st hd 2nd				
rev	£2	£6	£55	£100
1825 – –	£2	£5	£65	£100
1826 – –	£10	£35	£150	£225
1826 2nd hd 3rd				
rev	£2	£5	£60	£95

George IV 1825 sixpence

	F	VF	EF	Unc
1826 – – proof	*	*	*	£150
1827	£10	£35	£100	£225
1828	£3	£$12	£90	£135
1829	£2	£10	£65	£125

WILLIAM IV

	F	VF	EF	Unc
1831	£2	£9	£45	£95
1831 proof	*	*	*	£175
1834	£2	£9	£45	£95
1835	£2	£15	£70	£120
1836	£5	£35	£90	£135
1837	£2	£20	£90	£150

VICTORIA

	F	VF	EF	Unc
1838	£1	£5	£50	£75
1839	£1	£5	£50	£75
1839 proof	*	*	*	£150

SIXPENCES

	F	VF	EF	Unc
1840	£1	£9	£45	£80
1841	£1	£9	£45	£80
1842	£2	£10	£60	£110
1843	£1	£5	£50	£85
1844	£1	£5	£40	£70
1845	£1	£5	£40	£70
1846	£1	£5	£40	£70
1848	£5	£20	£175	£325
1848/6	£6	£25	£175	£325
1848/7	£6	£25	£175	£325
1850	£2	£10	£55	£110
1850 5 over 3	£10	£25	£150	£275
1851	£2	£10	£40	£85
1852	£2	£8	£40	£80
1853	£1	£5	£40	£75
1853 proof	*	*	*	£250
1854	£15	£50	£275	£400
1855	£1	£5	£40	£65
1856	£1	£5	£40	£65
1857	£1	£9	£45	£70
1858	£1	£9	£45	£70
1859	£1	£9	£40	£65
1859/8	£1	£9	£45	£75
1860	£1	£9	£45	£75
1862	£10	£35	£200	£350
1863	£5	£17	£90	£150
1864	£1	£8	£40	£70
1865	£1	£8	£40	£70
1866	£1	£8	£40	£70
1866 no die no.	*	*	*	*
1867	£5	£15	£50	£85
1868	£4	£15	£50	£85
1869	£5	£18	£60	£95
1870	£5	£15	£60	£100
1871	£2	£5	£40	£55
1871 no die no.	£3	£10	£40	£65
1872	£2	£8	£35	£65
1873	£1	£5	£30	£50
1874	£1	£5	£30	£50
1875	£1	£5	£30	£60
1876	£5	£15	£40	£75
1877	£2	£5	£30	£50
1877 no die no.	£2	£5	£30	£50
1878	£2	£5	£30	£50
1878 DRITANNIAR	£35	£100	£250	£375
1879 die no.	£5	£10	£40	£70
1879 no die no.	£2	£4	£30	£45
1880 2nd YH	£1	£4	£18	£35
1880 3rd YH	£1	£3	£15	£30
1881	£1	£3	£15	£30
1882	£3	£10	£30	£60
1883	£1	£3	£15	£30
1884	£1	£3	£15	£30
1885	£1	£3	£15	£30
1886	£1	£3	£15	£30
1887 YH	£1	£3	£15	£30
1887 JH shield rev	£1	£2	£4	£12

1887 Jubilee Head sixpence, withdrawn type

	F	VF	EF	Unc
1887 – proof	*	*	*	£75
1887 – new rev	£1	£2	£3	£10
1888	£1	£3	£12	£35
1889	£1	£3	£12	£35

SIXPENCES

	F	VF	EF	Unc
1890	£1	£3	£12	£35
1891	£1	£3	£12	£35
1892	£1	£3	£12	£35
1893	£100	£300	£750	*
1893 OH	£1	£3	£15	£35
1893 proof	*	*	*	£85
1894	£1	£3	£20	£35
1895	£1	£3	£20	£35
1896	£1	£3	£20	£35
1897	£1	£3	£18	£30
1898	£1	£3	£18	£30
1899	£1	£3	£20	£35
1900	£1	£3	£18	£30
1901	£1	£3	£18	£30

EDWARD VII

	F	VF	EF	Unc
1902	*	£2	£8	£15
1902 matt proof ...	*	*	*	£20
1903	£1	£5	£20	£40
1904	£2	£6	£22	£55
1905	£2	£6	£22	£45
1906	£1	£3	£12	£35
1907	£1	£5	£12	£35
1908	£2	£7	£22	£50
1909	£1	£4	£18	£40
1910	£1	£4	£9	£25

GEORGE V

	F	VF	EF	Unc
1911	*	*	£5	£20
1911 proof	*	*	*	£30
1912	*	*	£12	£35
1913	*	*	£15	£35
1914	*	*	£4	£14
1915	*	*	£4	£14
1916	*	*	£4	£14
1917	*	*	£12	£30
1918	*	*	£5	£12
1919	*	*	£6	£15
1920	*	*	£8	£25
1920 debased	*	*	£8	£25
1921	*	*	£6	£20
1922	*	*	£5	£20
1923	*	*	£7	£30
1924	*	*	£6	£20
1925	*	*	£6	£20
1925 new rim	*	*	£5	£18
1926 new rim	*	*	£8	£25
1926 mod effigy ...	*	*	£5	£18
1927	*	*	£3	£15
1927 new rev prf ...	*	*	*	£18
1928	*	*	£1	£7
1929	*	*	£1	£7
1930	*	*	£1	£8
1931	*	*	£1	£7
1932	*	*	£5	£15
1933	*	*	£1	£6
1934	*	*	£3	£10

George V 1935 sixpence

	F	VF	EF	Unc
1935	*	*	£1	£5
1936	*	*	£1	£4

GEORGE VI

	F	VF	EF	Unc
1937	*	*	*	£2
1937 proof	*	*	*	£4
1938	*	*	£2	£6
1939	*	*	£1	£3
1940	*	*	£1	£3
1941	*	*	£1	£3
1942	*	*	£1	£2
1943	*	*	*	£2
1944	*	*	*	£1
1945	*	*	*	£1
1946	*	*	*	£1
1947	*	*	*	£1
1948	*	*	*	£1
1949	*	*	*	£2
1950	*	*	*	£2
1950 proof	*	*	*	£3.50
1951	*	*	*	£2
1951 proof	*	*	*	£3.50
1952	*	£2	£8	£20

ELIZABETH II

	F	VF	EF	Unc
1953	*	*	*	£0.50
1953 proof	*	*	*	£2
1954	*	*	*	£2
1955	*	*	*	£0.60
1956	*	*	*	£0.60
1957	*	*	*	£0.30
1958	*	*	*	£2
1959	*	*	*	£0.20
1960	*	*	*	£1.50
1961	*	*	*	£1.50
1962	*	*	*	£0.25
1963	*	*	*	*
1964	*	*	*	*
1965	*	*	*	*
1966	*	*	*	*
1967	*	*	*	*

Groats (fourpences)

William IV 1836 groat
Earlier dates are included in Maundy sets

WILLIAM IV

	F	VF	EF	Unc
1836	*	£2	£15	£40
1836 proof	*	*	*	£350
1837	*	£5	£20	£50

Victoria 1842 groat

VICTORIA

	F	VF	EF	Unc
1838	*	£4	£12	£40
1838 8 over 8 on side	£1	£5	£25	£60
1839	*	£3	£15	£55
1839 proof	*	*	*	£125
1840	*	£2	£15	£55
1840 narrow 0	£2	£6	£30	*
1841	£3	£10	£25	£70
1841 I for last 1	*	*	*	*
1842	*	£3	£15	£50

	F	VF	EF	Unc
1842/1	£3	*	*	*
1843	*	£3	£15	£45
1844	*	£4	£25	£60
1845	*	£3	£15	£50
1846	*	£3	£15	£50
1847/6	£25	£40	£90	£135
1848 small date ...	*	£2	£15	£50
1848 large date ...	*	£2	£15	£50
1848/6	£2	£6	£18	£60
1848/7	£2	£6	£18	£60
1849	£2	£4	£18	£60
1849/8	£2	£8	£40	£80
1851	£5	£20	£150	£250
1852	£40	*	*	*
1853	£30	£65	£275	*
1853 proof	*	*	*	£250
1854	*	£2	£15	£55
1854 5 over 3	*	£2	£18	£70
1855	*	£2	£15	£55
1857 proof	*	*	*	£700
1862 proof	*	*	*	£450
1888 JH	£1	£3	£15	£35

Silver threepences

Earlier dates are included in Maundy sets

WILLIAM IV	F	VF	EF	Unc
1834	*	£3	£15	£60
1835	*	£3	£15	£60
1836	*	£3	£15	£50
1837	*	£6	£20	£65

Victoria threepence of 1848

VICTORIA				
1838	*	£4	£20	£50
1839	*	£7	£25	£60
1840	*	£5	£20	£60
1841	*	£5	£20	£60
1842	*	£5	£20	£65
1843	*	£5	£15	£45
1844	*	£6	£25	£65
1845	*	£3	£15	£40
1846	*	£6	£28	£75
1847	*	*	*	£350
1848	*	*	£275	*
1849	*	£6	£30	£75
1850	*	£3	£20	£50
1851	*	£3	£20	£50
1852	*	*	£275	*
1853	*	£6	£32	£100
1854	*	£3	£20	£50
1855	*	£5	£20	£55
1856	*	£2.50	£15	£45
1857	*	£5	£18	£45
1858	*	£3	£18	£45
1858/6	*	*	*	*
1859	*	£3	£18	£35
1860	*	£3	£18	£35
1861	*	£3	£18	£35
1862	*	£3	£15	£45
1863	*	£6	£25	£60
1864	*	£3	£20	£50
1865	*	£6	£25	£60
1866	*	£3	£20	£55
1867	*	£3	£25	£60

SILVER THREEPENCES

	F	VF	EF	Unc
1868	*	£3	£35	£55
1868 RRITANNIAR	£20	£40	£175	*
1869	*	*	£25	*
1870	*	£2	£15	£40
1871	*	£2	£15	£40
1872	*	£1.50	£12	£40
1873	*	£1.25	£12	£35
1874	*	£1.25	£12	£35
1875	*	£1.25	£10	£30
1876	*	£1.25	£10	£30
1877	*	£1.25	£10	£30
1878	*	£1.25	£10	£30
1879	*	£1.25	£10	£30
1880	*	£1.25	£10	£30
1881	*	£1	£10	£25
1882	*	£1.50	£12	£45
1883	*	£1	£8	£22
1884	*	£1	£8	£22
1885	*	£1	£8	£22
1886	*	£1	£8	£22
1887 YH	*	£3	£15	£40
1887 JH	*	£1.50	£3	£7
1887 proof	*	*	*	£40
1888	*	£1.50	£7	£20
1889	*	£1	£6	£15
1890	*	£1	£6	£15
1891	*	£1	£6	£15
1892	*	£1	£7	£15
1893	£10	£20	£60	£125
1893 OH	*	*	£3	£12
1893 OH proof	*	*	*	£50
1894	*	*	£4	£18
1895	*	*	£4	£18
1896	*	*	£4	£18
1897	*	*	£3	£15
1898	*	*	£3	£15
1899	*	*	£3	£15
1900	*	*	£3	£15
1901	*	*	£2	£12

EDWARD VII				
1902	*	*	£4	£10
1902 matt proof ...	*	*	*	£12
1903	*	£1.50	£6	£20
1904	*	£6	£14	£35
1905	*	£6	£14	£35
1906	*	£3	£10	£30
1907	*	£1.50	£5	£20
1908	*	£1.50	£6	£22
1909	*	£2	£6	£22
1910	*	£1.25	£4	£18

George V 1927 threepence, acorns on reverse

GEORGE V				
1911	*	*	£3	£12
1911 proof	*	*	*	£25
1912	*	*	£3	£12
1913	*	*	£3	£12
1914	*	*	£2	£10
1915	*	*	£2	£10
1916	*	*	£1.50	£8
1917	*	*	£1.50	£8
1918	*	*	£2	£8
1919	*	*	£2	£8

SILVER THREEPENCES

	F	VF	EF	Unc
1920	*	*	£2	£10
1920 debased	*	*	£2	£10
1921	*	*	£2	£12
1922	*	*	£2	£12
1925	*	£1	£6	£18
1926	*	£3	£10	£25
1926 mod effigy ...	*	£1	£6	£20
1927 new rev prf ...	*	*	*	£30
1928	*	£2	£6	£20
1930	*	£1.50	£5	£12
1931	*	*	£1	£6
1932	*	*	£1	£6
1933	*	*	£1	£6
1934	*	*	£1	£6
1935	*	*	£1	£6
1936	*	*	£1	£6

GEORGE VI

	F	VF	EF	Unc
1937	*	*	£0.75	£1.50
1937 proof	*	*	*	£5
1938	*	*	£0.50	£1
1939	*	£1	£3	£5
1940	*	*	£1	£2
1941	*	*	£1	£2
1942	£1	£2	£6	£8
1943	£1	£3	£7	£9
1944	£1.50	£5	£12	£20
1945[2]	*	*	*	*

[1]Threepences issued for use in the Colonies.
[2]All specimens of 1945 were thought to have been melted down but it appears that one or two still exist.

Small silver for Colonies

These tiny coins were struck for use in some of the Colonies – they were never issued for circulation in Britain. However, they are often included in collections of British coins and it is for this reason that prices for them are given here.

TWOPENCES

Other dates are included in Maundy sets.

VICTORIA	F	VF	EF	Unc
1838	*	£2	£10	£20
1838 2nd 8 like S ...	*	£6	£20	£40
1848	*	£2	£10	£20

THREEHALFPENCES

WILLIAM IV	F	VF	EF	Unc
1834	*	£2	£18	£30
1835	*	£2	£18	£30
1835/4	*	£8	£25	£60
1836	*	£2	£18	£30
1837	£10	£25	£90	£150

VICTORIA	F	VF	EF	Unc
1838	*	£2	£8	£25
1839	*	£1.25	£8	£20
1840	*	£5	£15	£40
1841	*	£2	£9	£30
1842	*	£2	£9	£25
1843	*	£1	£6	£20

1843 threehalfpence

	F	VF	EF	Unc
1843/34	£2	£8	£20	£60
1860	£1	£3	£15	£35
1862	£1	£3	£15	£35
1870 proof	*	*	*	£375

Maundy sets

EF prices are for evenly matched sets

Charles II 1670 Maundy set. The denomination is shown by one one, two, three of four Cs on the reverses

CHARLES II	F	VF	EF
1670	£50	£75	£200
1671	£50	£60	£150
1672	£50	£70	£200
1673	£50	£60	£150
1674	£50	£60	£150
1675	£50	£60	£150
1676	£50	£60	£150
1677	£50	£60	£150
1678	£50	£70	£250
1679	£50	£65	£150
1680	£50	£60	£150
1681	£50	£75	£225
1682	£50	£70	£175
1683	£50	£60	£150
1684	£50	£70	£175

JAMES II	F	VF	EF
1686	£50	£75	£150
1687	£50	£75	£175
1688	£50	£75	£175

WILLIAM AND MARY	F	VF	EF
1689	£250	£375	£600
1691	£80	£110	£225
1692	£95	£125	£275
1693	£85	£120	£300
1694	£80	£110	£200

WILLIAM III	F	VF	EF
1698	£60	£90	£200
1699	£60	£90	£200
1700	£60	£100	£225
1701	£60	£100	£200

ANNE	F	VF	EF
1703	£50	£80	£200
1705	£50	£80	£175
1706	£50	£75	£140
1708	£55	£85	£200
1709	£50	£75	£150
1710	£55	£85	£200
1713	£50	£75	£150

GEORGE I

	F	VF	EF
1723	£50	£80	£150
1727	£50	£80	£150

GEORGE II

	F	VF	EF
1729	£45	£65	£150
1731	£45	£65	£150
1732	£40	£60	£130
1735	£40	£60	£130
1737	£40	£60	£130
1739	£40	£60	£130
1740	£40	£60	£130
1743	£40	£70	£150
1746	£40	£60	£120
1760	£50	£70	£150

GEORGE III

	F	VF	EF	Unc
1763	£30	£40	£85	*
1766	£30	£50	£85	*
1772	£30	£50	£85	*
1780	£30	£50	£85	*
1784	£30	£50	£85	£125
1786	£30	£50	£85	£125
1792 wire type	*	£75	£150	£200

1792 wire type Maundy set, so called because of the wire-like style of the figures of value

1795	*	£50	£75	£130
1800	£30	£50	£65	£110
1817	*	£50	£75	£125
1818	*	£50	£75	£125
1820	*	£50	£75	£125

GEORGE IV

1822	*	£50	£80	£130
1823	*	£45	£70	£120
1824	*	£45	£75	£125
1825	*	£45	£70	£120
1826	*	£45	£70	£120
1827	*	£45	£70	£120
1828	*	£45	£70	£120
1829	*	£45	£70	£120
1830	*	£45	£70	£120

WILLIAM IV

1831	*	£50	£80	£150
1831 proof	*	*	*	£400
1832	*	£50	£75	£150
1833	*	£50	£75	£150
1834	*	£50	£75	£150
1835	*	£50	£75	£150

MAUNDY SETS

	F	VF	EF	Unc
1836	*	£50	£85	£175
1837	*	£50	£85	£175

VICTORIA

			EF	Unc
1838			£50	£75
1839			£50	£65
1839 proof			*	£300
1840			£50	£75
1841			£50	£80
1842			£50	£90
1843			£50	£75
1844			£50	£75
1845			£50	£65
1846			£50	£90
1847			£50	£75

Victoria 1847 Young Head Maundy set

			EF	Unc
1848			£50	£85
1849			£50	£90
1850			£50	£70
1851			£50	£70
1852			£60	£110
1853 proof			*	£500
1854			£50	£65
1855			£50	£60
1856			£50	£65
1857			£50	£70
1858			£50	£70
1859			£50	£65
1860			£50	£70
1861			£50	£70
1862			£50	£70
1863			£50	£70
1864			£50	£70
1865			£50	£70
1866			£50	£70
1867			£50	£70
1868			£50	£70
1869			£50	£70
1870			£45	£65
1871			£45	£65
1872			£45	£65
1873			£45	£65
1874			£45	£65
1875			£45	£65
1876			£45	£65
1877			£45	£65
1878			£45	£65
1879			£45	£65
1880			£45	£65
1881			£45	£65
1882			£45	£65
1883			£45	£65
1884			£45	£65
1885			£45	£65
1886			£45	£65
1887			£45	£65
1888 JH			£50	£60

MAUNDY SETS

	EF	Unc
1889	£50	£60
1890	£50	£60
1891	£50	£60
1892	£50	£60
1893 OH	£40	£50
1894	£40	£50
1895	£40	£50
1896	£40	£50
1897	£40	£50
1898	£40	£50
1899	£40	£50
1900	£40	£50
1901	£40	£50

EDWARD VII

	EF	Unc
1902	£35	£45
1902 matt proof	*	£55
1903	£35	£45
1904	£35	£45
1905	£35	£45
1906	£35	£45
1907	£35	£45
1908	£35	£45
1909	£50	£60
1910	£50	£65

GEORGE V

	EF	Unc
1911	£40	£55
1911 proof	*	£60
1912	£40	£55
1913	£40	£55
1914	£40	£60
1915	£40	£55
1916	£40	£55
1917	£40	£55
1918	£40	£55
1919	£40	£55
1920	£40	£55
1921	£40	£55
1922	£40	£55
1923	£40	£55
1924	£40	£55
1925	£40	£55
1926	£40	£55
1927	£40	£55
1928	£40	£55
1929	£40	£55
1930	£40	£55
1931	£40	£55
1932	£40	£55
1933	£40	£55
1934	£40	£55
1935	£45	£55
1936	£50	£65

GEORGE VI

	EF	Unc
1937	*	£50
1938	*	£55
1939	*	£50
1940	*	£50
1941	*	£50
1942	*	£50
1943	*	£50
1944	*	£50
1945	*	£50
1946	*	£50
1947	*	£55
1948	*	£60
1949	*	£55
1950	*	£55
1951	*	£55
1952	*	£55

ELIZABETH II

	EF	Unc
1953	£195	£275
1954	*	£50
1955	*	£50
1956	*	£50
1957	*	£50
1958	*	£55
1959	*	£50
1960	*	£50

1960 Maundy set of Elizabeth II

	EF	Unc
1961	*	£50
1962	*	£50
1963	*	£50
1964	*	£50
1965	*	£50
1966	*	£50
1967	*	£50
1968	*	£55
1969	*	£50
1970	*	£50
1971	*	£50
1972	*	£50
1973	*	£50
1974	*	£50
1975	*	£50
1976	*	£50
1977	*	£50
1978	*	£55
1979	*	£50
1980	*	£50
1981	*	£50
1982	*	£50
1983	*	£50
1984	*	£50
1985	*	£50
1986	*	£50
1987	*	£50
1988	*	£55
1989	*	£50
1990	*	£50
1991	*	£50
1992	*	£50
1993	*	£50
1994	*	£50
1995	*	£50
1996	*	£65
1997	*	£80

Nickel-brass threepences

1937 threepence of Edward VII, extremely rare

1977-dated Edward VIII threepences, struck in 1936 ready for issue, were melted after Edward's abdication. A few, however, escaped into circulation to become highly prized collectors' pieces. George VI 1937 threepences were struck in large numbers.

EDWARD VIII	F	VF	EF	BU
1937	*	* Highest rarity *		

1937 threepence of George VI

GEORGE VI				
1937	*	*	£1	£2
1938	*	*	£3	£10
1939	*	*	£4	£20
1940	*	*	£2	£4
1941	*	*	£1	£3
1942	*	*	£1	£2
1943	*	*	£1	£2
1944	*	*	£1	£3
1945	*	*	*	£3
1946	£2	£8	£35	£150
1948	*	*	£4	£6
1949	£2	£7	£35	£125
1950	*	*	£8	£25
1951	*	*	£8	£25
1952	*	*	*	£1.50

ELIZABETH II				
1953	*	*	*	£1
1954	*	*	*	£2
1955	*	*	*	£2
1956	*	*	£1	£2
1957	*	*	*	£2
1958	*	*	£2	£4
1959	*	*	*	£2
1960	*	*	*	£1.25
1961	*	*	*	*
1962	*	*	*	*
1963	*	*	*	*
1964	*	*	*	*
1965	*	*	*	*
1966	*	*	*	*
1967	*	*	*	*

Copper twopence

George III 1797 'cartwheel' twopence

GEORGE III	F	VF	EF	BU
1797	£6	£25	£135	£350

Copper pennies

GEORGE III	F	VF	EF	BU
1797 10 leaves	£1	£5	£65	£225
1797 11 leaves	£1	£6	£65	£225

1797 'cartwheel' penny

	F	VF	EF	BU
1806	£1	£4	£45	£120
1806 no incuse curl	£1	£4	£45	£125
1807	£1	£4	£45	£125

1806 penny of George III

GEORGE IV	F	VF	EF	BU
1825	£3	£8	£60	£175
1826	£1	£5	£50	£150
1826 thin line down				
St Andrew's cross	£2	£7	£55	£165
1826 thick line	£3	£8	£55	£175
1827	£80	£200	£950	*

COPPER PENNIES

William IV 1831 penny

	F	VF	EF	BU
1848	£2	£4	£25	£80
1848/6	£7	£18	£75	£150
1848/7	£2	£8	£35	£90
1849	£30	£75	£225	£475
1851 DEF far colon	£3	£7	£40	£90
1851 DEF close colon	£4	£8	£40	£100
1853 OT	£1	£4	£22	£75
1853 colon nearer F	£2	£5	£28	£90
1853 PT	£2	£5	£20	£65
1854 PT	£2	£5	£20	£65
1854/3	£12	£40	*	*
1854 OT	£2	£4	£20	£65
1855 OT	£2	£4	£20	£65
1855 PT	£2	£4	£20	£65
1856 PT	£15	£50	£120	£300
1856 OT	£8	£30	£85	£250
1857 OT	£1	£2	£18	£60
1857 PT	£1	£2	£18	£60
1857 small date ...	£1	£3	£18	£60
1858	£1	£2	£15	£60
1858 small date ...	£1	£2	£18	£70
1858/3 now thought to be 1858 9/8 (see below)				
1858/7	£1	£2.50	£17	£60
1858/6	£7	£20	£70	*
1858 no ww	£0.75	£2	£17	£60
1858 no ww (large 1 and 5 small 8s)	£2	£4	£18	£70
1858 9/8?	£4	£15	£35	£80
1858 9/8? large rose	£5	£18	£40	£100
1859	£1	£4	£30	£70
1859 small date ...	£2	£5	£35	£80
1860/59	*	£250	£600	*

Bronze pennies

For fuller details of varieties in bronze pennies see English Copper, Tin and Bronze Coins in the British Museum 1558-1958 *by C. W. Peck;* The Bronze Coinage of Great Britain *by M. J. Freeman and* The British Bronze Penny 1860-1970 *by Michael Gouby.*

VICTORIA	F	VF	EF	BU
1860 RB, shield crossed with incuse treble lines	*	£5	£25	£65
1860 RB, shield crossed with close double raised lines	£4	£8	£30	£75
1860 RB, double lines, but farther apart, rock to left of lighthouse	£10	£40	£100	£250
1860 RB obv/TB rev	£30	£80	£500	*
1860 TB obv/RB rev	£30	£70	£450	*

WILLIAM IV

	F	VF	EF	BU
1831	£3	£15	£150	*
1831.w.w incuse ...	£4	£20	£185	*
1831.w.w incuse ...	£5	£25	£200	*
1834	£5	£25	£175	*
1837	£7	£30	£220	*

Victoria 1841 copper penny

VICTORIA

	F	VF	EF	Unc
1839 proof	*	*	£125	£225
1841	£8	£22	£75	*
1841 no colon after REG	£1	£3	£30	£90
1843	£8	£30	*	*
1843 no colon after REG	£12	*	*	*
1844	£3	£7	£30	£90
1845	£4	£9	£50	£125
1846 DEF far colon	£2	£8	£30	£90
1846 DEF close colon	£3	£9	£40	£100
1847 DEF close colon	£3	£7	£30	£90
1847 DEF far colon	£3	£7	£35	£90

1860 penny, toothed border on obverse

1860 TB, L.C. WYON on truncation, L.C.W. incuse below

	F	VF	EF	BU
shield	*	£4	£25	£65

	F	VF	EF	BU
₹60 TB, same obv but ..C.W. incuse below foot	£15	£30	£175	£350
₹60 TB, as previous but heavy flan of 170 grains	*	£175	*	*
₹60 TB, LC, WYON below truncation, ..C.W. incuse below shield	*	£3	£25	£60
₹60 TB, no signature on obv. L.C.W. incuse below shield	*	£5	£40	£75
₹61 L.C. WYON on truncation, L.C.W. incuse below shield	£7	£20	£70	£150
₹61 same obv. no signature on rev	*	£6	£25	£60
₹61 L.C. WYON below truncation, L.C.W. incuse below shield	*	£5	£25	£60
₹61 similar, but heavy flan 170 grains)	*	*	*	*
₹61 same obv but no signature on rev	*	£4	£25	£70
₹61 no signature on obv, L.C.W. incuse below shield	*	£4	£25	£65
₹61-6/8	£15	£45	£250	£400
₹61 no signature either side	£1	£4	£25	£60
₹62	£1	£3	£25	£60
₹62 sm date figs ...	£12	£36	*	*
₹63	£1	£3	£25	£65
₹63 slender 3	*	*	*	*
₹63 die no. (2, 3 or 4) below date	£100	£175	*	*
₹64 plain 4	£6	£20	£150	£650
₹64 crossiet 4	£8	£25	£180	£750
₹65	*	£7	£30	£70
₹65/3	£10	£45	£225	£500
₹66	*	£4	£25	£75
₹67	*	£5	£30	£80
₹68	£3	£15	£85	£250
₹69	£10	£75	£450	£800
₹70	£2	£15	£100	£225
₹71	£6	£30	£150	£350
₹72	*	£4	£25	£65
₹73	*	£4	£25	£65
₹74 (1873 type) ...	*	£4	£25	£65
₹74 H (1873 type)	*	£3	£25	£70
₹74 new rev, lighthouse tall and thin	£5	£12	£25	£70
₹74 H as previous	£2	£5	£25	£60
₹74 new obv/1873 rev	*	£3	£25	£60
₹74 H as previous	*	£3	£20	£60
₹74 new obv/new rev	*	£3	£25	£60
₹74 H as previous	*	£3	£25	£50
₹75	*	£4	£25	£55
₹75 H	£10	£45	£200	£500
₹76 H	*	£3	£12	£40
₹77	*	£4	£12	£50
₹78	*	£6	£20	£60
₹79	*	*	£12	£50
₹80	*	*	£20	£70
₹81 (1880 obv)	*	*	£20	£50
₹81 new obv	*	£12	£35	£90
₹81 H	*	*	£12	£50
₹82 H	*	*	£14	£50
₹82 no H	£50	£175	£500	£1100
₹83	*	*	£10	£50
₹84	*	*	£10	£45
₹85	*	*	£10	£45
₹86	*	*	£8	£45
₹87	*	*	£9	£45

BRONZE PENNIES

	F	VF	EF	BU
1888	*	*	£80	£45
1889 14 leaves	*	*	£10	£50
1889 15 leaves	*	*	£10	£50
1890	*	*	£10	£40
1891	*	*	£10	£40
1892	*	*	£10	£45
1893	*	*	£10	£45
1894	*	*	£18	£65
1895 2mm	*	£25	£150	£250

Victoria old head penny of 1895

	F	VF	EF	BU
1895	*	*	£5	£35
1896	*	*	£3	£30
1897	*	*	£2.50	£25
1897 higher horizon	£2	£10	£125	£300
1898	*	£1.25	£6.50	£35
1899	*	£1	£3.50	£30
1900	*	*	£2.50	£12
1901	*	*	£1	£8

Edward VII 1902 penny, low horizon

EDWARD VII

	F	VF	EF	BU
1902 low horizon ...	*	£5	£25	£45
1902	*	*	£2	£8
1903	*	*	£2	£15
1904	*	*	£5	£20
1905	*	*	£3	£18
1906	*	*	£3	£15
1907	*	*	£2	£15

BRONZE PENNIES

	F	VF	EF	BU
1908	*	*	£5	£20
1909	*	*	£4	£20
1910	*	*	£3	£15

GEORGE V

	F	VF	EF	BU
1911	*	*	£3	£15
1912	*	*	£3	£15
1912 H	*	*	£12	£40
1913	*	*	£6	£30
1914	*	*	£3	£20
1915	*	*	£3.50	£20
1916	*	*	£3	£20
1917	*	*	£3	£20
1918	*	*	£3.50	£20
1918 H	*	£8	£75	£150
1918 KN	*	£10	£95	£200
1919	*	*	£3	£22
1919 H	*	£2	£60	£165
1919 KN	*	£6.50	£100	£275
1920	*	*	£3.50	£15
1921	*	*	£2	£15
1922	*	*	£7	£20
1922 rev as 1927 ext rare			*	*
1926	*	*	£10	£35
1926 mod effigy ...	£2	£25	£250	£600
1927	*	*	£3	£12
1928	*	*	£1	£10
1929	*	*	£1	£10
1930	*	*	£3.50	£15
1931	*	*	£4	£15
1932	*	*	£6	£30
1933			highest rarity	
1934	*	*	£6	£20
1935	*	*	£1	£5
1936	*	*	*	£4

GEORGE VI

	F	VF	EF	BU
1937	*	*	*	£1
1938	*	*	*	£1
1939	*	*	*	£2
1940	*	*	*	£5
1944	*	*	*	£4
1945	*	*	*	£3
1945 9 double (2 dies)	£2	£5	£20	*
1946	*	*	*	£2
1947	*	*	*	£1
1948	*	*	*	£2
1949	*	*	*	£2

Obverse used for George VI pennies from 1949 to 1951. IND: IMP: is omitted from the legend

	F	VF	EF	BU
1950	£1.50	£5	£9	£18
1951	£1.75	£5	£8	£15

ELIZABETH II

	F	VF	EF	BU
1953	*	£1	£1.80	£3
1953 proof	*	*	*	£5

	Fair	F	VF	EF
1961	*	*	*	£0.50
1962	*	*	*	*
1963	*	*	*	*
1964	*	*	*	*
1965	*	*	*	*
1966	*	*	*	*
1967	*	*	*	*

Copper halfpennies

All copper unless otherwise stated

Charles II 1975 halfpenny

CHARLES II

	Fair	F	VF	EF
1672	£4	£15	£60	£350
1672 CRAOLVS	£15	£50	£100	£400
1673	£4	£15	£60	£325
1673 CRAOLVS	£15	£40	£90	£350
1673 no stops on reverse	£5	£20	£70	£325
1673 no stops on obverse	£5	£20	£75	£325
1675	£5	£20	£75	£325
1675 no stops on obverse	£6	£25	£75	£325

James II 1685 tin halfpenny

JAMES II

	Fair	F	VF	EF
1685 (tin)	£25	£65	£200	£800
1686 (tin)	£30	£75	£250	£800
1687 (tin)	£25	£65	£200	£800
1687 D over D	*	*	*	*

WILLIAM AND MARY

	Fair	F	VF	EF
1689 (tin) ET on right	£65	£150	£400	*
1689 (tin) ET on left	*	*	*	*
1690 (tin) dated on edge	£25	£50	£250	£900
1691 (tin) date in exergue and on edge	£25	£50	£250	£900

	Fair	F	VF	EF
1691/2 (tin) 1691 in exergue 1692 on edge	£30	£55	£250	£900
1692 (tin) date in exergue and on edge	£20	£45	£250	*
1694	£5	£15	£50	£375

William and Mary 1694 halfpenny

	Fair	F	VF	EF
1694 GVLIEMVS ...	*	*	*	*
1694 no stop after MARIA	£15	£30	£95	£400
1694 BRITANNIA with last I over A	£10	£50	*	*
1694 no stop on reverse	£5	£15	£65	£350

WILLIAM III
Type 1 (date in exergue)
	Fair	F	VF	EF
1695	£3	£15	£50	£400
1695 thick flan	£25	£50	£120	*
1695 BRITANNIA ...	£3	£15	*	*
1695 no stop on reverse	£2	£14	£70	*
1696	£2	£14	£75	*
1696 GVLIEMVS, no stop on reverse ...	£15	*	*	*
1696 TERTVS	£5	£30	£120	*
1696 obv struck from doubled die	£10	£30	*	*
1697	£2	£10	£70	*
1697 no stops either side	£3	£16	£75	*
1697 I of TERTIVS over E	£5	£40	*	*
1697 GVLILMVS no stop on reverse ...	£6	£30	*	*
1697 no stop after TERTIVS	£2	£20	*	*
1698	£4	£16	*	*

Type 2 (date in legend)
	Fair	F	VF	EF
1698	£5	£20	£100	*
1699	£1	£25	£60	*
1699 BRITANNIA ...	£1.75	£10	£60	*
1699 GVLIEMVS ...	£3	£15	£75	*

Type 3 (Britannia's hand on knee, date in exergue)
	Fair	F	VF	EF
1699	£5	£12	£75	*
1699 stop after date ...	£7	£20	*	*
1699 BRITANNIA ...	£5	£12	£75	*
1699 GVILELMVS ...	£10	*	*	*
1699 TERTVS	£15	*	*	*
1699 no stop on reverse	£15	*	*	*
1699 no stops on obverse	£2	£8	£60	*

COPPER HALFPENNIES

	FAIR	F	VF	EF
1699 no stops after GVLIELMVS	£2	£8	£60	*
1700	£2	£8	£60	£500
1700 no stops on obverse	£2	£8	£60	*
1700 no stop after GVLIELMVS	£2	£9	£70	*
1700 BRITANNIA ...	£1	£7	£60	*
1700 no stops on reverse	£1	£8	£70	*
1700 GVLIELMS ...	£3	£16	£75	*
1700 GVLIEEMVS ...	£2	£12	£70	*
1700 TER TIVS	£1	£10	£70	*
1700 1 of TERTIVS over V	£10	£25	*	*
1701 BRITANNIA ...	£1	£7	£60	*
1701 no stops on obverse	£2	£10	£60	*
1701 GVLIELMVS TERTIVS	£5	£18	£80	*

GEORGE I
Type 1
	FAIR	F	VF	EF
1717	*	£4	£70	£250
1717 no stops on obverse	£1	£10	£90	*
1718	*	£4	£75	£275
1718 no stop on obverse	*	*	*	*
1719 no larger flan of type 2	*	*	*	*
1719 – edge grained	*	*	*	*

Type 2
	FAIR	F	VF	EF
1719 both shoulder straps ornate	£1	£4	£45	£250
1719 – edge grained	*	*	*	*
1719 bust with left strap plain	£1	£6	£50	*
1719 – edge grained	*	*	*	*
1720	*	£4	£45	£250
1721	*	£4	£45	£250
1721/0	£1	£6	£45	*
1721 stop after date ...	*	£6	£45	£250
1722	*	£6	£45	£250
1722 GEORGIVS ...	£1.50	£8	£45	*
1723	*	£6	£45	£250
1723 no stop on reverse	*	£8	£45	£275
1724	*	£6	£45	£250

George II 1729 halfpenny

GEORGE II
Young Head
	FAIR	F	VF	EF
1729	*	£4	£17	£120
1729 no stop on reverse	£1	£5	£20	£110

COPPER HALFPENNIES

	Fair	F	VF	EF
1730	*	£4	£10	£100
1730 GEOGIVS, no stop on reverse ...	£2	£6	£14	£110
1730 stop after date	*	£7	£13	£110
1730 no stop after REX or on reverse	£2	£8	£14	£110
1731	*	£4	£10	£110
1731 no stop on reverse	*	£6	£14	£90
1732	*	£3	£12	£90
1732 no stop on reverse	*	£6	£15	£90
1733	*	£2	£12	£90
1733 only obverse stop before REX ...	*	£4	£15	£90
1734	*	£2	£12	£90
1734/3	*	£4	£18	£90
1734 no stops on obverse	*	£2	£15	£85
1735	*	£2	£12	£85
1736	*	£2	£12	£85
1737	*	£2	£12	£85
1738	*	£2	£12	£85
1739	*	£2	£12	£85

Old Head

		F	VF	EF
1740		*	£2	£12	£80
1742	*	£4	£13	£80
1742/0	*	£8	£20	£80
1743	*	£2	£10	£80
1744	*	£2	£10	£80
1745	*	£2	£10	£80
1746	*	£3	£10	£80
1747	*	£3	£10	£80
1748	*	£2	£7	£80
1749	*	£2	£7	£80
1750	*	£3	£10	£80
1751	*	£3	£10	£80
1752	*	£3	£10	£80
1753	*	£3	£10	£80
1754	*	£3	£10	£80

GEORGE III

	F	VF	EF	BU
1770	£1	£6	£60	£200
1771	£1	£4	£50	£175
1771 no stop on reverse	£2	£6	£50	£175
1771 ball below spear head	£2	£6	£50	£175
1772	£2	£6	£50	£175
1772 GEORIVS	£7	£20	£85	£225
1772 ball below spear head	£2	£6	£50	£175
1772 no stop on reverse	£2	£10	£55	£175
1773	£2	£6	£50	£175
1773 no stop after REX	£2	£10	£50	£175
1773 no stop on reverse	£2	£11	£55	£200
1774	£2	£10	£50	£175
1775	£3	£10	£50	£175
1799 5 incuse gunports	*	*	£12	£50
1799 6 relief gunports	*	*	£12	£50
1799 9 relief gunports	*	*	£15	£50
1799 no gunports ...	*	*	£12	£50
1799 no gunports and raised line along hull	*	*	£12	£50
1806 no berries on olive branch	*	*	£12	£65

	F	VF	EF	B
1806 line under SOHO 3 berries	*	*	£12	£6
1807 similar but double-cut border bead between B and R	*	*	£12	£6

GEORGE IV

	F	VF	EF	B
1825	*	£2	£35	£9

George IV 1826 halfpenny

	F	VF	EF	B
1826 two incuse lines down cross	*	£2	£35	£11
1826 raised line down centre of cross ...	*	£4	£37	£10
1827	*	£2	£35	£10

WILLIAM IV

	F	VF	EF	B
1831	*	£5	£45	£12
1834	*	£5	£45	£12
1837	*	£4	£40	£12

VICTORIA

	F	VF	EF	B
1838	*	£1	£12	£4
1839 proof	*	*	*	£12
1839 proof, rev inv ...	*	*	*	£15
1841	*	£1	£10	£4
1843	£3	£8	£40	£9
1844	£1	£3	£30	£7
1845	£18	£40	£250	£65
1846	£2	£4	£30	£6
1847	£1	£6	£30	£6
1848	£1	£3	£30	£6
1848/3	£15	£25	*	
1848/7	£1	£2	£12	£5
1851	£1	£2	£12	£6
1851 7 incuse dots on and above shield	*	£2	£12	£6
1852	*	£2	£12	£6
1852 7 incuse dots on and above shield	*	£2	£12	£5
1853	*	£1	£10	£4
1853/2	£3	£8	£45	
1854	*	£1	£8	£4

Victoria 1854 copper halfpenny

	F	VF	EF	B
1855	*	£1	£8	£4
1856	*	£2	£15	£6
1857	*	£2	£15	£4

	F	VF	EF	BU
1857 7 incuse dots on and above shield	*	£2	£12	£55
1858	*	£2	£12	£55
1858/6	£2	£8	£30	£75
1858/7	£1	£3	£15	£55
1858 small date	£1	£3	£15	£55
1859	£1	£2	£15	£55
1859/8	£3	£8	£40	*
1860	*	*	*	£2000

Bronze halfpennies

VICTORIA

	F	VF	EF	BU
1860	*	£3	£15	£40
1860 TB 7 berries in wreath	*	£3	£15	£40
1860 TB4 berries in wreath	*	£3	£15	£40
1860 TB similar but centres of four of leaves are double incuse lines	£5	£8	£25	£75
1861 obv 4 berries, 15 leaves, raised leaf centres, rev L.C.W. on rock	*	£2	£15	£55
1861 same obv, rev no signature			ext. rare	
1861 same but lighthouse has no vertical lines	£6	£10	£25	£75
1861 obv 4 berries, 4 double incuse leaf centres, rev L.C.W. on rock ...	*	£2	£12	£35
1861 same obv, rev no signature	£5	£8	£25	£80
1861 obv 7 double incuse leaf centres, rev L.C.W on rock	*	£2	£12	£45
1861 same obv, rev no signature	*	£2	£12	£30
1861 obv 16 leaves, rev lighthouse has rounded top	*	£2	£12	£30
1861 same obv, rev lighthouse has pointed top	*	£2	£12	£30
1861 no signature ...	*	£2	£10	£30
1862 L.C.W. on rock	*	£4	£10	£50
1862 letter (A,B or C) left of lighthouse base ...	£35	£85	£350	*
1863	*	£2	£12	£30
1864	*	£4	£15	£50
1865	*	£2	£15	£50
1865/3	£10	£40	£150	*
1866	*	£2	£12	£40
1867	*	£2	£12	£45
1868	*	£2	£12	£45

Victoria 1871 bronze halfpenny

BRONZE HALFPENNIES

	F	VF	EF	BU
1869	*	£5	£18	£65
1870	*	£4	£15	£45
1871	£10	£25	£100	£295
1872	*	£2	£12	£30
1873	*	£5	£18	£55
1874	*	£8	£25	£65
1874H	*	£2	£12	£30
1875	*	£2	£12	£30
1875H	*	£6	£16	£45
1876H	*	£2	£10	£35
1877	*	£2	£10	£35
1878	*	£15	£35	£150
1879	*	£2	£10	£30
1880	*	£2	£10	£30
1881	*	£2	£10	£30
1881H	*	£2	£10	£30
1882H	*	£2	£10	£30
1883	*	£2	£10	£30
1884	*	£2	£10	£30
1885	*	£2	£10	£30
1886	*	£1.50	£10	£30
1887	*	£1	£10	£30
1888	*	£1	£10	£30
1889	*	£1	£10	£30
1889/8	*	£8	£20	£60
1890	*	£1	£6	£35
1891	*	£1	£8	£30
1892	*	£1	£7	£30
1893	*	*	£7	£30
1894	*	£2	£10	£35
1895 OH	*	*	£2	£30
1896	*	*	£2	£30
1897 normal horizon	*	*	£2	£28
1897 higher horizon	*	*	£2	£28
1898	*	*	£5	£30
1899	*	*	£3	£30
1900	*	*	£1	£10
1901	*	*	£1	£10

EDWARD VII

	F	VF	EF	BU
1902 low horizon ...	*	£5	£28	£65
1902	*	*	£2	£10
1903	*	*	£3	£25
1904	*	*	£5	£30
1905	*	*	£3	£20
1906	*	*	£3	£20
1907	*	*	£3	£20
1908	*	*	£3	£20
1909	*	*	£4	£25
1910	*	*	£4.25	£25

GEORGE V

	F	VF	EF	BU
1911	*	*	£2.75	£12
1912	*	*	£2	£12

George V 1912 halfpenny

	F	VF	EF	BU
1913	*	*	£5	£20
1914	*	*	£3	£15
1915	*	*	£3	£15

BRONZE HALFPENNIES

	FAIR	F	VF	EF
1916	*	*	£2	£15
1917	*	*	£2	£15
1918	*	*	£2	£15
1919	*	*	£2	£15
1920	*	*	£2	£15
1921	*	*	£2	£15
1922	*	*	£3	£15
1923	*	*	£2	£15
1924	*	*	£3	£15
1925	*	*	£4	£15
1925 mod effigy ...	*	*	£4	£20
1926	*	*	£4	£15
1927	*	*	£2.50	£12
1928	*	*	£2	£12
1929	*	*	£2	£12
1930	*	*	£2	£12
1931	*	*	£2	£12
1932	*	*	£2	£12
1933	*	*	£2	£15
1934	*	*	£2	£15
1935	*	*	£1.75	£7
1936	*	*	£1.50	£5

GEORGE VI

	FAIR	F	VF	EF
1937	*	*	*	£1
1938	*	*	*	£2
1939	*	*	*	£2
1940	*	*	*	£2.75
1941	*	*	*	£3
1942	*	*	*	£1
1943	*	*	*	£1
1944	*	*	*	£2
1945	*	*	*	£1
1946	*	*	£2	£4
1947	*	*	*	£3
1948	*	*	*	£1
1949	*	*	*	£1
1950	*	*	*	£4
1951	*	*	*	£4.50
1952	*	*	*	£1.50

ELIZABETH II

	FAIR	F	VF	EF
1953	*	*	*	£1.75
1954	*	*	*	£2.50
1955	*	*	*	£3
1956	*	*	*	£3
1957	*	*	*	£1
1958	*	*	*	£0.50
1959	*	*	*	£0.25
1960	*	*	*	£0.20
1962	*	*	*	*
1963	*	*	*	*
1964	*	*	*	*
1965	*	*	*	*
1966	*	*	*	*
1967	*	*	*	*

Copper farthings

Copper unless otherwise stated

CHARLES II

	FAIR	F	VF	EF
1671 patterns only	*	*	£100	£350
1672	£1	£4	£30	£200
1672 no stop on obverse	£2.75	£6	£40	£225
1672 loose drapery at Britannia's elbow	£2	£6	£40	£225
1673	£1	£5 -	£25	£200

Charles II 1673 farthing

	FAIR	F	VF	E
1673 CAROLA	*	*	*	
1673 BRITANNIA ...	*	*	*	
1673 no stops on obverse	£2	£5	£50	£22
1673 no stop on reverse	£2	£5	£50	£22
1674	£1	£4	£40	£20
1675	£1	£2.75	£30	£20
1675 no stop after CAROLVS	*	*	*	
1676	*	*	*	
1679	£1.50	£4	£50	£22
1679 no stop on reverse	*	*	*	
1684 (tin) various edge readings	£12	£25	£150	£80
1685 (tin)	£15	£70	£175	£82

JAMES II

	FAIR	F	VF	E
1684 (tin)	£30	£80	£175	£80
1685 (tin) various edge readings	£20	£35	£120	
1686 (tin) various edge readings	£20	£50	£125	
1687 (tin)	*	*	*	
1687 (tin) draped bust, various readings	*	*	*	

WILLIAM AND MARY

	FAIR	F	VF	E
1689 (tin) date in exergue and on edge, many varieties ...	£15	£45	£135	
1689/90 (tin) 1689 in exergue, 1690 on edge	*	*	*	
1689/90 (tin) 1690 in exergue, 1689 on edge	*	*	*	
1690 (tin) various types	£12	£30	£125	£80
1691 (tin) small and large figures	£12	£30	£125	£80
1692 (tin)	£15	£35	£125	£80
1694 many varieties	£2	£15	£45	£25

WILLIAM III
Type 1, date in exergue

	FAIR	F	VF	E
1695	£3	£7	£50	£35
1695 M over V	*	*	*	
1696	£2	£5	£45	£35
1697	£2	£5	£40	£35

William III 1697 farthing

	FAIR	F	VF	E
1698	£5	£12	£50	
1699	£2	£5	£45	£40
1700	£2	£5	£35	£37

COIN MARKET VALUE

	Fair	F	VF	EF
Type 2, date in legend				
1698	£4	£10	£40	£400
1699	£2	£10	£35	£400

Anne 1714 pattern farthing

George II 1730 farthing

ANNE

	Fair	F	VF	EF
1714 patterns (**F**) ...	£40	£150	£225	£350

GEORGE II	Fair	F	VF	EF
1730	*	£3	£10	£110
1731	*	£3	£12	£110
1732	*	£5	£12	£110
1733	*	£3	£9	£110
1734	*	£2	£10	£110
1734 no stops on obverse	*	£3	£14	£120
1735	*	£2	£10	£110
1735 3 over 3	*	£8	£25	£120
1736	*	£3	£10	£110
1736 triple tie-riband	*	*	*	*
1737 sm date	*	£2	£10	£110
1737 lge date	*	£3	£12	£110
1739	*	£2	£10	£80
1739/5	*	*	*	*
1741 Old Head	*	£3	£10	£50
1744	*	£2	£10	£45
1746	*	£2	£9	£45
1746 V over U	*	*	*	*
1749	*	£2	£8	£45
1750	*	£2	£8	£45
1754/0	*	£12	£35	*
1754	*	£2	£8	£40

George I 'dump' farthing of 1717

GEORGE I
'Dump Type'

	Fair	F	VF	EF
1717	£12	£20	£70	£275
1718 silver proof ...	*	*	*	£600

Larger flan

	Fair	F	VF	EF
1719 large lettering on obverse	£3	£10	£30	£200
1719 small lettering on obverse	£3	£10	£45	£225
1719 – last A of BRITANNIA over I	*	*	*	*

GEORGE III	F	VF	EF	BU
1771	*	£15	£65	£165
1773	*	£3	£35	£135
1774	*	£3	£35	£135
1775	*	£3	£40	£135
1799	*	*	£5	£40
1806	*	£1	£8	£50
1807	*	£2	£10	£45

GEORGE IV				
1821	*	£1	£20	£50
1822	*	£1	£20	£50
1823	*	£2	£20	£50
1825	*	£2	£20	£50
1825 D of DEI over U	£2	£5	£50	*
1826 date on rev ...	*	£1	£20	£50
1826 date on obv ...	*	£2	£25	£65
1826 I for 1 in date	*	*	*	*
1827	*	£2	£25	£65
1828	*	£2	£30	£90
1829	*	£3	£30	£90
1830	*	£2	£25	£75

George I 1719 farthing

	Fair	F	VF	EF
1719 legend continuous over bust	£7	£25	*	*
1720 large lettering on obverse	£3	£10	£30	£220
1720 small lettering on obverse	£2	£5	£28	£220
1721	£2	£4	£25	£220
1721/0	£10	£30	*	*
1722 large lettering on obverse	£4	£10	£30	£220
1722 small lettering on obverse	£3	£8	£28	£220
1723	£2	£5	£25	£200
1723 R of REX over R	£8	*	*	*
1724	£5	£10	£30	£250

WILLIAM IV				
1831	*	£2	£30	£90
1834	*	£2	£30	£90
1835	*	£2	£35	£110
1836	*	£2	£35	£110
1837	*	£2	£30	£90

VICTORIA				
1838	*	£2	£8	£40
1839	*	£2	£6	£35

COPPER FARTHINGS

	F	VF	EF	BU
1840	*	£2	£8	£40
1841	*	£2	£2	£30
1842	*	£4	£12	£45
1843	*	£2	£5	£35
1843 1 for 1	*	£5	£22	£100
1844	£10	£30	£150	*
1845	*	£3	£10	£50
1846	*	£5	£15	£60
1847	*	£2	£8	£50
1848	*	£3	£10	£55
1849	*	£7	£36	£175
1850	*	£2	£8	£50
1851	*	£6	£20	£90
1851 D over D	£5	*	*	*
1852	*	£7	£20	£100
1853 w.w. raised	*	£1	£6	£35
1853 ww inc	*	£2	£8	£40
1854 ww inc	*	£2	£8	£40
1855 ww inc	*	£2	£8	£45
1855 ww raised	*	£4	£12	£50
1856	*	£3	£20	£60
1856 R over E	£5	*	*	*
1857	*	£2	£5	£30
1858	*	£1	£5	£30
1859	*	£7	£20	£70
1860 proof	*	*	*	£3500

Bronze farthings

VICTORIA	F	VF	EF	BU
1860 RB	*	£2	£10	£30
1860 TB/RB (mule)	£25	£60	100	*
1860 TB	*	£1	£8	£30
1861	*	£1	37	£30
1862 small 8	*	£2	£7	£25
1862 large 8	*	£3	£9	£28
1863	£8.30	£20	£50	*
1864	*	£2	£7	£28
1865 large 8	*	£1	£7	£28
1865–5/2	*	£3	£8	£30
1865–5/3	*	£2	£10	£35
1865 small 8	*	£1	£6	£30
1865–5/3	*	£2	£10	£35
1866	*	*	£6	£25
1867	*	£1	£6	£25
1868	*	£2	£8	£28
1869	*	£2	£9	£35
1872	*	£2	£9	£28
1873	*	£2	£5	£38
1874 H	*	£2	£5	£25
1874 H both Gs over	£30	*	*	*
1875 5 berries/large date	£5	£10	£20	*
1875 5 berries/small date	*	*	*	*
1875 4 berries/small date	£6	£12	£25	*
1875 H 4 berries/small date	*	*	£4	£25
1876 H	*	£5	£14	£40
1877 proof	*	*	*	£1450
1878	*	*	£5	£25
1879	*	£1	£6	£25
1879 large 9	*	£2	£7	£25
1880 4 berries	*	£2	£7	£25
1880 3 berries	*	£5	£12	£40
1881 4 berries	*	£5	£15	£40
1881 3 berries	*	£2	£6	£18

	F	VF	EF	E
1881 H 3 berries	*	£2	£6	£
1882 H	*	£1	£5	£
1883	*	£3	£8	£
1884	*	*	£3	£
1886	*	*	£3	£
1887	*	*	£7	£
1890	*	*	£5	£
1891	*	*	£5	£
1892	*	£3	£9	3
1893	*	*	£2	£
1894	*	*	£2	£
1895	*	£7	£25	£
1895 OH	*	*	£1	£

Victoria 1896 Old Head farthing

	F	VF	EF	
1897 bright finish	*	*	£2	£
1897 black finish higher horizon	*	*	£1	£
1898	*	*	£2	£
1899	*	*	£1	£
1900	*	*	£1	£
1901	*	*	£1	

Edward VII 1907 farthing

EDWARD VII	F	VF	EF	
1902	*	*	£1	
1903 low horizon	*	*	£2	£
1904	*	*	£2	£
1905	*	*	£2	£
1906	*	*	£2	£
1907	*	*	£2	£
1908	*	*	£2	£
1909	*	*	£2	£
1910	*	*	£3	£

GEORGE V	F	VF	EF	
1911	*	*	*	
1912	*	*	*	
1913	*	*	*	
1914	*	*	*	
1915	*	*	*	
1916	*	*	*	
1917	*	*	*	
1918 black finish	*	*	*	
1919 bright finish	*	*	*	
1919	*	*	*	
1920	*	*	*	
1921	*	*	*	
1922	*	*	*	
1923	*	*	*	
1924	*	*	*	
1925	*	*	*	

94

	F	VF	EF	BU
1926 modified effigy	*	*	*	£4
1927	*	*	*	£4
1928	*	*	*	£2
1929	*	*	*	£2
1930	*	*	*	£2
1931	*	*	*	£2
1932	*	*	*	£2
1933	*	*	*	£2
1934	*	*	*	£3
1935	*	*	£1.50	£5
1936	*	*	*	£1

George VI 1937 farthing, wren on reverse

GEORGE VI

	F	VF	EF	BU
1937	*	*	*	£1
1938	*	*	*	£2
1939	*	*	*	£1
1940	*	*	*	£2
1941	*	*	*	£1
1942	*	*	*	£1
1943	*	*	*	£1
1944	*	*	*	£1
1945	*	*	*	£1
1946	*	*	*	£1
1947	*	*	*	£1
1948	*	*	*	£1
1949	*	*	*	£1
1950	*	*	*	£1
1951	*	*	*	£1
1952	*	*	*	£1

ELIZABETH II

	F	VF	EF	BU
1953	*	*	*	£0.50
1954	*	*	*	£0.35
1955	*	*	*	£0.35
1956	*	*	*	£1

Fractions of farthings

COPPER HALF FARTHINGS

GEORGE IV	F	VF	EF	BU
1828 Britannia breaks legend	£3	£6	£35	£100
1828 Britannia below legend	£5	£8	*	*
1830 lge date	£3	£7	£40	£110
1830 sm date	£4	£10	*	*

WILLIAM IV	F	VF	EF	BU
1837	£12	£40	£250	*

Victoria 1839 half farthing

BRONZE FARTHINGS

	F	VF	EF	BU
VICTORIA				
1839	*	£2	£15	£50
1842	*	£2	£10	£40
1843	*	*	£1	£10
1844	*	*	£1	£8
1844 E over N	£3	£12	£50	*
1847	*	£3	£10	£40
1851	*	£3	£12	£45
1852	*	£3	£20	£50
1853	*	£4	£35	£75
1854	*	£4	£40	£95
1856	*	£5	£50	£110
1856 large date	£6	£25	*	*
1868 bronze proof	*	*	*	£150
1868 copper-nickel proof	*	*	*	£300

COPPER THIRD FARTHINGS

GEORGE IV	F	VF	EF	BU
1827	*	£3	£12	£45

WILLIAM IV				
1835	*	£3	£15	£50

VICTORIA				
1844	*	£8	£25	£50
1844 RE for REG	£20	£35	£95	*
1844 large G in REG	*	£8	£25	£60

BRONZE THIRD FARTHINGS

VICTORIA	F	VF	EF	BU
1866	*	*	£4	£20
1868	*	*	£3	£20
1876	*	*	£4	£25
1878	*	*	£3	£20
1881	*	*	£4	£17
1884	*	*	£2	£10
1885	*	*	£2	£10

Edward VII 1902 third farthing

EDWARD VII				
1902	*	*	£1	£5

GEORGE V				
1913	*	*	£2	£7

COPPER QUARTER FARTHINGS

VICTORIA				
1839	£3	£10	£20	£50

Victoria 1839 quarter farthing

1851	£4	£12	£28	£60
1852	£3	£10	£20	£50
1853	£5	£12	£25	£60
1868 bronze-proof	*	*	*	£200
1868 copper-nickel proof	*	*	*	£350

Decimal coinage

f denotes face value

ELIZABETH II

BRITANNIAS

A new United Kingdom gold bullion coin introduced in the autumn of 1987 contains one ounce of 22ct gold and has a face value of £100. There are also half ounce, quarter ounce and one-tenth ounce versions, with face values of £50, £25 and £10 respectively. All are legal tender.

The Britannia coins bear a portrait of The Queen on the obverse and the figure of Britannia on the reverse.

	BU
1987, 1988, 1989, 1991, 1992, 1993, 1994, 1995, 1996, 1997 1oz, proof ...	£550
1987 to 1997 inclusive ½oz, proof	*
1987 to 1997 inclusive ¼oz, proof	*
1987 to 1997 inclusive ⅒oz, proof	£65
(½ and ¼ oz issued only in sets)	

FIVE POUNDS

1984 gold, BU	£400
1985 – –	£425
1986 – –	£425
1987 – new uncoupled effigy	£425
1988 – –	£425
1989 – BU, 500th anniversary of the sovereign	£450
1990 gold, BU	£435
1990 Queen Mother's 90th birthday, gold, proof	£600
1990 – silver, proof	£35
1990 – cu-ni, BU	£10
1991 gold, BU	£450
1992 gold, BU	£450
1993 40th Anniversary of The Coronation gold, proof	£700
1993 – silver, proof	£32
1993 – cu-ni, BU	£10
1993 gold BU	£475
1994 gold BU	£500
1995 gold BU	£535
1996 Queen's 70th birthday, gold, proof	£645
1996 – silver, proof	£33
1996 – cu-ni, BU	£10
1996 – gold, BU	£575
1997 Golden Wedding, gold, proof	£650
1997 – silver, proof	£32
1996 – cu-ni, BU	£10
1997 – gold, BU	£535

(Gold versions also listed in FIVE POUNDS section of milled gold.) In 1984 the Royal Mint issued the first of an annual issue of Brilliant Uncirculated £5 coins. These bear the letter 'U' in a circle.

TWO POUNDS

1983 gold, proof	£225
1986 Commonwealth Games (Nickel brass), unc in folder, BU	£6
1986 silver unc	£15
1986 – – proof	£20
1986 gold, proof	£225
1987 gold, proof	£250
1988 gold, proof	£250
1989 Bill of Rights, in folder, BU	£6
1989 – silver, proof	£23
1989 Claim of Right, in folder, BU ...	£6
1989 – silver, proof	£23
(For 1989 £2 piedforts see sets)	
1989 500th anniversary of the sovereign, gold, proof	£275
1990 gold, proof	£250
1991 proof	£250
1993 gold, proof	£250
1994 Bank of England, gold, proof	£425
1994 gold 'mule', proof	£600
1994 silver, proof	£30
1994 silver piedfort, proof	£50
1994 in folder, BU	£8
1995 50th Anniversary of end of Second World War, silver, proof	£27
1995 ditto, in folder, BU	£8
1995 –, silver, piedfort, proof	£50
1995 –, gold, proof	£375
1995 50th Anniversary of United Nations, gold, proof	£300
1995 –, in folder, BU	£6
1995 –, silver, piedfort, proof	£50
1995 –, proof	£30
1996 European Football, gold, proof ...	£350
1996 –, silver, proof	£27
1996 –, silver, piedfort	£50
1996 –, in folder, BU	£6
1997 Bimetal, gold, proof	£350
1997 –, silver, proof	£29
1997 –, in folder, BU	£6

(Gold versions are also listed in TWO POUNDS section of milled gold.)

ONE POUND

1983	£2
1983 Unc, in folder	£5
1983 silver, proof	£30
1983 – – piedfort	£120
1983 Scottish reverse	£2
1984 – Unc, in folder	£5
1984 – silver, proof	£20
1984 – – piedfort	£50
1985 New portrait, Welsh reverse	£2
1985 – – Unc, in folder	£5
1985 – – silver, proof	£22
1985 – – piedfort	£50
1986 – Northern Ireland reverse	£2
1986 – Unc, in folder	£5
1986 – silver, proof	£25
1986 – – – piedfort	£50
1987 English reverse	£2
1987 – Unc, in folder	£3
1987 – silver, proof	£20
1987 – – – piedfort	£50
1988 Royal Arms reverse	£2
1988 – Unc, in folder	£5
1988 – silver, proof	£30
1988 – – – piedfort	£50
1989 Scottish rev as 1984, silver, proof	£20
1989 – – – piedfort	£40
1990 Welsh rev as 1985, silver, proof	£25

1991 Northern Ireland rev as 1986, silver, proof	£25
1992 English rev as 1987, silver, proof	£25
1993 Royal Coat of Arms (reverse as 1983), silver, proof	£30
1993 – – – piedfort	£50
1994 Scottish Lion, silver, proof	£35
ditto, Unc. in folder	£5
1994 – silver, piedfort	£50
1995 Welsh dragon, silver, proof	£25
ditto, Unc in folder, English version ...	£5
1995 – silver, piedfort	£50
1996 Northern Ireland Celtic Ring	
Unc in folder	£5
Silver, proof	£27
Silver, piedfort	£50
1997 English Lions Unc, in folder	£5
silver, proof	£25
silver, piedfort	£45

Note that the edge inscriptions on £2 and £1 appear either upright or inverted in relation to the obverse. Sovereign and half sovereign prices are not listed here but in the main listings under milled gold.)

FIFTY PENCE

1969	£1
1970	£1
1973 EEC	£1
1973 – proof	£3
1976-1981	f
1982 rev changed to FIFTY PENCE instead of NEW PENCE	f
1983-1985	f
1992 European Community	f
1992 – silver, proof	£30
1992 – silver, proof piedfort	£55
1992 – gold, proof	£400
1994 Normandy landing	f
1994 – silver, proof	£28
1994 – silver, piedfort	£50
1994 – gold, proof	£400
1997 new size (27.3mm diameter)	
silver, proof	£27
silver, piedfort	£46
1997 old and new size, silver proofs	£50

TWENTY-FIVE PENCE

1972 Silver Wedding	£1
1972 – silver, proof	£25
1977 Jubilee	£1
1977 – silver, proof	£20
1980 Queen Mother's 80th birthday	£1
1980 – in blister pack	£3
1980 – silver, proof	£32
1981 Royal Wedding	£1
1981 – in folder	£3
1981 – silver, proof	£30

TWENTY PENCE

1982	f
1982 silver, proof piedfort	£40
1983, 1984, 1985, 1987, 1988-1996	f

TEN PENCE

1968	£0.25
1969	£0.25
1970	£0.20
1971	£0.20
1973	£0.20
1974-1977, 1979-1981	f
1992 new size (24.5mm diameter) silver, proof, piedfort	£30

1992 old and new size, silver, proofs	£30
1992, 1995, 1996 – cu-ni	f

FIVE PENCE

1968-1971	*
1975, 1977-1980, 1987, 1988, 1989	f
1990 silver, proof, old and new	£26
1990, 1991, 1992, 1994–1996 – cu-ni ...	f

TWO PENCE

1971	*
1975-1981	f
1985 new portrait, rev changed to TWO PENCE instead of NEW PENCE ...	f
1986-1996	f

ONE PENNY

1971	*
1973-1981	f
1982 rev changed to ONE PENNY instead of NEW PENNY	f
1983, 1984	f
1985 new portrait	f
1986-1996	f

HALF PENNY

1971	*
1973-81	*
1982 rev changed to HALFPENNY instead of 1/2 NEW PENNY	*
1983	*

Proof and Specimen Sets

Proof or specimen sets have been issued since 1887 by the Royal Mint in official cases. Prior to that date, sets were issued privately by the engraver. Some sets are of currency coins, easily distinguishable from proofs which have a vastly superior finish. The two 1887 sets frequently come on to the market, hence their place in this list. The 1953 'plastic' set, though made up of currency coins, is official. It was issued in a plastic packet, hence the name. Apart from the seats stated, as being uncirculated, currency or specimen, all those in the following listing are proof sets.

GEORGE IV   FDC
New issue, **1826.** Five pounds to farthing (11 coins) £17000

WILLIAM IV
Coronation, **1831.** Two pounds to farthing (14 coins) £13500

VICTORIA
Young head, **1839.** 'Una and the Lion' five pounds plus sovereign to farthing (15 coins) £20000
Young head, **1853.** Sovereign to quarter farthing, including 'Gothic' crown (16 coins) £16000
Jubilee head, Golden Jubilee, **1887.** Five pounds to Threepence ('full set' – 11 coins) £5000
As above, currency set (unofficial) £1250
Jubilee head, Golden Jubilee, **1887.** Crown to threepence ('short set' – 7 coins) £750
As above, currency set (unofficial) £150
Old head, **1893.** Five pounds to threepence ('full set)' – 10 coins) £5500
Old head, **1893.** Crown to threepence ('short set' – 6 coins) £900

EDWARD VII
Coronation, **1902.** Five pounds to Maundy penny – matt proofs (13 coins) £1350
Coronation, **1902.** Sovereign to Maundy penny – matt proofs (11 coins) £400

GEORGE V
Coronation, **1911.** Five pounds to Maundy penny (12 coins) £2250
Coronation, **1911.** Sovereign to Maundy penny (10 coins) £600
Coronation, **1911.** Halfcrown to Maundy penny (8 coins) £250
New types, **1927.** Crown to threepence (6 coins) £200

GEORGE VI
Coronation, **1937.** Gold set, five pounds to half sovereign (4 coins) £1350
Coronation, **1937.** Silver and bronze set, crown to farthing including Maundy money (15 coins) £120
Mid-century, **1950.** Halfcrown to farthing (9 coins) £40
Festival of Britain, **1951.** Crown to farthing (10 coins) £50

ELIZABETH II
Coronation, **1953.** Crown to farthing (10 coins) £55
Coronation, **1953.** Currency ('plastic') set, official, halfcrown to farthing (9 coins) £15
Specimen decimal set, **1968.** 10p, 5p; **1971** 2p, 1p, ½p in wallet (5 coins) £1
Last £sd decimal set, **1970.** (sets issued 1971-73). Halfcrown to Halfpenny (8 coins) £15
Proof decimal set, **1971.** (issued 1973), 50p, 10p, 5p, 2p, 1p, ½p (6 coins) £15
Proof decimal set, **1972.** 50p, Sliver Wedding, 25p, 10p, 5p, 2p, 1p, ½p (7 coins) £15
Proof decimal sets, **1973, 1974, 1975, 1976.** 50p, to ½p (6 coins) £9
Proof decimal set, **1977.** 50p to ½p, plus Jubilee crown (7 coins) £13
Proof decimal set, **1978.** 50p to ½p (6 coins) £15
Proof decimal set, **1979.** 50p to ½p (6 coins) £15
Proof decimal set, **1980.** 50p to ½p (6 coins) £11
Proof gold set, **1980.** Five pounds, two pounds, sovereign, half sovereign (4 coins) £700
Commemorative proof coin set, **1981.** Five pounds, sovereign, Royal Wedding Silver crown,
50p to ½p (9 coins) £600
Commemorative set, **1981.** Sovereign and Royal Wedding silver crown (2 coins) £125
Proof decimal set, **1981.** 50p to ½p (6 coins) £11
Proof gold set, **1982.** Five pounds, two pounds, sovereign, half sovereign (4 coins) £725
Proof decimal set, **1982.** 50p to ½p including 20p (7 coins) £14
Uncirculated decimal set, **1982.** 50p to ½p including 20p (7 coins) £8
Proof gold set, **1983.** Two pounds, sovereign, half sovereign (3 coins) £325
Proof decimal set, **1983.** £1 to ½p (8 coins) £18
Uncirculated decimal set, **1983.** £1 to ½p (8 coins) £12
Proof gold set, **1984.** Five pounds, sovereign, half sovereign (3 coins) £575
Proof decimal set, **1984.** £1 (Scottish rev) to ½p (8 coins) £15
Uncirculated decimal set, **1984.** £1 (Scottish rev) to ½p (8 coins) £13
Proof goldl set, **1985.** new portrait. Five pounds, two pounds, sovereign, half sovereign (4 coins) £750
Proof decimal set, **1985.** new portrait. £1 (Welsh rev) to 1p (7 coins) in de luxe case £20
Proof decimal set, **1985.** As above, in standard case £15
Uncirculated decimal set, **1985.** £1 (Welsh rev) to 1p (7 coins) £12
Proof gold set, **1986.** Commonwealth Games two pounds, sovereign, half sovereign (3 coins) £350
Proof decimal set, **1986.** Commonwealth Games £2, Northern Ireland £1.50p to 1p (8 coins),
de luxe case £25
Proof decimal set, **1986.** As above in standard case £20
Uncirculated decimal set, **1986.** As above, in folder £12
Proof gold Britannia set, **1987.** One ounce, half ounce, quarter ounce tenth ounce (4 coins) £650
Proof decimal set, **1987.** Quarter ounce, tenth ounce (2 coins) £150

PROOF AND SPECIMEN SETS

	FDC
Proof gold set, **1987**. Two pounds, sovereign, half sovereign (3 coins)	...£325
Proof decimal set, **1987**. £1 (English rev) to 1p (7 coins) in de luxe case	...£23
Proof decimal set, **1987**. As above, in standard case	...£18
Uncirculated decimal set, **1987**. As above, in folder	...£10
Proof gold Britannia set, **1988**. One ounce, half ounce, quarter ounce, tenth ounce (4 coins)	...£615
Proof gold Britannia set, **1988**. Quarter ounce, tenth ounce (2 coins)	...£150
Proof gold set, **1988**. Two pounds, sovereign, half sovereign (3 coins)	...£325
Proof decimal set, **1988**. £1 (Royal Arms rev) to 1p (7 coins) in de luxe case	...£26
Proof decimal set, **1988**. As above, in standard case	...£19
Uncirculated decimal set, **1988**. As above, in folder	...£11
Proof gold Britannia set, **1989**. One ounce, half ounce, quarter ounce, tenth ounce (4 coins)	...£700
Proof gold Britannia set, **1989**. Quarter ounce, tenth ounce (2 coins)	...£150
Proof gold set, **1989**. 500th anniversary of the sovereign. Five pounds, two pounds, sovereign, half sovereign (4 coins)	...£900
Proof gold set, **1989**. 500th anniversary of the sovereign. Two pounds, sovereign half sovereign (3 coins)	...£450
Proof decimal set, **1989**. Bill of Rights £2. Claim of Right £2, £1 (Scottish rev as 1984), 50p to 1p (9 coins) in de luxe case	...£32
Proof decimal set, **1989**. As above, in standard case	...£27
Proof silver, Bill of Rights £2. Claim of Right £2. **1989**. (2 coins)	...£40
Proof silver piedfort, **1989**. £2 as above (2 coins)	...£80
Uncirculated, **1989**. As above (2 coins) in folder	...£10
Uncirculated decimal set, **1989**. £1 (Scotish rev as 1984) to 1p (7 coins)	...£15
Proof gold Britannia set, **1990**.	...£775
Proof gold set, **1990**. Five pounds, two pounds, sovereign, half-sovereign (4 coins)	...£800
Proof gold set, **1990**. Two pounds, sovereign, half sovereign (3 coins)	...£375
Proof silver set, **1990**. Five pence (23.59mm diam) and five pence (18mm diam, new size)	...£24
Proof decimal set, **1990**. £1 (Welsh rev as 1985) to 1p including large and small 5p (8 coins) in deluxe case	...£30
Proof decimal set, **1990**. As above, in standard case	...£25
Uncirculated decimal set, **1990**. £1 (Welsh rev as 1985) to 1p including large and small 5p (8 coins)	...£15
Proof gold Britannia set, **1991**.	...£775
Proof gold set, **1991**. Five pounds, two pounds, sovereign, half sovereign (4 coins)	...£900
Proof gold set, **1991**. Two pounds, sovereign, half sovereign (3 coins)	...£450
Proof decimal set, **1991**. £1 to 1p (7 coins) in deluxe case	...£30
Proof decimal set, **1991**. As above, in standard case	...£25
Uncirculated decimal set, **1991**. (7 coins)	...£15
Proof gold Britannia set, **1992**.	...£800
Proof gold set, **1992**. Five pounds, two pounds, sovereign, half sovereign (4 coins)	...£950
Proof gold set, **1992**. Two pounds, sovereign, half sovereign (3 coins)	...£450
Proof decimal set, **1992**. £1 (English rev as 1987) to 1p (two 50p, new 10p) (9 coins) in deluxe case	...£32
Proof decimal set, **1992**. As above, in standard case	...£28
Proof gold Britannia set, **1993**.	...£900
Proof gold set, **1993**. Five pounds, two pounds, sovereign, half sovereign (4 coins)	...£975
Proof gold set, **1993**. Two pounds, sovereign, half sovereign (3 coins)	...£450
Proof decimal set, **1993**. Coronation Anniversary £5, £1 to 1p (8 coins) in deluxe case	...£35
Proof decimal set, **1993**. As above, in standard case	...£30
Uncirculated decimal set, **1993**. (with two 50p, no £5) (8 coins)	...£12
Proof gold Britannia set, **1994**.	...£900
Proof gold set, **1994**. Five pounds, two pounds Bank of England, Sovereign, half sovereign (4 coins)	£1025
Proof gold set, **1994**. Two pounds Bank of England, sovereign, half sovereign (3 coins)	£550
Proof decimal set, **1994**. £2 Bank of England, £1 (Scottish rev), 50p D-Day to 1p (8 coins) in deluxe case	£34
Proof decimal set, **1994**. As above, in standard case	...£28
Uncirculated decimal set, **1994**.	...£14
Proof gold Britannia set, **1995**.	...£1000
Proof gold set, **1995**. Five pounds, two pounds Peace, sovereign, half sovereign (4 coins)	...£1100
Proof gold set, **1995**. Two pounds Peace, sovereign, half sovereign (3 coins)	...£500
Proof decimal set, **1995**. Two pounds Peace, £1 (Welsh rev) to 1p (8 coins) in deluxe case	...£36
Proof decimal set, **1995**. As above, in standard case	...£29
Uncirculated decimal set, **1995**.	...£12
Proof gold Britannia set, **1996**.	...£1050
Proof gold set, **1996**. Five pounds, two pounds, sovereign, half sovereign (4 coins)	...£1175
Proof gold set, **1996**. Two pounds, sovereign, half sovereign (3 coins)	...£500
Proof silver decimal set, **1996**. £1 to 1p (7 coins)	...£100
Proof decimal set, **1996**. 60th Birthday £5, £2 football, £1 (Northern Irish rev) to 1p (9 coins) in deluxe case	...£38
Proof decimal set, **1996**. As above, in standard case	...£32
Uncirculated decimal set, **1996**. £2 to 1p (8 coins)	...£11
Proof gold set, **1997**. Five pounds, two pounds (bimetal), sovereign, half sovereign (4 coins)	...£1175
Proof gold set, **1997**. Two pounds (bimetal), sovereign, half sovereign	...£500
Proof decimal set, **1997**. Golden Wedding £5, £2 bimetal, £1 (English rev) to 1p, with new 50p	...£40
Proof decimal set, **1997**. As above, in standard case	...£35
Uncirculated decimal set, **1997**. As above but no £5 (9 coins)	...£11
Proof gold Britannia set, **1997**.	...£1050

Scottish Coins

Based on a map of actual and supposed mints prepared by Spink and Son Ltd.

The number of mints which have been in operation in Scotland can be seen from the map above. The mints of the first coinage of Alexander III are the greatest number ever working together in Scotland, and it is this area that really attracts the collector of the different mint issues. For this reason, when we deal with this reign later on, we give a price for issues of each mint town, but not for any other reign.

MINT TOWN	KING(S)
ABERDEEN	Alexander III, David II
	Robert III, James I, II, III
AYR	Alexander III
BAMBOROUGH	Henry
BERWICK	David I, Malcom IV,
	William I, Alexander II, III
	Robert Bruce, James III
CARLISLE	David I, Henry
CORBRIDGE	Henry
DUMBARTON	Robert III

DUMFRIES	Alexander III
DUNBAR	William I ?, Alexander II
DUNDEE	William I ?, Alexander I
DUNFERMLINE	William I
FORFAR	Alexander III
FORRES	Alexander III
GLASGOW	Alexander III
INVERNESS	Alexander III
JEDBURGH	Malcom IV
KELSO	Alexander II
KINGHORN	Alexander III
LANARK	Alexander III
LINLITHGOW	James I, II
MONTROSE	Alexander III
PERTH	William I, Alexander III,
	Robert II to James II
RENFREW	Alexander III
ROXBURGH	Alexander III
ST ANDREWS	Alexander III
STIRLING	Alexander III, James I,
	Mary Stuart

Prices are for the commonest coins in each case.
Collectors should expect to pay these amounts and
upwards. For further details see The Scottish
Coinage, by I. Stewart (Spink, 1967, reprint 1975) and
Standard Catalogue, Volume 2 (Seaby, 1984). Gold
coins are indicated. All other coins are silver unless
another metal is stated.

	F	VF
DAVID I 1124-53		
Pennies	£450	£950

Four different groups; struck at the
mints of Berwick, Carlisle, Roxburgh and
Edinburgh

*This superb David I penny of Carlisle realised
£1,210 in Spink's Douglas auction in 1997*

HENRY 1136-52
(Earl of Huntingdon and Northumberland)
Pennies ... £950 *
Three types; struck at the mints of Corbridge,
Carlisle and Barnborough.

MALCOLM IV 1153-65
Pennies ... £3500 *
Five types; struck at the mints of
Roxburgh and Berwick.

WILLIAM THE LION 1165-1214
Pennies ... £60 £140
Three issues; struck at the mints of Roxburgh,
Berwick, Edinburgh, Dun (Dunfermline?), Perth

ALEXANDER II 1214-49
Pennies ... £700 £1500
Mints of Berwick and Roxburgh, varieties of bust.

*Halfpenny and farthing of Alexander III
and penny of Robert Bruce*

ALEXANDER III 1249-86
1st coinage pennies 1250-80
Mints

	F	VF
Aberdeen	£100	£300
Ayr	£100	£275
Berwick	£40	£90
'DUN'	£125	£350
Edinburgh	£35	£100
Forfar	£120	£350
Fres	£120	£350
Glasgow	£150	£400
Inverness	£150	£400
Kinghorn	£150	£400
Lanark	£150	£400
Montrose	£250	*
Perth	£50	£130

SCOTTISH COINS

	F	VF
Renfrew	£160	*
Roxburgh	£35	£120
St. Andrews	£80	£200
Stirling	£100	£300
'TERWILANER' (uncertain name)	£150	*

2nd coinage c. 1280 –
Many types and varieties

	F	VF
Pennies	£15	£35
Halfpennies	£60	£170
Farthings	£150	£400

JOHN BALIOL 1292-6
1st coinage (rough surface issue)

	F	VF
Pennies	£90	£250
Halfpennies		Very rare

2nd coinage (smooth surface issue)

	F	VF
Pennies	£120	£300
Halfpennies	£200	£450

ROBERT BRUCE 1306-29

	F	VF
Pennies	£250	£600
Halfpennies	£300	£750
Farthings		ext. rare

Probably all struck at Berwick.

David II groat

DAVID II 1329-71

	F	VF
Nobles (gold)		ext. rare
Groats	£70	£200
Halfgroats	£50	£160
Pennies	£40	£95
Halfpennies	£150	£350
Farthings	£500	*

Three issues, but these denominations were not
struck for all issues. Edinburgh and Aberdeen
mints.

ROBERT II 1371-90

	F	VF
Groats	£50	£170
Halfgroats	£70	£180
Pennies	£60	£140
Halfpennies	£130	£400

Some varieties. Struck at mints of Dundee,
Edinburgh, Perth.

ROBERT III 1390-1406

	F	VF
Lion or crowns (gold)	£400	£900
Demy lions or halfcrowns (gold)	£350	£800
Groats	£60	£150
Halfgroats	£100	£300
Pennies	£150	£300
Halfpennies	£250	*

Three issues, many varieties. Struck at mints of
Edinburgh, Aberdeen, Perth, Dumbarton.

JAMES I 1406-37

	F	VF
Demies (gold)	£300	£650
Half demies (gold)	£400	£850
Groats	£130	£270

SCOTTISH COINS

	F	VF
Billon pennies	£75	*
Billon halfpennies	£100	*

Mints, Aberdeen, Edinburgh,
Inverness, Linlithgow, Perth, Stirling.

JAMES II 1437-60
Demies (gold) from	£375	£750
Lions (gold) from	£500	£1250
Half lions (gold) from		Very rare
Groats	£150	£500
Halfgroats	£375	*
Billon pennies	£150	*

Two issues, many varieties. Mints: Aberdeen,
Edinburgh, Linlithgow, Perth, Roxburgh, Stirling.

ECCLESIASTICAL ISSUES C 1452-80
Bishop Kennedy copper pennies ...	£75	£170
Copper farthings	£150	*

Different types, varieties

JAMES III 1460-88
Riders (gold) from	£700	£1500
Half riders (gold)	£800	£1600
Quarter riders (gold)	£900	£1800
Unicorns (gold)	£750	£1600
Groats ... ...from	£150	£350

*James III groat and
James V one-third groat*

Halfgroats from	£350	*
Pennies from	£80	£250
Billon placks from	£35	£90
Billon half placks from		Very rare
Billon pennies from	£70	*
Copper farthings from	£150	*

Many varieties. Mints: Edinburgh, Berwick,
Aberdeen.

JAMES IV 1488-1513
Unicorns (gold)	£650	£1500
Half unicorns (gold)	£500	£1000
Lions or crowns (gold)	£850	£2000
Half lions (gold)	£1500	£3500
Pattern angel (gold)		unique
Groats	£260	£700
Halfgroats	£300	*
Pennies (light coinage)	£350	*
Billon placks	£25	£70
Billon half placks	£90	*
Billon pennies	£50	£100

Different types, varieties. Mint: Edinburgh only.

James V 'Bonnet' piece of 1540

JAMES V 1513-42
	F	
Unicorns (gold)	£800	£17
Half unicorns (gold)	£1500	£45
Crowns (gold)	£500	£12
'Bonnet' pieces or ducats (gold) ...	£1400	£30
Two-thirds ducats (gold)	£1800	£25
One-third ducats (gold)	£2000	£45
Groats from	£90	£2
One-third groats	£140	£3

James V groat

Billon placks	£20	£
Billon bawbees	£20	£
Billon half bawbees	£75	£1
Billon quarter bawbees		uniq

Different issues, varieties. Edinburgh mint.

*Note: from here on all Scottish coins were struc
at Edinburgh.*

MARY 1542-67
1st Period 1542-58
Crown (gold)	£850	£22
Twenty shillings (gold)	£1800	£27
Lions or forty-four shillings (gold)	£800	£16

*Extremely rare Francis and Mary ducat which
realised £77,000 at a Spink auction in March 19*

Half lions or twenty-two shillings (gold)	£475	£13
Ryals or £3 pieces (gold) 1555, 1557, 1558	£1750	£40
Half ryals 1555,1557,1558 ...	£2700	
Portrait testoons, 1553	£1000	£35
Non-portrait testoons, 1555-8	£120	£3
– half testoons, 1555-8	£130	£3
Billon bawbees	£25	£
– half bawbees	£65	£1
– pennies (facing bust)	£150	£4
– pennies (no bust) 1556	£100	£4
– lions, 1555, 1558	£25	£
– placks, 1557	£25	£

2nd period (Francis and Mary) 1558-60
Ducats or sixty shillings (gold) (One fetched £77,000 (including 10%) at the Spink auction on 4 March 1997)		ext. ra
Non-portrait testoons, 1558-61 ...	£150	£4
– half testoons, 1558-60	£150	£4
Twelvepenny groats (Nonsunt) 1558-9	£90	£2.
– lions, 1559-60	£18	£

3rd period (widowhood) 1560-5
Crown (gold) 1562 (Probably a pattern)		uniqu

		F	VF
Portrait testoons, 1561-2		£750	£2500
– half testoons, 1561-2		£850	*

4th period (Henry and Mary) 1565-7

Portrait ryals, 1565 ... ...   ext. rare
The only available specimen was sold at
Glendining's in December 1990. It realised £48,000

		F	VF
Non-portrait ryals, 1565-7		£175	£500

Mary and Henry non-porait ryal, 1565

		F	VF
– two thirds ryals, 1565-7		£190	£550
– – undated		£400	£950
– one-third ryals, 1565-6		£170	£450
– testoons, 1565			ext.rare

5th period (2nd widowhood) 1567

		F	VF
_ Non portrait ryals, 1567		£190	£450
– two thirds ryals, 1567		£190	£500
– one third ryals, 1566-7		£200	£500

Mints: Edinburgh, Stirling (but only for some bawbees

JAMES VI
Before English accession 1567-1603
1st coinage 1567-71

		F	VF
Ryals 1567-71		£180	£475
Two-third ryals –		£150	£450
One-third ryals –		£170	£475

Superb gold £20 piece of 1575 realised £30,800 in Spink auction in March 1997

2nd coinage 1571-80

		F	VF
Twenty pounds (gold)		£9000	£18,000
Nobles, 1572-7, 1580		£45	£350
Half nobles –		£70	£220
Two merks, 1578-80 –		£950	*
Merks, 1579-80		£900	*

3rd coinage 1580-81

		F	VF
Ducats (gold), 1580		£2750	£5500
Sixteen shillings, 1581		£900	£3000

		F	VF
Eight shillings, 1581		£900	*
Four shillings, 1581		very rare	
Two shillings, 1581		ext. rare	

4th coinage 1582-88

		F	VF
Lion nobles (gold)		£2000	£4500
Two-third lion nobles (gold)		£2500	£6000
One-third lion nobles (gold)		£3000	£7500
Forty shillings, 1582		£2500	£7500
Thirty shillings, 1582-6		£180	£750
Twenty shillings, 1582-5		£130	£400
Ten shillings, 1582-4		£100	£250

James VI twenty shillings, 1582

5th coinage 1588

		F	VF
Thistle nobles (gold)		£1250	£2750

6th coinage 1591-93

		F	VF
Hat pieces (gold) 1591-3		£2500	£4000
Balance half merks, 1591-3		£170	£400
Balance quarter merks, 1591		£250	£600

7th coinage 1594-1601

		F	VF
Riders (gold)		£450	£850
Half riders (gold)		£350	£750
Ten shillings, 1593-5, 1598-1601 ...		£90	£275
Five shillings, 1593-5, 1598-1601 ...		£100	£250
Thirty pennies, 1595-6, 1598-9, 1601		£75	£180
Twelve pennies, 1594-6		£60	£150

8th coinage 1601-4

		F	VF
Sword and sceptre pieces (gold) ...		£275	£550
Half sword and sceptre pieces (gold)		£220	£375
Thistle-merks, 1601-4		£50	£150
Half thistle merks –		£40	£120
Quarter thistle-merks –		£35	£100
Eighth thistle-merks, 1601-3		£35	£150

Billon and copper issues

		F	VF
Billon placks or eight penny groats		£20	£75
Billon half packs		£100	*
Billon hardheads		£25	£80
Billon saltire placks		£125	*
Copper twopence 1597		very rare	
Copper penny 1597		very rare	

After English accession 1603-25

		F	VF
Units (gold)		£400	£800
Double crowns (gold)		£450	£1200
Britain crowns (gold)		£350	*
Halfcrowns (gold)		£300	*
Thistle crowns (gold)		£250	*
Sixty shillings		£250	£700
Thirty shillings		£75	£200
Twelve shillings		£80	£180
Six shillings		£100	*
Two shillings		£50	*
One shilling		£60	*

SCOTTISH COINS

*James VI Gold Unit
(after English accession)*

	F	VF
Sixpences	*	*
Copper twopences	£10	£50
Copper pennies	£20	£60

*Charles I
Scottish
unit by
Briot*

CHARLES 1652-49
1st coinage 1625-36
	F	VF
Units (gold)	£450	£900
Double crowns (gold)	£950	*
Britain crowns (gold)	ext. rare	
Sixty shillings	£275	£800
Thirty shillings	£60	£200
Twelve shillings	£60	£175
Six shillings	very rare	
Two shillings	£70	*
One shillings	ext. rare	

2nd coinage 1636
	F	VF
Half merks	£35	£150
Forty penny pieces	£40	£100
Twenty penny pieces	£40	*

3rd coinage 1637-42
	F	VF
Units (gold)	£475	£1000
Half units (gold)	£700	*
Britain crowns (gold)	£400	£950
Britain half crowns (gold)	£200	£600
Sixty shillings	£300	£800
Thirty shillings	£50	£150
Twelve shillings	£50	£150
Six shillings	£50	£140
Half Merks	£50	£150
Forty pennies	£20	£70
Twenty pennies	£12	£30
Three shillings	£40	£90
Two shillings	£40	£100
Copper twopences (lion)	£10	£50
– pennies –		rare
– twopences (CR crowned)	£10	£50
– twopences (Stirling turners) ...	£10	£40

CHARLES II 1660-85
1st coinage
Four merks

	F	
1664 thistle above bust	£250	
1664 thistle below bust	£270	
1665	*	
1670	£170	
1673	£175	
1674 F below bust	£300	£7
1675	£150	£4

Two merks

	F	
1664 thistle above bust	£175	£5

*Charles II two merks, 1664
(thistle above bust)*

	F	
1664 thistle below bust	£170	
1670	£120	£4
1673	£120	£4
1673 F below bust	£200	
1674	£250	
1674 F below bust	£200	
1675	£150	£4

Merks

	F	
1664	£35	£1
1665	£35	£1
1666	£100	
1668	£40	£1
1669	£40	£1
1670	£35	£2
1671	£60	£2
1672	£30	£1
1673	£30	£1
1674	£50	£2
1674 F below bust	£50	£2
1675 F below bust	£50	£2
1675	£95	£2

Half merks

	F	
1664	£50	£1
1665	£50	£1
1666	£75	£1
1667	£50	£1
1668	£50	£1
1669	£75	£1
1670	£90	
1671	£50	£2
1672	£40	£1
1673	£40	£1
1675 F below bust	£35	£1
1675	£45	£1

2nd coinage
Dollars

	F	
1676	£170	£4
1679	£170	£4
1680	£250	
1681	£120	£5
1682	£120	£3

Half dollars

	F	
1675	£150	£4
1676	£190	£4
1681	£70	£4

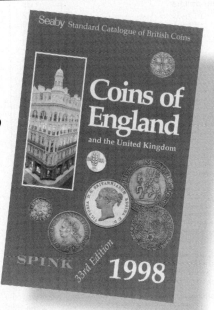
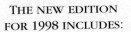

Quarter dollars		F	VF
1675	....	£50	£2
1676	....	£50	£200
1677	....	£75	*
1678	....	£50	£200
1679	....	£75	*
1680	....	£50	£200
1681	....	£75	£200
1682	....	£50	£200

Eighth dollars			
1676	....	£50	£150
1677	....	£50	£150
1678/7	....	*	*
1679	....	*	*
1680	....	£75	£150
1682	....	£100	*

Sixteenth dollars			
1677	....	£35	£90
1678/7	....	£100	*
1679/7	....	£100	*
1680	....	£80	£200
1681	....	£35	£100

Copper twopence CR"			
crowned		£20	£90
Copper bawbees, 1677-9		£35	£100
Copper turners, 1677-9		£20	£90

JAMES VII 1685-9
		F	VF
Sixty shillings 1688 proof only[1]		FDC	£950
– gold proof only[1]		FDC	*

([1]Struck in 1828, not contemporary)

Forty shillings			
1887	... ...	£80	£300
1688	... ...	£150	£400

Ten shillings			
1687	... ...	£80	£275
1688	... ...	£90	£300

WILLIAM AND MARY 1689-94
Sixty shillings			
1691	... ...	£150	£500
1692	... ...	£100	£400

Forty shillings			
1689	... ...	£95	£300
1690	... ...	£90	£280
1691	... ...	£70	£270
1692	... ...	£90	£280
1693	... ...	£100	*
1694	... ...	£100	*

Twenty shillings			
1693	... ...	£90	£280
1694	... ...	£200	*

Ten shillings			
1689	... ...	*	*
1690	... ...	£100	£250
1691	... ...	£70	£200
1692	... ...	£40	£120
1694	... ...	£150	£400

William and Mary 1694 five shillings

Five shillings			
1691	... ...	£70	£250
1694	... ...	£60	£200
Copper bawbee 1691-4		£40	£100
Copper bodle 1691-4		£30	£75

SCOTTISH COINS

WILLIAM II 1694-1702
		F	VF
Pistole (gold) 1701	... ...	£1600	£3500
Half pistole (gold) 1701		£1500	£3500

Sixty shillings			
1699	... ...	*	*

Forty shillings			
1695	... ...	£70	£300
1696	... ...	£50	£200
1697	... ...	£75	£300
1698	... ...	£60	£200
1699	... ...	£100	*
1700	... ...	£200	*

Twenty shillings			
1695	... ...	£50	£170
1696	... ...	£50	£170
1697	... ...	*	*
1698	... ...	£80	£250

1698 ten shillings

		F	VF
1699	... ...	*	*

Ten shillings			
1695	... ...	£75	*
1696	... ...	£70	£200
1697	... ...	£70	*
1698	... ...	£70	*
1699	... ...	£100	£350

Five shillings			
1695	... ...	£50	*
1696	... ...	£50	*
1697	... ...	£20	£80
1699	... ...	£80	*
1700	... ...	£40	*
1701	... ...	£70	*
1702	... ...	£60	£200
Copper bawbee 1695-7		£20	£100
Copper bodle 1695-7		£30	£120

ANNE 1702-14
Pre-Union 1702-7
Ten shillings			
1705	... ...	£50	£150
1706	... ...	£100	£300

Five shillings			
1705	... ...	£15	£70
1706	... ...	£20	£80

Post-Union 1707-14
see under British milled series

JAMES VIII 1688-1766 (The Old Pretender)
		F	VF
Guinea 1716, gold	... ...	FDC	£3000
– silver	... ...	FDC	£800
– bronze	... ...	FDC	£1200
Crown 1709			unique
Crown 1716, silver	... ...	FDC	£900
– gold			ext. rare
– bronze	... ...		ext. rare

NB: All the 1716-dated pieces were struck in 1828 from original dies.

Irish Coins

Hammered Issues 995-1661

Prices are for the commonest coins in each case. It should be remembered that most of the Irish coins of these times are in fairly poor condition and it is difficult to find specimens in VF condition upwards. For more details see The Guide Book to the Coinage of Ireland AD 995 to the present day, *by Anthony Dowle and Patrick Finn (ref. DF in the following lists): Seaby's* Coins of Scotland, Ireland and the Islands, *which is volume Two of Seaby's Standard Catalogue (ref Sby in price list): and also Patrick Finn's* Irish Coin Values.

All coins are silver unlesss otherwise stated

HIBERNO-NORSEMEN OF

	F	VF
DUBLIN 995-1150		
Pennies, imitative of English coins, many types and varieties ...from	£100	£150

Hiberno-Norse penny, c 1015-1035

JOHN, as Lord of Ireland
c 1185-1199

	F	VF
Halfpennies, with profile portrait	extremely rare	
Halfpennies, with facing head	£40	£80
Farthings	£200	£450
Different types,varieties, mints, moneyers.		

JOHN DE COURCY
Lord of Ulster 1177-1205

Halfpenny		unique
Farthings	£400	£800
Different types,varieties, mints, moneyers.		

Triangle type, penny of King John

JOHN as King of England and
Lord of Ireland c 1199-1216
Rex/Triangle types

	F	VF
Pennies ... ...from	£40	£90
Halfpennies	£75	£160
Farthings	£175	£400
Different types,varieties, mints, moneyers.		

HENRY III 1216-1272

Pennies (c 1251-1254) ... ...from	£35	£85
Dublin only, moneyers DAVI and RICHARD. many varieties.		

Edward I Waterford penny

EDWARD I 1272-1307

	F	VF
Pennies ... ...from	£20	£40
Halfpennies	£60	£150
Farthings	£130	£300
Dublin,Waterford and Cork. Many different issues.		

EDWARD III 1327-1377

Halfpennies Dublin mint	ext. rare

There were no Irish coins struck for Edward II, Richard II, Henry IV or Henry V.

HENRY VI 1422-1461

Pennies, Dublin mint	ext. rare

Edward IV untitled crown groats

EDWARD IV 1461-1483

	F	VF
Untitled crown groats ... ...from	£250	£500
– pennies	£500	*
Titled crown groats	£850	*
– halfgroats		ext. rare
– pennies		very rare
Cross on rose/-sun groats	£500	*
– – pennies	£400	*
Bust/rose-sun double groats	£1400	£3500
– – groats	£1800	*
– – halfgroats		ext.rare
– – pennies		ext.rare
'English style' groats	£50	£150
– halfgroats	£200	£400
– pennies	£60	£130
– halfpennies		ext.rare
Butt/rose groats	£350	£750
– – pennies	£75	£150
copper issues		
Crown/cross farthing	£800	*
– – half farthing	£550	*
PARTICIUS/SALVATOR		
Farthing	£500	£1000
3 crowns/sun half-farthing		very rare

This is, of course, a very abbreviated listing of the issues of Edward IV which are numerous and complicated, and still pose numismatics many problems. There are also many varieties and different mints.

IRISH COINS

	F	VF
RICHARD III 1483-1485		
Bust/rose-cross groats	£700	£1800
— halfgroat		unique
— penny		unique
Cross and Pellet Penny	£500	*
Three-crown groats	£400	£850
Different mints, varieties, etc.		

HENRY VII 1485-1509
Early issues

Three-crown groats	£65	£170
— halfgroats	£140	£350
— pennies	£300	£650
— halfpennies		ext. rare
Different mints, varieties, etc.		

LAMBERT SIMNEL (pretender) 1487

Three-crown groats	£950	£2500
Different mints, varieties.		

HENRY VII 1485-1509
Later issues

Facing bust groats	£75	£160
— halfgroats		ext. rare
— pennies		very rare
Crowned H pennies		very rare

Many varieties. Mainly Dublin. Waterford is extemely rare.

Henry VIII 'harp groat, initials HA

HENRY VIII 1509-1547

'Harp' groats	£30	£90
— halfgroat	£250	£550

These harp coins carry crowned initials, e.g., HA (Henry and Anne Boleyn), HI (Henry and Jane Seymour), HK (Henry and Katherine Howard), HR (Henricus Rex).

Henry VIII portrait groat

Posthumous issues

Portrait groats current for 6 pence	£60	£150
— halfgroats ...current for 3 pence	£90	£200
— pennies current for 3 halfpence	£150	*
— halfpennies current for 3 farthings	£250	*
Different busts, mintmarks etc.		

EDWARD VI 1547-1553

Base shillings 1552 (MDLII)	£500	£1000
— contemporary copy	£40	£150

Mary 1553 shilling

MARY 1553-1558	F	V
Shillings 1553 (MDLIII)	£450	£100
Shillings 1554 (MDLIIII)		ext. rar
Groats		very rar
Halfgroats		ext. ra
Pennies		ext. rar
Several varieties of the shillings and groats.		

PHILIP AND MARY 1554-1558		
Base shillings	£150	£40
— groats	£50	£14
Several minor varieties.		

ELIZABETH I 1558-1603		
Base portrait shillings	£130	£47
— groats	£100	£30

Elizabeth I 1561 shilling

Fine portrait shillings 1561	£95	£40
— groats –	£250	£60
Base shillings arms-harp	£95	£30
— sixpences –	£75	£17
— threepences –	£140	£38
— pennies –	£15	£7
— halfpennies –	£35	£14

JAMES I 1603-1625		
Shillings	£50	£15
— Sixpences	£40	£12
Different issues, busts and mintmarks.		

CHARLES I 1625-1649
Seige money of the Irish Rebellion 1642-1649
Siege coins are rather irregular in size and shape

Kilkenny Money 1642

Copper halfpennies (**F**)	£150	£35
Copper farthings (**F**)	£150	£40

Inchiquin Money 1642-1646
(The only gold coins struck in Ireland. Of the ve few known specimens there is only one private owned; the others are in museums.)

Gold double pistoles		ext. ra
Gold pistoles (**F**)		ext. ra
Crowns	£750	£150

Inchiquin shilling

	F	VF
Halfcrowns	£1250	*
Shillings	£1600	*
Ninepences	ext. rare	
Sixpences	£1500	*
Groats (F)	£1500	*
Threepences	ext. rare	

Three issues and many varieties.

Ormonde Money 1643

	F	VF
Crowns (F)	£275	£600
Halfcrowns (F)	£190	£500
Shillings	£75	£160

Ormonde sixpence

	F	VF
Sixpences (F)	£60	£160
Groats (F)	£50	£150
Threepences	£35	£90
Halfgroats (F)	£220	£475

Many varieties.

Rebel Money 1643

	F	VF
Crowns	£1500	*
Halfcrowns	ext. rare	*

Town Pieces 1645-1647
Bandon

	F	VF
Copper farthings (F)	£100	*

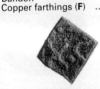

Kinsale copper farthing

Kinsale

	F	VF
Copper farthings (F)	£90	*

Youghal

	F	VF
Copper farthings (F)	£100	£750
Brass twopences	ext. rare	
Pewter threepences	ext. rare	

Cork

	F	VF
Shillings (F)	£950	*
Sixpences (F)	£500	£1000
Copper halfpennies	ext. rare	
Copper farthings	£80	*
Elizabeth I shillings countermarked CORKE (F)	ext. rare	

Youghal farthing

'Blacksmith's' Money 1649
(Based in English Tower halfcrown)

	F	VF
Halfcrown, varieties	£350	£1200

Dublin Money 1649

	F	VF
Crowns	£1250	£2500
Halfcrowns	£1400	£3000

CHARLES II 1660-1685
Armstrong issues 1660-1661

	F	VF
Copper farthings	£45	£300

Charles II to George IV

This series, of which all the issues except Bank of Ireland tokens were struck in base metal, features a large number of varieties, many of which are unpublished, but there is space here for only the main types and best-known variants. A number of rare proofs have also been omitted.

Except for the 'gunmoney' of James II, Irish copper coins are notably hard to find in the top grades, especially the so-called 'Voce populi' issues and specimens of Wood's coinage (which are reasonably common in the lower grades, apart from the rarities).

We have listed some of the 'gunmoney' of James II in only three grades – Fair, Fine and VF. The majority of these hastily produced coins were not well struck and many pieces with little substantial wear are, arguably, not EF in the strictest sense.

Finally, a note on the dating of gunmoney. In the calendar used up to 1723 the legal or civil year commenced on March 25 in Great Britain and Ireland, so December 1689 came before, not after January, February and March 1689. Coins dated March 1689 and March 1690 were struck in the same month.

CHARLES II	Fair	F	VF	EF
St Patrick's coinage				
Halfpenny	£65	£140	*	*
— star in rev legend	£75	£170	*	*
Farthing	£40	£90	*	*
— stars in rev legend	£50	£100	£300	*
— cloud around			*	*
St Patrick	*	*	*	*
— martlet below king	*	*	*	*
— annulet below king	*	*	*	*

St Patrick's farthing

IRISH COINS

Regal coinage	Fair	F	VF	EF
Halfpennies				
1680 large letters				
small cross	£25	£60	£130	*
1680 large letters,				
pellets	£5	£25	£100	£250
1681 large letters	£5	£25	£100	£250
1681 small letters	*	*	*	*
1682 large letters	*	*	*	*
1682 small letters	£6	£15	£100	£250
1683	£5	£12	£100	£250
1684	£12	£35	£150	*

JAMES II				
Regal coinage				
Halfpennies				
1685	£1	£10	£100	£250
1686	£1	£10	£100	£250
1687	*	*	*	*
1688	£10	£35	£180	*

Emergency coinage				
Gunmoney				
Crowns				
1690	£15	£35	£100	*
1690 'chubby'				
horseman, sword				
to E (Sby 6577) ...	£20	£70	£200	*
1690 similar (DF 373)	£20	£50	£180	*

James II gunmoney crown

Large halfcrowns				
1689 July	£4	£20	£70	*
1689 August	£2	£15	£45	*
1689 September ...	£2	£15	£50	*
1689 October	£2	£15	£45	*
1689 November ...	£2	£15	£45	*
1689 December ...	£2	£15	£45	*
1689 January	£2	£15	£50	*
1689 February	£2	£15	£45	*
1689 March	£2	£15	£45	*
1690 March	£2	£15	£45	*
1690 April	£4	£15	£60	*
1690 May	£4	£15	£60	*

Small halfcrowns				
1690 April	*	*	*	*
1690 May	£2	£15	£45	*
1690 June	£2	£15	£45	*
1690 July	£2	£15	£45	*
1690 August	£4	£20	£50	*
1690 September ...	*	*	*	*
1690 October	£70	*	*	*

Large shillings				
1689 July	£2	£12	£40	£120
1689 August	£2	£12	£40	£120
1689 September ...	£2	£10	£35	£100
1689 April	£2	£10	£35	£100
1689 November ...	£2	£10	£40	£100
1689 December ...	£2	£10	£40	£100
1689 January	£2	£10	£40	£100
1689 February	£2	£10	£40	£100

	Fair	F	VF	E
1689 March	£2	£10	£40	£10
1690 March	£2	£10	£40	£10
1690 April	£2	£10	£40	£10
Small shillings				
1690 April	£2	£10	£30	£10
1690 May	£2	£10	£30	£10
1690 June	£2	£10	£30	£10
1690 July	*	*	*	*
1690 August	*	*	*	*
1690 September ...	*	*	*	*

Gunmoney sixpence February 1689

Sixpences				
1689 June	£1	£10	£35	£95
1689 July	£1	£10	£35	£95
1689 August	£1	£10	£35	£95
1689 September ...	£1	£10	£35	£95
1689 October	*	*	*	*
1689 November ...	£1	£10	£35	£95
1689 December ...	£1	£10	£35	£95
1689 January	£1	£10	£35	£95
1689 February	£4	£12	£45	£110
1689 March	*	*	*	*
1690 March	*	*	*	*
1690 April	*	*	*	*
1690 May	£12	£20	£90	*
1690 June	*	*	*	*
1690 October	*	*	*	*

Pewter Money				
Crown	£190	£350	£1000	*
Groat	£95	£220	£700	*
Penny large bust ...	£100	£200	£500	*
Penny small bust	£100	£200	£500	*
Halfpenny large bust	£50	£100	£250	*
Halfpenny small bust	£50	£120	£350	*

Limerick Money halfpenny

Limerick Money				
Halfpenny	£8	£40	£95	*
Farthing reversed N	£10	£50	£100	*
— normal N	£15	£55	£120	*

1693 halfpenny

	Fair	F	VF	EF
WILLIAM AND MARY				
Halfpennies				
1692	£2	£15	£90	*
1693	£2	£25	£100	*
1694	£2	£20	£90	*
WILLIAM III				
1696 Halfpenny draped				
bust	£10	£30	£120	*
1696 Halfpenny crude				
undraped bust ...	£25	£100	*	*
GEORGE I				
Wood's coinage				
1722 harp left	£15	£70	£200	*
1722 harp right ...	£3	£12	£100	£350
1723	£2	£8	£80	£250
1723 obv Rs altered				
Bs	£2	£8	£80	£250
1723 no stop after				
date	£2	£8	£80	£250
1723/2	£6	£20	£100	*
1723 star in rev				
legend	*	*	*	*
1723 no stop before				
HIBERNIA	£4	£10	£100	£250
1724 head divides rev				
legend	£4	£10	£100	£220
1724 legend continuous				
over head	£5	£15	£140	£350

George I Wood's farthing, 1723

Farthings				
1722 harp left	£20	£70	£350	£600
1723 D: G:	£10	£30	£120	£400
1723 DEI GRATIA ...	£4	£10	£90	£300
1724	£5	£25	£140	£350

GEORGE II				
halfpennies				
1736	*	£5	£35	£150
1737	*	£5	£35	£150
1738	*	£5	£30	£120
1741	*	£5	£30	£120
1742	*	£5	£30	£120
1743	*	£5	£30	£140
1744	*	£5	£30	£140
1744/43	*	£5	£30	£120
1746	*	£10	£40	£150
1747	*	£5	£30	£140
1748	*	£5	£30	£120
1749	*	£5	£30	£120
1750	*	£5	£30	£120
1751	*	£5	£30	£120
1752	*	£5	£30	£120
1753	*	£5	£30	£120
1755	*	£10	£70	£200
1765	*	£5	£35	£120
Farthings				
1737	*	£4	£40	£100
1738	*	£2	£30	£90
1744	*	£5	£40	£100
1760	*	£5	£40	£10

IRISH COINS

Voce populi halfpenny, 1760

	Fair	F	VF	EF
GEORGE III				
Voce populi coinage				
Halfpennies (1760)				
Type 1 (DF 565) ...	£16	£40	£120	£250
Type 2 (DF 566)	£12	£35	£160	*
Type 3 (DF 567)	£14	£45	£170	*
Type 4 (DF 569)	£12	£40	£170	*
Type 5 (DF 570)	£12	£40	£170	*
Type 6 (DF 571)	£12	£50	£170	*
Type 7 (DF 572)	£12	£40	£170	*
Type 8 (DF 573)	£12	£40	£170	*
Type 9 (DF 575)	£12	£50	£170	*
Type 9, P before head				
(DF 576)	£14	£50	£16	*
Type 9, P under head				
(DF 577)	£14	£50	£10	*
Farthings (1760)				
Type 1 loop to				
truncation	£45	£100	£350	£750
Type 2 no loop ...	*	*	*	*
London coinage				
Halfpennies				
1766	*	£2	£30	£120
1769	*	£2	£30	£120
1769 2nd type	*	£2.50	£30	£120
1775	*	£2	£30	£120
1776	*	*	*	*
1781	*	£3	£30	£120
1782	*	£3	£30	£120
Soho coinage				
Penny 1805		£3	£30	£140
Halfpenny 1805 ...		£3	£30	£120
Farthing 1806		£1	£25	£100
Bank of Ireland token coinage				
Six shillings 1804 ...	£10	£45	£275	£900

1804 six shilling Bank of Ireland

IRISH COINS

	Fair	F	VF	EF
Thirty pence 1808	£2	£10	£50	£200
Ten pence 1805 ...	£1	£8	£30	£100
Ten pence 1806 ...	£1	£6	£30	£70
Ten pence 1813 ...	£1	£5	£20	£60
Five pence 1805 ...	£1	£5	£15	£50
Five pence 1806 ...	£2	£8	£25	£75

Bank of Ireland ten pence token, 1813

GEORGE IV

		F	VF	EF
Penny 1822...	*	£3	£30	£140
Penny 1823...	*	£3	£30	£140
Halfpenny 1822 ...	*	£2	£25	£120
Halfpenny 1823 ...	*	£2	£25	£120

Free State and Republic

Proofs exist for nearly all dates of the modern Irish coinage. However, only a few dates have become available to collectors or dealers and apart from the 1928 proofs, are all very rare. They have therefore been omitted from the list.

TEN SHILLINGS	F	VF	EF	Unc
1966	*	£2.50	£5	£7.50
1966	*	*	*	£15

HALFCROWNS				
1928	£3	£6	£12	£25
1928 proof	*	*	*	£40

Reverse of halfcrown

1930	£3	£10	£75	£200
1931	£6	£20	£100	£250
1933	£3	£15	£80	£200
1934	£3	£15	£15	£100
1937	£30	£75	£300	£650
1939	£3	£6	£10	£30
1940	£3	£5	£10	£30
1941	£4	£6	£15	£35
1942	£4	£6	£15	£30
1943	£70	£150	£600	£1300
1951	*	£1	£5	£25
1954	*	£1	£5	£25
1955	*	£1	£5	£15
1959	*	£1	£5	£10
1961	*	£1	£5	£15

	F	VF	EF	Unc
1961 mule (normal) obv/pre-1939 rev)	£5	£12	£200	*
1962	*	*	*	£5
1963	*	*	*	£5
1964	*	*	*	£5
1966	*	*	*	£3
1967	*	*	*	£3

FLORINS

1928	£2	£4	£8	£20
1928 proof	*	*	*	£30
1930	£3	£6	£50	£200
1931	£3	£10	£80	£200
1933	£3	£10	£60	£200
1934	£10	£25	£100	£350
1935	£3	£10	£35	£150
1937	£3	£15	£70	£200
1939	£2	£4	£10	£20
1940	£2	£5	£12	£20
1941	£2	£5	£12	£30
1942	£2	£5	£12	£30
1943	£1500	£3000	£6000	£10000
1951	*	*	£3	£10
1954	*	*	£3	£10
1955	*	*	£3	£10
1959	*	*	£3	£10
1961	*	£3	£6	£20
1962	*	*	£3	£10
1963	*	*	£3	£10
1964	*	*	*	£3
1965	*	*	*	£3
1966	*	*	*	£3
1968	*	*	*	£3

SHILLINGS

1928	*	£3	£8	£12
1928 proof	*	*	*	£25
1930	£2	£10	£50	£150
1931	£2	£10	£50	£150
1933	£3	£10	£20	£150
1935	£2	£5	£20	£50
1937	£5	£25	£150	£450
1939	*	£3	£6	£15
1940	*	£3	£8	£20
1941	£2	£5	£8	£20
1942	£2	£5	£8	£20
1951	*	£1	£3	£10
1954	*	*	£3	£10
1955	*	£2	£5	£15
1959	*	*	£3	£10
1962	*	*	*	£3
1963	*	*	*	£2
1964	*	*	*	£3
1966	*	*	*	£2
1968	*	*	*	£2

1968 shilling

SIXPENCES

1928	*	£1	£3	£10
1928 proof	*	*	*	£20
1934	*	£1	£8	£30
1935	*	£3	£12	£50
1939	*	£1	£5	£20

112

	F	VF	EF	Unc
1940	*	£1	£5	£20
1942	*	*	£5	£20
1945	*	£5	£25	£60
1946	£1	£5	£50	£170
1947	*	£2	£20	£50
1948	*	*	£8	£25
1949	*	*	£5	£25
1950	*	£2	£15	£60
1952	*	£1	£4	£15
1953	*	£1	£4	£15
1955	*	£1	£4	£15
1956	*	*	£3	£10
1958	*	£1	£5	£35
1959	*	*	£2	£6
1960	*	*	£2	£6
1961	*	*	£2	£6
1962	*	*	£3	£30
1963	*	*	*	£3
1964	*	*	*	£3
1966	*	*	*	£3
1967	*	*	*	£3

1968 sixpence

	F	VF	EF	Unc
1968	*	*	*	£2
1969	*	*	*	£3

THREEPENCES

	F	VF	EF	Unc
1928	*	£1	£3	£8
1928 proof	*	*	*	£12
1933	£1	£3	£20	£150
1934	*	£1	£5	£30
1935	£1	£3	£15	£65
1939	£1	£5	£50	£200
1940	*	*	£5	£25
1942	*	*	£5	£20
1943	*	*	£5	£40
1946	*	*	£5	£15
1948	*	£2	£15	£50
1949	*	*	£5	£20
1950	*	*	£2	£6
1953	*	*	£2	£5
1956	*	*	£1	£4
1961	*	*	*	£3
1962	*	*	*	£3
1963	*	*	*	£3
1964	*	*	*	£3
1965	*	*	*	£3
1966	*	*	*	£3

1967 threepence

	F	VF	EF	Unc
1967	*	*	*	*
1968	*	*	*	*

PENNIES

	F	VF	EF	Unc
1928	*	*	£3	£10
1928 proof	*	*	*	£30
1931	*	£2	£10	£50

	F	VF	EF	Unc
1933	*	£3	£15	£70
1935	*	*	£6	£20
1937	*	*	£9	£60
1938 (unique?)	*	*	*	*
1940	£2	£6	£60	*
1941	*	£1	£6	£15
1942	*	*	£3	£10
1943	*	*	£5	£15
1946	*	*	£3	£10
1948	*	*	£3	£10
1949	*	*	£3	£10
1950	*	*	£3	£10
1952	*	*	£2	£5
1962	*	*	£2	£4
1963	*	*	*	£2
1964	*	*	*	£2
1965	*	*	*	£1
1966	*	*	*	£1
1967	*	*	*	£1
1968	*	*	*	£1

HALFPENNIES

	F	VF	EF	Unc
1928	*	£3	£6	£20
1928 proof	*	*	*	£20
1933	£1	£5	£30	£150
1935	*	£5	£15	£50
1937	*	*	£4	£8
1939	£4	£10	£25	£60
1940	*	£3	£20	£35
1941	*	*	£5	£10
1942	*	*	£2	£10
1943	*	*	£3	£10
1946	*	*	£5	£20
1949	*	*	£3	£5
1953	*	*	*	£3
1964	*	*	*	£2
1965	*	*	*	£2
1966	*	*	*	£2
1967	*	*	*	£1.50

FARTHINGS

	F	VF	EF	Unc
1928	*	*	£3	£6
1928 proof	*	*	*	£10
1930	*	*	£5	£8
1931	£1	£3	£8	£18
1932	£1	£3	£10	£20
1933	*	£2	£5	£10
1935	*	£5	£12	£25
1936	*	£6	£15	£30
1937	*	£2	£5	£12
1939	*	*	£3	£5
1940	*	£3	£6	£20
1941	*	£1	£3	£5
1943	*	£1	£3	£6
1944	*	£1	£3	£6
1946	*	£1	£3	£5
1949	*	£2	£5	£8
1953	*	*	£3	£5
1959	*	*	£1	£3
1966	*	*	£2	£5

DECIMAL COINAGE
50p, 10p, 5p, 2p, 1p, ½p
All issues face value only.

SETS

	F	VF	EF	Unc
1928 (in card case)	*	*	FDC	£120
1928 (in leather case)	*	*	FDC	£200
1966 unc. set	*	*	*	£10
1971 specimen set in folder	*	*	*	£5
1971 proof set	*	*	*	£9

The Anglo-Gallic Series

Chronological table of the Kings of England and France in the period 1154-1453

Henry II 1154-89
He was Duke of Normandy and Count of Anjou, Maine and Touraine. Through his marriage in 1152 with Eleanor of Aquitaine he became Duke of Aquitaine and Count of Poitou. He relinquished both these titles to his son Richard who in 1169 did homage to Louis VII of France. In 1185 he forced Richard to surrender Aquitaine and Poitou to ELEANOR who later – during Richard's absence – actually governed her provinces.

Louis VII 1137-80

Philip II (Augustus) 1180-1223

Richard I (Coeur de Lion) 1189-99
After his homage to the French King, he was, in 1172, formally installed as Duke of Aquitaine and Count of Poitou. Although his father forced him in 1185 to surrender Aquitaine and Poitou to his mother he retained actual government. Later Eleanor ruled in his absence.

John 1199-1216
He lost all provinces of the Angevin Empire except Aquitaine and part of Poitou.

Henry III 1216-72
In 1252 he ceded Aquitaine to his son Edward.

Louis VIII 1223-26
Louis IX (Saint Louis) 1226-70
Philip III 1270-85

Edward I 1272-1307
He governed Aquitaine since 1252. In 1279 he became Count of Ponthieu in the right of his wife, Eleanor of Castile. When she died in 1290 the county went to his son Edward.

Philip IV 1285-1314

Edward II 1307-27
He was Count of Ponthieu as from 1290. In 1325 he relinquished the county of Ponthieu and the Duchy of Aquitaine to his son Edward.

Louis X 1314-16
Philip V 1316-22
Charles IV 1322-28

Edward III 1327-77
He was Count of Ponthieu and Duke of Aquitaine as from 1325. At the outbreak of the war in 1337 he lost Ponthieu which was restored to him in 1360. In 1340 he assumed the title of King of France, which he abandoned again in 1360 as a result of the Treaty of Calais. He then obtained Aquitaine in full sovereignty and consequently changed his Aquitanian title from Duke (dux) to Lord (dominus) as the first one implied the overlordship of the French King. He gave Aquitaine as an apanage to his son, the Prince of Wales, better known as Edward The Black Prince, b.1330, d.1376, who was Prince of Aquitaine from 1362 till 1372, although he actually ruled from 1363 till 1371. In 1369, after war broke out again Edward reassumed the French title, which was henceforth used by the Kings of England until the Treaty of Amiens in 1802.

Philip VI (de Valois) 1328-50

John II (The Good) 1350-64

Charles V 1364-80

Richard II 1377-99
The son of The Black Prince succeeded his grandfather, Edward III, as King of England and as Lord of Aquitaine.

Charles VI 1380-1422

Henry IV 1399-1413
He adopted the same titles Richard II had, whom he ousted from the throne.

Henry V 1413-22
From 1417 until 1420 he used the title 'King of the French' on his 'Royal' French coins. After the Treaty of Troyes in 1420 he styled himself 'heir of France'.

Henry VI 1422-61
He inherited the title 'King of the French' from his grandfather Charles VI. He lost actual rule in Northern France in 1450 and in Aquitaine in 1453.

Charles VII 1422-61

'All Kings of England in the period 1154-1453 had interests in France. They were Dukes or Lords of Aquitaine, Counts of Poitou or Ponthieu, Lords of Issoudun or they were even or pretended to be, Kings of France itself, and, in those various capacities, struck coins. These coins, together with the French coins of their sons, and of their English vassals, are called Anglo-Gallic coins'.

So starts the introduction of the Bourgey-Spink book by E.R. Duncan Elias on this series. We would also like to thank Messrs Bourgey and Spink for allowing us to use some of the illustrations from the book, as well as the chronological table of the Kings of England and France during the period.

The Anglo-Gallic Coins by E.R.D. Elias is still available from Spink and Son Ltd, London (see Some Useful Books on page 11).

Henry II
Denier,
Aquitaine

HENRY II 1152-68	F	VF
Denier	£40	£120
Obole	£100	£280

RICHARD THE LIONHEART 1168-99

Aquitaine

Denier	£40	£140
Obole	£40	£150

Poitou

Denier	£35	£90
Obole	£60	£220

Issoudun

Denier	ext. rare

ELEANOR 1199-1204

Denier	£40	£120
Obole	£275	*

Edward I
Denier au lion,
during his
father's
lifetime

EDWARD I

During the lifetime of his father 1252-72

Denier au lion	£40	£130
Obole au lion	£50	£150

After succession to the English throne 1272-1307

Denier au lion	£120	£250
Obole au lion	£160	*

Edward I
Obole au lion,
after succession

Denier á la croix longue	£100	£150
Denier au léopard, first type	£45	£90
Obole au léopard, first type	£60	£140
Denier á la couronne		ext. rare

The coinage of PONTHIEU (Northern France) under the Edwards

Edward I	F	VF
Denier	£100	£220
Obole	£120	£250

Edward III		
Denier	£130	£275
Obole		ext. rare

EDWARD II

Gros Turonus Regem		ext. rare
Maille blanche		ext. rare
Maille blanche Hibernie	£75	£190

EDWARD III

Gold coins

Ecu d'or	£1250	£3000
Florin	£4500	£8500
Léopard d'or, 1st issue		ext. rare
Léopard d'or, 2nd issue	£1500	£3500

Edward III Léopard d'or, 2nd issue

Léopard d'or, 3rd issue	£1000	£2500
Léopard d'or, 4th issue	£1750	£4500
Guyennois d'or, 1st type	£10000	£20000
Guyennois d'or, 2nd type	£2250	£4500
Guyennois d'or, 3rd type	£1900	£3750

Silver coins

Gros aquitainaie au léopard	£180	£490
Gros tournois à la crois mi-longue	£200	£550
Gros tournois à la croix longue	£100	£290
Sterling	£75	£250
Demi-sterling	£150	£375
Gros au léopard passant		ext. rare
Gros à la couronne	£150	£390
Gros au châtel aquitainique	£150	£390
Gros tournois au léopard au-dessus	£80	£200
Gros à la porte	£80	£20
Gros acquitainaie au léopard au-dessous	£180	*
Blanc au léopard sous couronne	£60	£150
Gros au léopard sous couronne	£250	£500
Gros à la couronne avec léopard	£170	£400
Sterling à la tête barbue	£325	£950
Petit gros de Bordeaux		ext. rare
Gros au lion	£160	£475
Demi-gros au lion	£120	£275
Guyennois of argent (sterling)	£130	£350
Gros au buste	£700	£1500
Demi-gros au buste	£500	£1350

Black coins

Double à la couronne, 1st type	£100	*
Double à la couronne, 2nd type	£100	£200
Double à la couronne, 3rd type	£100	*
Double au léopard	£80	£170
Double au léopard sous couronne	£40	£100
Double guyennois		ext. rare
Denier au léopard, 2nd type	£35	£100
Obole au léopard, 2nd type		ext. rare
Denier au léopard, 3rd type	£45	£120
Denier au léopard, 4th type	£50	£200

THE ANGLO-GALLIC SERIES

	F	VF
Obole au léopard, 4th type	£50	£120
Denier au lion	£35	£80

N.B. Some issues of the deniers au léopard of the 2nd and 3rd type are very rare to extremely rare and therefore considerably more valuable.

The coinage of BERGERAC
Henry, Earl of Lancaster 1347-51

Gros tournois à la croix longue ...	£800	*
Gros tournois à la couronne	£500	*
Gros au châtel aquitainque		ext. rare
Gros tournois au léopard au-dessus	£500	*
Gros à la couronne	£800	*
Gros à fleur-de-lis		ext. rare
Gros au léopard passant		ext. rare
Double		ext. rare
Denier au léopard		ext. rare

Henry, Duke of Lancaster 1351-61

Gros tournois à la couronne avec léopard	£600	*
Gros au léopard couchant	£700	*
Sterling à la tête barbue		ext. rare
Gros au lion		ext. rare

EDWARD THE BLACK PRINCE 1362-72
Gold Coins

Léopard d'or	£950	£2000
Guyennois d'or	£1800	*
Chaise d'or	£1800	£3500
Pavillon d'or 1st issue	£1500	£3000
Pavillon d'or 2nd issue	£1500	£3000
Demi-pavillon d'or		ext. rare
Hardi d'or	£1500	£3000

Edward the Black Prince Hardi d'or of Bordeaux

Silver Coins

Gros	£750	£1500
Demi-gros	£95	£230
Sterling	£80	£175
Hardi d'argent...	£35	£95

Edward the Black Prince Hardi d'argent

Black Coins

Double guyennois	£100	£200
Denier au lion...	£50	£120
Denier	£50	£120

RICHARD II 1377-99
Gold Coins

Hardi d'or	£1000	£2750
Demi-hardi d'or		ext. rare

	F	
Silver Coins		
Double Hardi d'argent	£450	
Hardi d'argent...	£70	£1...
Black Coins		
Denier	£70	£1...

HENRY IV 1399-1413
Silver Coins

Double Hardi d'argent	£800	

Henry IV Double Hardi d'argent

Hardi d'argent...	£60	£1
Hardi aux genêts...		ext. ra...
Black Coins		
Denier	£40	£1...
Denier aux genêts		ext. ra...

HENRY V 1413-22
Gold Coins

Agnel d'or		ext. ra...
Salut d'or	£9000	£250...

Silver Coins

Florette, 1st issue	£100	£2...
Florette, 2nd issue	£150	£3...
Florette, 3rd issue	£70	£1...
Florette, 4th issue	£70	£1...
Guénar	£250	£5...
Gros au léopard	£300	

Black Coins

Mansiois		ext. ra...
Niquet	£60	£1...
Denier tournois	£60	£1

HENRY VI 1422-53
Gold Coins

Salut d'or	£350	£7...

Henry VI Salut d'or, Dijon mint

Angelot	£1500	£30...

Silver Coins

Grand Blanc aux ècus	£40	£1...
Petit Blanc	£140	£3...
Trésin...		ext. ra...

Black Coins

Denier Parisis, 1st issue	£60	£1...
Denier Parisis, 2nd issue	£60	£1...
Denier tournois	£40	£1...
Maille tournois	£65	£1...

N.B. The prices of the saluts and grand blancs are for the mints of Paris, Rouen and Saint Lô; coins other mints are rare to very rare and consequenth more valuable.

Island Coinages

CHANNEL ISLANDS

From the date of their introduction onwards, proofs have been struck for a large number of Channel Islands coins, particularly in the case of Jersey. Except for those included in the modern proof sets these are mostly at least very rare and in the majority of cases have been omitted from the list. A number of die varieties which exist for several dates of the earlier 19th century Guernsey eight doubles have also been excluded. For further information in both cases the reader is referred to The Coins of the British Commonwealth of Nations, Part I, European Territories *by F. Pridmore, published by Spink and Son Ltd.*

GUERNSEY

	F	VF	EF	BU
TEN SHILLINGS				
1966	*	*	*	£1
THREEPENCE				
1956	*	*	*	£1
1959	*	*	*	£1
1966 proof only ...	*	*	*	£1
EIGHT DOUBLES				
1834	*	£8	£25	£100
1858	*	£8	£25	£100
1864	*	£8	£30	*
1868	*	£4	£30	*
1874	*	£4	£30	*
1885 H	*	*	£8	£25
1889 H	*	*	£6	£20
1893 H	*	*	£6	£20
1902 H	*	*	£6	£20
1903 H	*	*	£6	£20
1910 H	*	*	£8	£25
1911 H	*	*	£8	£30
1914 H	*	*	£8	£25
1918 H	*	*	£8	£30
1920 H	*	*	£4	£10
1934 H	*	*	£4	£10
1934 H prooflike ...	*	*	*	£50
1938 H	*	*	*	£5
1945 H	*	*	*	£5
1947 H	*	*	*	£4
1949 H	*	*	*	£4
1956	*	*	*	£1
1959	*	*	*	£1
1966 proof only ...	*	*	*	£3
FOUR DOUBLES				
1830	*	*	£20	£60
1858	*	*	£25	£70

Guernsey 1864 four doubles

	F	VF	EF	BU
1864	*	£5	£35	*
1868	*	£5	£35	*

	F	VF	EF	BU
1874	*	*	£30	*
1885 H	*	*	£8	£25
1889 H	*	*	£5	£20
1893 H	*	*	£4	£15
1902 H	*	*	£4	£15
1903 H	*	*	£4	£15
1906 H	*	*	£4	£15
1908 H	*	*	£4	£15
1910 H	*	*	£3	£15
1911 H	*	*	£3	£15
1914 H	*	*	£3	£15
1918 H	*	*	£3	£15
1920 H	*	*	*	£10
1945 H	*	*	*	£4
1949 H	*	*	*	£5
1956	*	*	*	£1
1966 proof only ...	*	*	*	£1
TWO DOUBLES				
1858	*	£4	£25	*
1868	*	£4	£30	*
1874	*	£4	£20	*
1885 H	*	*	£6	£15
1889 H	*	*	£4	£10
1899 H	*	*	£4	£10
1902 H	*	*	£5	£10
1903 H	*	*	£5	£15
1906 H	*	*	£4	£15
1908 H	*	*	£4	£20
1911 H	*	*	£4	£15
1914 H	*	*	£4	£18
1917 H	*	£10	£30	£60
1918 H	*	*	£2	£6
1920 H	*	*	£3	£8
1929 H	*	*	£2	£5
ONE DOUBLE				
1830	*	*	£10	£25
1868	*	£5	£20	*
1868/30	*	£5	£20	*
1885 H	*	*	£4	£10
1889 H	*	*	£2	£5
1893 H	*	*	£2	£5
1899 H	*	*	£2	£5
1902 H	*	*	£2	£5
1903 H	*	*	£2	£5
1911 H	*	*	£2	£8
1911 H new type ...	*	*	£2	£8
1914 H	*	*	£3	£8
1929 H	*	*	£1	£2
1933 H	*	*	£1	£2
1938 H	*	*	£1	£2

ISLAND COINAGES

DECIMAL COINAGE
The word 'NEW' was omitted from coins issued after December 1976, being replaced by the word for the denomination.

f denoted face value

TWENTY-FIVE POUNDS
	BU
1994 50th Anniversary Normandy Landings gold	£175
1995 Queen Mother, gold, proof	£200
1996 Queen's 70th Birthday, gold, proof	£200
1996 European Football, gold, proof	£200
1997 Golden Wedding, gold, proof	£200

FIVE POUNDS
1995 Queen Mother, cu-ni	£7
1995 Queen Mother silver, proof	£37
1996 Queen's 70th Birthday, cu-ni	£7
1996 Queen's 70th Birthday, silver, proof ...	£37
1996 European Football, cu-ni	£7
1996 European Football, silver, proof	£37
1997 Golden Wedding, cu-ni	£7
1997 Golden Wedding, silver, proof	£40
1997 Castle Cornet, silver, proof	£00
1997 Caernarfou Castle, silver, proof	£41
1997 Leeds Castle, silver, proof	£41

TWO POUNDS
1985 Liberation 40th Anniversary, crown size, in blister pack	£3.45
1985 – – silver, proof	£28.75
1986 Commonwealth Games, plastic case	£3.50
1986 – in presentation folder	£4
1986 – .500 silver, B. Unc	£15
1986 – .925 silver, proof	£28.75
1987 90th Anniversary of death of William the Conqueror, cu-ni, in presentation folder	£4
1987 gold, proof	£90
1987 – silver, proof	£28.75
1988 William the Second, cu-ni in presentation folder	£4
1988 – silver, proof	£28.75
1989 Accession of Henry I cu-ni in presentation folder	£4.25
1989 – silver, proof	£28.75
1989 Royal Visit, cu-ni	£2
1989 – – in plastic case	£3.50
1989 – silver, proof	£28.75
1990 Queen Mother's 90th Birthday, cu-ni	£2
1990 – – in plastic case	£3.50
1990 – silver, proof	£28.75
1991 Henry II, cu-ni	£5
1991 – – silver, proof	£30
1993 40th Anniversary of the Coronation, silver, proof	£28.75
1994 Normandy Landings	f
1994 – silver, proof	£30
1995 50th Anniversary of Liberation, silver, proof	£35
1995 –, silver, piedfort, proof	£60
1995 – cu-ni	£5

ONE POUND
1981 copper, zinc, nickel	£2
1981 gold proof (8 grammes)	£85
1981 gold piedfort (16 grammes)	£250
1983 new specification, new reverse	f
1985 new designs (in folder)	£1.20
1995 Queen Mother, silver, proof	£22
1996 Queen's 70th Birthday, silver, proof ...	£22
1997 Golden Wedding, silver, proof	£22
1997 Tower of London, silver, proof	£22

FIFTY PENCE
1969	£1

1970	
1971 proof (from set)	
1981	
1982	
1985 new designs	
Other dates	

TWENTY-FIVE PENCE
1972 Silver Wedding (cupro-nickel)	
1972 – proof (silver)	
1977 Jubilee	£1.
1977 – silver, proof	£
1978 Royal visit (cu-ni)	£1.
1978 – silver, proof	
1980 Queen Mother's 80th birthday (cu-ni)	£1.
1980 – silver, ...	£
1981 Royal Wedding (cu-ni)	
1981 – silver, proof	£

OTHER DECIMAL COINAGE
20p, 10p, 5p, 2p, 1p, 1/₂p. All issues face value on (the 5p and 10p were issued in a reduced size in 1992 and 1993 respectively.)

SETS
1956 proof	£.
1966 proof	
1971 proof	£7.
1979 proof	
1981 proof (including £1)	£
1985 new designs, £1 to 1p, (7 coins)	
1985 – £2 Liberation crown to 1p proof (8 coins)	£.
1986 BU set in folder, £1 to 1p (7 coins) ...	
1986 £2 Commonwealth Games to 1p, proof (8 coins)	£
1987 BU set in folder, £1 to 1p (7 coins) ...	
1987 £2 William the Conqueror to 1p, proof (8 coins)	£
1988 BU set in folder £1 to 1p (7 coins)	
1988 £2 William the Second to 1p, proof (8 coins)	£
1989 BU set in folder, £1 to 1p (7 coins)	£
1989 £2 Henry I to 1p, proof (8 coins)	£
1990 £2 Queen Mother's 90th birthday to 1p, proof (8 coins)	£
1990 BU set as above (8 coins)	£1
1944 Normandy Landings, £100, £50, £25, £10 gold	£10(
1995 50th Anniversary of Liberation, £100, £50, £25, £10	£100
1995 Queen Mother, £25 gold, £5 silver, £1 proof (3 coins)	£25
1996 Queen's 70th Birthday, £25 gold, £5 + £1 silver, proof (3 coins)	£25
1997 Golden Wedding, £25 gold, £5 + £1 silver, proof (3 coins)	£25
1997 Three £5 + £1 silver, proof (4 coins) ...	£13

ALDERNEY

TWENTY FIVE POUNDS
1993 Coronation, gold proof	£22

FIVE POUNDS
1995 Queen Mother, cu-ni	£7.5
1995 – silver proof	£3
1995 – piedfort	£6
1995 – gold proof	£80
1996 – Queens 70th Birthday, cu-ni	£7.5
1996 – silver proof	£3
1996 – piedfort	£6
1996 – gold proof	£80

TWO POUNDS

1989 Royal Visit, cu-ni	£3
1989 – in plastic case	£5
1989 – silver, proof	£30
1989 – piedfort	£60
1989 gold, proof...	£800
1990 Queen Mother's 90th birthday, cu-ni	£3
1990 – in plastic case	£5
1990 – silver, proof	£30
1990 – – – piedfort	£60
1990 – gold, proof	£800
1992 Accession, cu-ni	£3
1992 – , plastic case	£5
1992 – , silver, proof	£30
1992 – , piedfort	£60
1992 – , gold, proof	£800
1993 Coronation, cu-ni	£3
1993 – – , plastic case	£5
1993 – , silver, proof	£35
1993 – – , piedfort	£60
1994 D-Day, cu-ni	£3
1994 – , card pack	£6
1994 – , silver proof	£35
1994 – – , piedfort	£60
1995 VE/Libration, cu-ni	£3
1995 – – , plastic case	£5
1995 – , silver proof	£33
1995 – – , piedfort	£60
1995 – , gold proof	£800
1997 Golden Wedding, cu-ni	£3
1997 Golden Wedding, silver, proof	£38
1997 WWF, Puffin, silver, proof	£3
1997 WWF, Puffin, silver, proof	£32

ONE POUND

1993 Coronation, silver, proof	£30
1995 VE/Liberation, silver, proof	£22
1995 – , gold, proof	£300

SETS

1994 £100, £50, £25, £10, D-Day gold, proof (4 coins)	£1000
1994 £50, £25, £10, D-Day gold, proof (3 coins)	£500

JERSEY

CROWN	F	VF	EF	BU
1966	*	*	*	£1
1966 – proof	*	*	*	£3

1/4 OF A SHILLING				
1957	*	*	*	£2
1960 proof only	*	*	*	£5
1964	*	*	*	£0.30
1966	*	*	*	£0.75

1/2 OF A SHILLING				
1877 H	*	*	£7	£40
1881	*	*	£9	£50
1888	*	*	£8	£40
1894	*	*	£7	£30
1909	*	*	£8	£40
1911	*	*	£5	£25
1913	*	*	£5	£20
1923	*	*	£5	£25
1923 new type	*	*	£7	£20
1926	*	*	£5	£18
1931	*	*	£2	£10
1933	*	*	£3	£10
1935	*	*	£2	£10
1937	*	*	*	£5

ISLAND COINAGES

	F	VF	EF	BU
1945' (George VI)[1] ...	*	*	*	£3
'1945' (Elizabeth II)[1] ...	*	*	*	£2
1946	*	*	*	£4
1947	*	*	*	£3
1957	*	*	*	£0.40
1960	*	*	*	£0.20
1964	*	*	*	£0.15
1966	*	*	*	£0.15

[1]The date 1945 on one-twelfth shillings commemorates the year of liberation from German occupation. The coins were struck in 1949, 1950, 1952 and 1954.

1/13 OF A SHILLING				
1841	*	*	£30	£100
1844	*	*	£35	£120
1851	*	*	£40	£100
1858	*	*	£35	£110
1861	*	*	£40	£100
1865 proof only	*	*	*	£350
1866	*	*	£20	£60
1870	*	*	£25	£60
1871	*	*	£25	£60

1/24 OF A SHILLING				
1877 H	*	*	£4	£30
1888	*	*	£4	£25
1894	*	*	£4	£25
1909	*	*	£3	£20
1911	*	*	£3	£20
1913	*	*	£3	£20
1923	*	*	£2	£15
1923 new type	*	*	£2	£15
1926	*	*	£2	£15
1931	*	*	£1	£5
1933	*	*	£1	£5
1935	*	*	£1	£5
1937	*	*	£1	£5
1946	*	*	£1	£5
1947	*	*	£1	£5

1/26 OF A SHILLING				
1841	*	*	£18	£75
1844	*	*	£18	£75
1851	*	*	£18	£75
1858	*	*	£18	£75
1861	*	*	£16	£65
1866	*	*	£15	£60
1870	*	*	£15	£50
1871	*	*	£18	£50

1/48 OF A SHILLING				
1877 H	*	£8	£30	£75

1/52 OF A SHILLING				
1841	*	£12	£50	£100
1841 proof	*	*	*	£300
1861 proof only	*	*	*	£400

DECIMAL COINAGE

f denotes face value

FIVE POUNDS	BU
1990 50th Anniversary of the Battle of Britain, silver, proof	£85
1997 Golden Wedding, silver, proof	£38

TWO POUNDS	
1981 Royal Wedding, nickel silver (crown size)	f

ISLAND COINAGES

	BU
1981 – in presentation pack	£2.75
1981 – silver, proof	£15
1981 – gold, proof	£300
1985 40th anniversary of liberation, (crown size)	f
1985 – in presentation pack	£3.75
1985 – silver, frosted proof	£28.75
1985 – gold, frosted proof	£1000
1986 Commonwealth Games	£2
1986 – in presentation case	£3
1986 – .500 silver, B. Unc	£14.95
1986 – .925 silver, proof	£28.75
1987 World Wildlife Fund 25 years cu-ni in blister pack	£3.25
1987 – silver, proof	£30
1989 Royal Visit cu-ni in de luxe presentation case	£4
1989 – silver, proof	£28.75
1990 Queen Mother's 90 birthday, cu-ni...	£4
1990 – silver, proof	£28.75
1990 – gold, proof	£402.50
1990 50th Anniversary of the Battle of Britain, silver, proof	£28.75
1993 40th Anniversary of the Coronation silver, proof	£30
1995 50th Anniversary of Liberation, silver, proof	£35
1995 –, silver, piedfort, proof...	£60
1995 – cu-ni	£4
1996 Queen's 70th Birthday, cu-ni	£5
1996 – – – silver, proof	£33

ONE POUND

1981 cu-ni	£2.25
1981 silver, proof	£25
1981 gold, proof	£150

In 1983 Jersey issued a one pound coin with the specification changed to conform with that of the UK one pound coin. The reverse initially bore the emblem of St Helier Parish, but this was changed regularly to represent, in rotation, each of the 12 parishes of Jersey, the others being: St Saviour, St Brelade, St Clement, St Lawrence, St Peter, Grouville, St Martin, St Ouen, Trinity, St John and St Mary, in order of size of the population.

1983 new specification, new designs (both sides), on presentation card (St Helier)	£4
1983 silver, frosted proof, in case –	£23
1983 gold, frosted proof, in case –...	£345
1984 in presentation wallet (St Saviour)	£4
1983 silver, frosted proof –	£23
1984 gold, frosted proof –...	£345
1984 in presentation wallet (St Brelade)	£4
1984 silver, frosted proof –	£23
1984 gold, frosted proof –	£345
1985 in presentation wallet (St Clement)	£4
1985 silver, frosted proof –	£23
1985 gold, frosted proof –	£345
1985 in presentation wallet (St Lawrence)	£4
1985 silver, frosted proof –	£23
1985 gold, frosted proof –	£345
1986 in presentation wallet (St Peter)	£4
1986 silver, frosted proof –	£23
1986 gold, frosted proof –	£345
1986 in presentation wallet (Grouville)	£4
1986 silver, frosted proof –	£23
1986 gold, frosted proof –	£345
1987 in presentation wallet (St Martin)	£4
1987 silver, frosted proof –	£23
1987 gold, frosted proof –	£345
1987 in presentation wallet (St Ouen)	£4
1987 silver, frosted proof –	£23

1987 gold, frosted proof –	£3
1988 in presentation wallet (Trinity)	
1988 silver, frosted proof –	£
1988 gold, frosted proof –	£3
1988 in presentation wallet (St John)	
1988 silver, frosted proof –	£
1988 gold, frosted proof –	£3
1988 in presentation wallet (St Mary)	
1988 silver, frosted proof –	£
1988 gold, frosted proof –	£3

In 1991 Jersey launched a series of six coins featuring ships built on the island during the second half of the 19th century.

1991 Silver, frosted proof 'Tickler'	£
1991 Gold, frosted proof 'Tickler'	£3
1991 Silver, frosted proof 'Percy Douglas'	£25.
1991 Gold, frosted proof 'Percy Douglas'	£3
1992 Silver, proof 'The Hebe'	£.
1992 Gold, frosted proof 'The Hebe'	£3
1992 Silver, proof Coat of Arms	£.
1992 Gold, frosted proof Coat of Arms	£3
1992 Silver, proof 'The Gemini'	£
1992 Silver, proof 'The Century'	£
1992 Silver, proof 'The Resolute'	£
1992 Gold, proof 'The Resolute'	£3

FIFTY PENCE

1969	
1983 new obv, new rev...	
1985 40th anniversary of liberation	

TWENTY-FIVE PENCE

1977 Jubilee	£1.
1977 – Silver, proof	£17.

TWENTY PENCE

1982 date on rocks on rev (cased)	£0.
1982, silver, proof, piedfort	£
1983 new obv, with date, rev no date on rocks	
Later dates	

OTHER DECIMAL COINAGE

10p, 5p, 2p, 1p, ½p (to 1982). All face value only.

1983 10p, 5p, 2p, 1p: new obv and rev designs...	
Later dates	

SETS

	B
1957	£
1960	£
1964	£
1966 (4 coins) proof	
1966 (2 crowns)	
1968/7 1 decimal coins	
1972 Silver Wedding (5 gold, 4 silver coins)	£4
1972 – – proof	£4
1972 – – (4 silver coins)	£2
1980 50p to ½p	£
1980 – frosted proof	£
1981 £1 to ½p, in presentation pack	
1981 – base metal, proof	£13.
1983 £1 to 1p (7 coins)	£3.
1983 – silver frosted proof, in album	£
1987 £1 to 1p, in folder (7 coins)	£
1990 50th Anniversary of the Battle of Britain, gold coins with face values of £100, £50, £25 and £10 (4 coins)	£10
1992 £1 to 1p (7 coins)	£
1995 50th Anniversary of Liberation, £100, £50 £25 and £10 (4 coins)	£10
1997 £2 to 1p incl. 2 x 50p (9 coins)	£

ISLE OF MAN

*Contemporary forgeries of several of the earlier
Isle of Man coins exist.*

COPPER AND BRONZE 1709-1839

PENNIES	F	VF	EF	Unc
1709	£10	£35	£90	*
1733	*	£10	£65	£125
1733 proof	*	*	£125	£200
1733 silver	*	*	£200	£300
1758	*	£5	£50	£175
1758 proof	*	*	*	*
1758 silver	*	*	£275	£400
1786	*	£5	£40	£100
1786 plain edge proof	*	*	£120	£250
1798	*	£5	£45	£100
1798 bronzed proof	*	*	£90	£175
1798 AE gilt proof ...	*	*	£300	*
1798 silver proof	*	*	*	*
1813	*	£5	£45	£100
1813 bronzed proof ...	*	*	£90	£175
1839	*	*	£25	£60
1839 proof	*	*	*	*

HALFPENNIES				
1709	£8	£20	£60	*
1733	*	£5	£50	£100
1733 proof	*	*	£80	£150
1733 silver	*	£60	£120	£200
1758	*	£8	£50	£120
1758 proof	*	*	*	*
1786	*	£4	£30	£65
1786 plain edge proof	*	*	£110	£200
1798	*	£5	£35	£85
1798 proof	*	*	£65	£100
1798 AE gilt proof ...	*	*	*	*
1813	*	£5	£35	£90
1813 proof	*	*	£65	£100
1839 proof	*	*	£15	£40

FARTHINGS				
1839	*	£14	£18	£50
1839 proof	*	*	*	*

ISSUES SINCE 1965

*Prices for the gold series, £5 to half sovereign,
plus 'angels', and platinum 'nobels' are directly
governed by day-to-day prices in their respective
bullion markets, to which reference should be
made for current valuations.
Since 1973 there have been many changes to the
designs of the circulating coins and these have
often been accompanied by special sets in gold,
platinum and silver. In addition there have been
many commemorative crowns struck in base
metal and in precious metal. A full list of the
complete coinage is beyond the scope of this
publication.*

Forgeries

MOST collectors know that there have been forgeries since the earliest days of coin production, so it is only to be expected that some new forgeries appear on the scene every year. It seems that there is always someone willing to deceive the collector and the dealer. However, nowadays very few forgers end up making much money. As a result of the actions of the British Numismatic Trade Association, the trade is much more tightly knit than ever before, and anxious to stamp out new forgeries before they have a chance to become a serious menace.

They were last a matter of serious concern in the late 1960s and early 1970s, when an enormous number of 1887 £5 pieces and United States $20 manufactured in Beruit came on to the market. Also in the early 1970s the group of Dennington forgeries could have made a serious impact on the English hammered gold market, but for lucky early detection. (Unfortunately we have noticed a number of these are still in circulation, and so we will deal with them later in this article.)

In the late 1970s a crop of forgeries of Ancient British coins came to light causing a panic in academic and trade circles. This caused a lack of confidence in the trade and it has taken a number of years for everyone to feel happy that there was no further problem. The BNTA firmly pursues any mention of forgeries and one hopes that a new spate of copies of Anglo-Saxon coins from the West Country are not allowed to develop. They are being sold as replicas, but they are still deceptive in the wrong hands. Bob Forrest compiled a list of these and it was published by the IAPN Bulletin of Forgeries in 1995/6 Vol.20 No.2. He has now done an update of this which will be available at the end of the year.

The worrying forgeries

We mentioned earlier the 'Dennington' forgeries. It is now many years since the trial of Anthony Dennington at the Central Criminal Court, where he was found guilty of six charges of 'causing persons to pay money by falsely pretending that they were buying genuine antique coins' *The Times*, July 10, 1969). There is a small number of these pieces still circulating in the trade, and since they have deceived some collectors and dealers, we thought we should record them more fully here. The following is a list of the pieces which appeared in the IBSCC Bulletin in August 1976.

1 Henry III gold penny
2 Edward III Treaty period noble
3 Another, with saltire before King's name
4 Henry IV heavy coinage noble
5 Henry V noble, Class C (mullet at King's sword arm)
6 Henry V/VI mule noble
7 Henry V/VI noble, annulet issue, London
8 Edward IV ryal, Norwich
9 Another, York
10 Elizabeth I Angel

Dennington forgeries: Edward III noble (top) and Mary Fine Sovereign

11 Mary Fine Sovereign 1553
12 James I unite, mintmark mullet
13 James I rose ryal, 3rd coinage,
    mint mark lis
14 James I 3rd coinage laurel
15 Commonwealth unite 1651
16 Commonwealth half unite 1651
17 Charles II touch piece

One can only reiterate that these copies are generally very good and you must beware of them. The following points may be useful.

1   The coins are usually slightly 'shiny' in appearance, and the edges are not good, since they have been filed down and polished.

2   They are usually very 'hard' to touch, whereas there is a certain amount of 'spring' in the genuine articles.

3   They usually feel slightly thick, but not always, not quite like an electrotype but certainly thicker than normal.

4   Although the Mary Fine sovereign reproduction is heavy, at 16.1986 gr, these pieces are usually lighter in weight than the originals.

As far as forgeries of modern coins are concerned, the most worrying aspects has been the enormous increase in well produced forgeries in the last 25 years.

They are so well produced that it is often impossible for the naked eye to detect the difference, and it has therefore become the job of the scientist and metallurgist. Many of these pieces have deceived dealers and collectors, although they do not seem to have caused too great a crisis of confidence. This increase in the number of modern counterfeits has been due to the enormous rise in coin values since the 1960s.

It is well known that the vast majority of these modern forgeries has emanated from the Middle East, as we have suggested earlier, where it is *not* illegal to produce counterfeits of other countries' coins. It has proved to be very good business for a lot of these small forgers in Beruit, and one can only rely on the alertness of the coin trade so that reports are circulated quickly whenever a new forgery is spotted.

Unfortunately, the main problem is still that the forger has every encouragement to continue production of copies, when one thinks of the profit involved. At the time of writing, it only takes about £290 worth of gold to make an 1887-dated five pound piece of correct composition, valued at around £650. We cannot, therefore, be complacent.

There is not enough space here to tell you in detail what to look for, and anyway detecting forgeries requires specialist knowledge, so a list of faults would not help. If you turn to the catalogue section of COINS MARKET VALUES you will find that as far as British coins are concerned we have placed **(F)** beside a number of coins which we know have been counterfeited, and which frequently turn up. However, you should watch out for sovereigns, in particular, of which there are forgeries of every date from 1900 to 1932 and even recent dates such as 1957 and 1976.

A list follows of the pieces you should be particularly careful about, especially if you notice that they are being offered below the normal catalogue value. Most modern forgeries of, say, Gothic crowns, seem to be offered at prices which are 10 per cent or 20 per cent below the current market price. The moral is, do not automatically think you have a bargain if the price is low – it could be a forgery!

Modern cast copies of Anglo-Saxon pennies: Ceolwulf 1st above, and Ceonwulf below

1738, 1739 two guineas
1793, 1798 guineas (there could also be other dates)
1820 pattern two pounds
1839 five pounds (in particular the plain edge variety)
1887 five pounds
1887 (two pounds (there seem to be many forgeries of these)
1893 five pounds, two pounds
1902 five pounds, two pounds
1911 five pounds, two pounds
    1817, 1819, 1822, 1825, 1827, 1887, 1889, 1892, 1892M, 1908C, 1913C sovereigns; also every date from 1900 to 1932 inclusive, plus 1957, 1959, 1963, 1966, 1967, 1974, 1976
1847 Gothic crowns
1905 halfcrowns

Other safeguards against forgery

(a) The best method of protection against purchasing forgeries is to buy your coins from a reputable dealer who is a member of the British Numismatic Trade Association or the International Association of Professional Numismatists, or one who will unconditionally guarantee that all his coins are genuine.

(b) Legal tender coins, which include five and two pound pieces, sovereigns, half sovereigns and crowns, are protected by the Forgery and Counterfeiting Act, and it is the responsibility of the police to prosecute in cases where this Act has been contravened.

(c) If your dealer is unhelpful over a non legal tender item which you have purchased and which you think has been falsely described, you can take legal action under the Trades Description Act 1968. However, we should warn you that it can be a tedious and long-winded business, but if you want to proceed in this you should contact your local Trading Standards Office or Consumer Protection department.

THE INAFB

The best known professional opponent of the forger in the British Isles is E.G.V. Newman, formerly of the Royal Mint. He has been providing an excellent service to traders and collectors for many years now, and is expert, especially on modern machine-made coins, and in particular gold £5, £2, sovereigns and so on. Mr Newman's organisation, the INAFB (International Numismatic Anti-Forgery Bureau) is a completely independent body.

Members of the public may send coins to MNC Ltd, PO Box 52, Farnham, Surrey GU10 4JR.

The INAFB charges are, per item:

Insured value of coin	Charge
Up to £100	£3
£101-£1,000	3% of insured value
£1,001-£2,500	£35
£2,501-£5,000	£40
£5,001-£10,000	£45
Over £10,000	£50

A charge will be made for return registered postage, packing and intransit insurance from £5 upwards according to destination.

Note that no legal responsibility in respect of any claim made as a result of this opinion will be accepted by the Director or the INAFB.

A 'Behra' counterfeit of the 1950s. The last of a series bearing the dates 1902 to 1920, where the original pattern piece was a genuine South African sovereign of unknown date but post 1924. An attempt was made to remove the SA mint mark on the tool used to prepare the dies but traces still remained and were transferred to all the dies.

The different types of forgery

There are many different forgeries, but essentially they can be divided into two main groups. First of all there are contemporary forgeries intended to be used as face-value money (as in the cases, some years ago, of the counterfeit 50p pieces, which even worked in slot machines), and secondly forgeries intended to deceive collectors.

Contemporary forgeries, those pieces struck in imitation of currency coins, are obviously not a serious problem to numismatists. The recent ones cause more trouble to bank clerks, anyway, and are not of sufficiently good standard to deceive numismatic experts. In general, those produced in the Middle Ages were base (which was how the forger made a profit), consisting wholly of base metal or occasionally having a thin coating of the proper metal on the outside. Sometimes they were struck, but more often they were cast. Whatever the problems they caused at the time of issue, they are now often as interesting as the regular coins of the period.

However, one can be less light-hearted about copies which are made to deceive collectors. The following five methods of reproduction have been used.

1. Electrotyping. These copies would not normally deceive an expert.

2. Casting. Old casts are easily recognisable, having marks made by air bubbles on the surface, and showing a generally 'fuzzy' effect. Much more of a problem are the modern cast copies, produced by sophisticated 'pressure-casting', which can be extremely difficult for all but most expert to distinguish from the originals (more of this later).

3. The fabrication of false dies. With hammered coins counterfeits are not difficult for an expert to detect. However, the sophisticated die production techniques used in Beiruit have resulted in the worrying features of modern gold and silver coins described later.

4. The use of genuine dies put to some illegal use such as restriking (a mintmaster in West Germany was convicted in 1975 of that very issue).

5. Alteration of a genuine coin. (Ask your dealer how many George V pennies he has seen with the date altered to 1933 - it does happen!)

Literature on forgery

The back numbers of Spink's Numismatic Circulars are useful sources of information on forgeries that have been recorded over the years. The now defunct IBSCC (set up by the IAPN in 1975 under the auspices of Vincent Newman), also produced a series of important forgery bulletins on mainly modern coins, and are very useful if you can find them on the second-hand shelves.

As far as hammered coins are concerned, still the most useful work is that by L.A. Lawrence in the *British Numismatic Journal* as long ago as 1905! ('Forgery in relation to Numismatics', BNJ 1905-1907, a series of articles).

Treasure Trove

Change in the law

In recent years a much needed overhaul of the medieval law of treasure trove has been undertaken. The Treasure Act which received the Royal Assent on July 4 1996 extends the protection afforded by the old treasure trove law to a wider range of archaeological finds and removes many of the anachronisms of it.

In the past, before an object could be declared treasure trove and therefore be the property of the crown, it had to pass three tests: it had to be made substantially of gold or silver, it had to have been deliberately hidden with the intention of recovery, and its owner or his heirs had to be unknown. If then a museum wanted to keep the coins (or artefacts) the **lawful** finder normally received the full market value (Assessed by the Treasure Trove Reviewing Committee), if not, the coins were returned to the finder.

The new Act removes the need to establish that objects were hidden with the intention of being recovered, it sets out the precious metal content required for a find to qualify as treasure, and it extends the definition of treasure. It simplifies the task of coroners in determining whether or not a find is treasure and it includes a new offence of non-declaration of treasure. Finally it states that lawful occupiers and landowners will have the right to be informed of finds of treasure from their land and that they will be eligible for reward.

The Committee

The Treasure Trove Reviewing Committee was established in 1977 as an independent body to advise Ministers on the valuation of treasure trove finds. The committee seek out independent valuations for finds that are referred to them, and their reports are now delivered very quickly. There is an annual report of the commitee's finding published and available from the Department of National Heritage. [A very useful publication which is also available from the Book Dept. of Spink and Son Ltd.].

The current committee consists of:

Lord Stewartby (Chairman)
Mr John Casey
Mr Patrick Finn
Dr Jack Ogden
Professor Norman Palmer

Dealers who display this symbol are Members of the

BRITISH NUMISMATIC TRADE ASSOCIATION

The primary purpose of the Association is to promote and safeguard the highest standards of professionalism in dealings between its Members and the public. In official consultations it is the recognised representative of commercial numismatics in Britain.

For a free Membership Directory please send a first class stamp to the address below.

The BNTA will be organising the following international coin fairs in 1998:

**SPRING COINEX, The Queen Hotel, Chester
28 March 1998**

oOo

**COINEX LONDON, Hotel Mattiott, Grosvenor Sq, W1
9/10 October 1998**

oOo

For further information contact:
Mrs Carol Carter, General Secretary, BNTA
PO Box 474A, Thames Ditton, Surrey KT7 0WJ
Tel: 0181 398 4290 - Fax: 0181 398 4291

THESE ARE THE CURRENT MEMBERS OF THE BNTA

LIST OF MEMBERS IN COUNTY ORDER

(Those members with retail premises are indicated with an *)

LONDON AREA
*A. H. Baldwin & Sons Ltd.
Beaver Coin Room
*W. & F. C. Bonham & Sons Ltd.
Chelsea Coins
*Philip Cohen Numismatics
Andre de Clermont
Michael Dickinson
*Dix Noonan Webb
*Dolphin Coins
Christopher Eimer
*Glendining's
Harrow Coin & Stamp Centre
Ian Jull
*Knightsbridge Coins
*Lennox Gallery
Lubbock & Son Ltd.
C. J. Martin Coins Ltd.
*Colin Narbeth & Son Ltd.
*George Rankin Coin Co.
*Seaby Coins/C.N.G. Inc.
R. D. Shah
*Simmons Gallery
*Spink & Son Ltd.
Surena Ancient Art & Numismatic
*Vale Coins
*Italo Vecchi
West Essex Coin Investments
BERKSHIRE
Frank Milward
BUCKINGHAMSHIRE
Europa Numismatics
CORNWALL
Frank Milward
CUMBRIA
Patrick Finn
DORSET
*Dorset Coin Co Ltd.
ESSEX
E. J. & C. A. Brooks
Mark J. Vencenzi
GLOUCESTERSHIRE
R J B Coins
HAMPSHIRE
*SPM Jewellers
Raymond Sleet
Studio Coins
HERTFORDSHIRE
KB Coins
David Miller

KENT
C. J. Denton
*Peter Morris
LANCASHIRE
*B. J. Dawson (Coins)
*Colin De Rouffignac
*Liverpool Medal Co.
*Peter Ireland Ltd.
*R & L Coins
LINCOLNSHIRE
John Cummings Ltd.
Grantham Coins
NORFOLK
*Clive T. Dennett
Chris Rudd
NORTHUMBERLAND
*Corbitt Stamps Ltd.
OXFORDSHIRE
S. R. Porter
SHROPSHIRE
*Collectors Gallery
SUFFOLK
*Schwer Coins
SURREY
*G. & L. Monk
SUSSEX
*Brighton Coin Co.
A. G. Wilson
WEST MIDLANDS
David Fletcher Mint Coins
*Format of Birmingham Ltd.
WORCESTERSHIRE
Whitmore
YORKSHIRE
Airedale Coins
Paul Clayton
Paul Davis Ltd.
*C. J. & A. J. Dixon Ltd.
SCOTLAND
*Edinburgh Coin Shop
WALES
Lloyd Bennett
*North Walers Coins Ltd.
C. Rumney
REPUBLIC OF IRELAND
*Coins & Medals, Dublin

CLASSICAL COINS

For 20 years we have been selling Greek, Roman, Judaean, Byzantine, Medieval European and British coins (and books about them). We purchase daily in the international marketplace - if you have something to sell we are interested. With our contacts in Europe and at our London office of Seaby Coins, we acquire some of the finest coins on the market today. Request a complimentary copy of our fixed price list - The *Classical Numismatic Review* - or our latest auction catalogue and see for yourself. We publish at least eight times a year. Our staff in the US (Victor, Kerry, Barry, Peter, Karen, Carol, Liz and Cathy) or London (Eric, Wendy, Tina and Helen) are glad to be of help. An annual subscription to our publications is reasonable at £36/$55 to all United Kingdom and United States addresses, all others £55/$85. Call or write today. A copy of our latest publication is complimentary for the asking.

SEABY COINS
Eric J. McFadden, Senior Director
14 Old Bond Street
London W1X 3DB
(0171) 495-1888, Fax (0171) 499-5916

CLASSICAL NUMISMATIC GROUP, INC.
Victor England, Senior Director
Post Office Box 479
Lancaster, Pennsylvania 17608-0479
(717) 390-9194; Fax (717) 390-9978